The Indian Mutiny Letters of Colonel H P Pearson CB

(then a Sub-Altern in the 84th Foot
The York & Lancaster Regiment)

August 1856–March 1859

Edited by
T A Heathcote

ROYAL ▪ ARMOURIES

Published in association with the York and Lancaster Regimental Museum,
Rotherham Metropolitan Borough Council.

Royal Armouries
Armouries Drive
Leeds LS10 1LT

ISBN 978-0-948092-57-2

Typeset & printed in the United Kingdom by Henry Ling Limited, at the Dorset Press, Dorchester, DT1 1HD

Contents

Introduction

The 67 letters in this previously unpublished collection were written by Hugh Pearce Pearson variously to his father ('Chaper') and mother ('Macher'), his ten-year-old sister Emily ('Emmie') and his aunt, Frances Elizabeth Ashby ('Taty'), wife of the future General Thomas Hooke Pearson ('Uncle Key'), then commanding the 12th Lancers. The writer joined the Army in February 1856 as an ensign on the strength of the 57th (West Middlesex) Regiment of Foot, at that time stationed in Malta. It is clear, however, that he never intended actually to join this corps, but merely to use it in a paper transaction as a stepping-stone for an exchange to the 84th (York and Lancaster) Regiment, a unit that had been in India since 1842 and was at that time stationed in Burma (the modern Myanmar).

Five months after his arrival in the East Indies, his regiment was fighting in a major war, the Indian Mutiny, a military revolt that within days of its outbreak became an insurgency affecting great tracts of northern India. Pearson's own regimental experiences of the war began at Barrackpur, near Calcutta, attending the disbandment of two regiments of Bengal Native Infantry for refusing to handle cartridges that they believed to be polluted, and the execution of the first two Indian soldiers (both named Pande) to die in the revolt. He then took part in the operations that re-established British authority in Varanasi and Allahabad, followed by a series of conventional battles on the way to Kanpur (reached too late) and Lucknow. He served in the reinforcement, continued defence, and final recovery of that city, and ended the war in counter-insurgency operations in Eastern Awadh and Bihar. From first to last, he was on active duty for two years, the entire duration of major operations in his theatre.

Like many people of his class and time, when letters were the normal (indeed the only) means of communication over any distance, Pearson wrote good clear English, and was able to describe his experiences and interests in a series of vivid pen-pictures. As an 18-year-old junior regimental officer, he had nothing to say about policy-making decisions or the conduct of war at the operational level, but as a record of the struggle on the ground his letters are of the greatest interest. He writes of the sickening stench of flesh when mutineers were executed by being blown away from guns, of the crunch made by a ball hitting a bone, of how he held the leg of one of his men while it was being amputated, and of how his right-hand man was shot through the head while talking to him. In one battle he was grazed on the temple by an enemy missile that knocked him senseless for a few seconds and gave him 'a rattling good headache for 2 days' (*Letter 16, 19 June 1857*). In the same fight, other missiles passed through both legs of his trousers, just below the knee. He wrote also of the other privations endured on campaign, with men (including his best friend) dying around him of cholera or the effects of the heat. Some of his concerns, such as peer pressure to take up smoking, or the danger of casualties from what is now called 'friendly fire', still remain with the Army 150 years later. Yet his letters also show his interest in the country around him and in the unfamiliar animals and birds of India, and he delighted to tell his young sister about his pet monkeys, and to ask her about the family's companion animals at home.

The first five letters, written from Chatham while Ensign Pearson was waiting to embark for India, are dated between 14 August and 28 December 1856. Thereafter, at his father's suggestion, he gave each letter a number, as service personnel in distant stations often still do, so that if several reached their destination at the same time, they could be read in their correct sequence. In some cases, especially in the stressful conditions of active service, Pearson gave the wrong number, or used the same number twice, but on the whole he kept his system most creditably in order. Eight letters are missing from the numbered series, either because they never arrived or were subsequently mislaid, and another one was so badly damaged in the loss of the mail steamer *Ava* that, though eventually delivered, it was indecipherable. Despite such gaps, this collection gives a fascinating insight into the life of a junior infantry officer during the British Army's most important campaign between the Crimean and South African Wars.

Hugh Pearce Pearson was the son of the then Lieutenant Hugh Pearson of the 49th (Princess Charlotte of Wales's, or Hertfordshire Regiment) of Foot, who had purchased his first commission as an ensign in July 1833 and his promotion to lieutenant in May 1835. In June 1837, in Calcutta, where the 49th had been stationed since 1829, Lieutenant Pearson married Jane Augusta Atkinson, then aged 33 (five years older than him), who may possibly have gone to India, where middle-class Englishwomen of marriageable age were always in short supply, to find a husband. Their first child was born when she was nearly 35, an age making her an 'elderly primip' even in modern medical terminology. Childbirth, hazardous at any age, was especially so in the insanitary conditions of early-Victorian India, but she survived this and the subsequent birth of their daughter, Emily Jane Augusta, in Darton in her native county of Yorkshire, by which time she was 42. She lived to be 89, predeceasing her husband by three and a half years.

The newly-married Pearsons moved with their regiment to Dinapore, Bihar (north-western Bengal), in December 1838 and Hugh Pearce Pearson was born there on 4 March 1839. From there, in February 1840, the 49th Foot returned to Calcutta and embarked for the First China War, 'the Opium War'. Lieutenant Pearson accompanied his regiment and served in the capture of Canton (Guangzhou), in May 1841, where he was wounded, and Chusan (Zhoushan) in October 1841. Late in 1843 the 49th returned to England, where Pearson purchased his captaincy on 3 July 1844. In 1846, when the regiment was ordered to Ireland, he sold his commission and became adjutant of the West Essex Militia. This, like all Militia regiments at that time, existed only as a cadre, with the adjutant as its only full-time officer. In response to successive invasion panics, the Militia was reformed and expanded during 1852–53, and Captain Pearson ended his service with the West Essex in May 1855, shortly after it was embodied following the outbreak of the Crimean War.

His son, Hugh Pearce Pearson, began his military career as a subaltern in the Essex Rifles (the East Essex Militia), sister regiment of the West Essex Militia, and became a lieutenant at the age of 16 on 6 July 1855. Several of his letters refer to other officers of the Essex Rifles, such as his friend William Drage (who later joined the 85th Foot) and the adjutant, Captain Stewart Northey. Colonels of militia regiments were usually members of prominent families within their counties and as such had great parliamentary influence. The colonel of the Essex Rifles at this time was a local aristocrat, the Hon C H Maynard, late of the Household Cavalry. Militia commissions were issued not by the Horse Guards (the term used, from its location, for the headquarters of the Commander-in-Chief of the British Army), but by the Lord Lieutenant of the county to which each regiment belonged. Normally, a local property qualification was required, at a level rising with each rank. It is reasonable to assume that the grant of the young Pearson's commissions, first in the Militia and then in the Army (for which the Militia was a recognised source of recruits), was helped by his father's service in these two forces.

Appointments and promotions

In every walk of life it is natural for individuals of any spirit to seek to advance as far as they can in their chosen career. In the military profession, with its hierarchy of distinct ranks, each offering their own rewards in terms of pay and status, ambition is a particularly powerful motivator. As Sir Francis Bacon put it, 'to take a soldier without ambition is to pull off his spurs'. It is not surprising, therefore, that almost one-third of the letters of this collection include references by Pearson to his promotion prospects and the extent to which these were affected by the death or departure of other officers in his regiment. Indeed, to students of the history of the British Army, they are just as valuable as evidence of the working of the promotion system as they are of the battles in which he fought.

At this time, the accepted way for officers in the British cavalry and infantry to gain their first commissions and subsequent promotion, up to and including the rank of lieutenant colonel, was by purchase. In the Household Cavalry and Foot Guards, officers held commissions in the Army at a rank higher than their regimental commissions. In the Royal Artillery and Royal Engineers, the purchase system did not apply. Officers in these two corps were granted their first commissions as second lieutenants and thereafter promoted by seniority according to the order in which they had graduated as gentlemen cadets from the Royal Military Academy at Woolwich. Officers of the East India Company's three armies were appointed as cadets by the Company's Court of Directors and thereafter were promoted within their respective regiments, by seniority, as vacancies occurred among themselves.

For officers with meritorious service to their credit, there was the possibility of promotion without purchase, by brevet, to ranks for which there was no vacancy on the establishment of their regiments. In such cases they enjoyed the status and title that went with their brevet rank, and the pay of any staff post to which they thereby became eligible, but retained their existing seniority within their regiment until promoted to a post on its rolls. Thus Lieutenant Colonel John Impett of the 74th Highlanders, a Waterloo veteran of whom Pearson speaks very warmly (*Letter 1 ,1 January 1857*) and who was commandant of the depot for the Queen's (i.e. British Army) troops in Madras, was a lieutenant colonel by brevet, but still, after 43 years' commissioned service, only a regimental captain. At the time when Pearson was writing, there were no regimental majors in the Royal Artillery or Royal Engineers, so that Francis Maude, whom he mentions in his account of the first advance to Lucknow and who commanded the artillery of Havelock's column, became a brevet major in the Army but never rose above his regimental rank of captain.

It was always the case in the British Army that a number of first commissions, either as cornets (in the cavalry) or ensigns (in the infantry), were available for issue without purchase. Such commissions derived from various sources, but were most commonly granted in wartime, when new units were being raised, or as replacements for battle casualties. Thus in 1855 (the year before Pearson was first commissioned), at the height of the Crimean War, 1,387 cornets or ensigns were granted their commissions without purchase, and only 345 by purchase. In peacetime, the situation was reversed and in 1860, the year after Pearson ended his Mutiny campaign, only 159 free first commissions were granted, compared with 351 by purchase. In wartime, the purchase system could almost collapse, as many candidates, either for promotion or first appointment, preferred to wait until campaign casualties created vacancies that, by custom, were filled without purchase. In principle, priority for the grant of free commissions was given to men who had distinguished themselves while serving in the ranks and to gentlemen cadets graduating from the Royal Military College at Sandhurst. In practice, they were more often given to candidates who had an influential patron, and especially to the sons of former military officers who otherwise would have found it difficult to produce the necessary funds for purchase.

Officers who were too poor to purchase promotion when their name came to the top of their regimental seniority list were obliged to remain in their existing rank while wealthier officers were promoted over their heads. Their best hope lay in the occurrence of campaign casualties, when promotion (including consequential promotion to any vacancies thus created) was given free, by regimental seniority. As remains the case in any profession where promotion depends upon casual vacancies arising in a fixed establishment, advancement in the Army at this time was very much a matter of chance. In a regiment that was not in the right place at the right time when a war began, or was not sent to take part in it or, even if it was, suffered few deaths among its officers, a good officer might languish at a junior level for years. Henry Havelock, under whom Pearson served in the first relief and subsequent defence of Lucknow, was one example of an officer who had studied his profession and had several campaigns to his credit, but who, for lack of funds for purchase, and lack of vacancies from battle casualties, only obtained promotion late in his career. On the other hand, officers on whom fortune smiled and who chose their regiments carefully could avoid the need to purchase. Pearson himself, in the course of a single campaign, rose in this way from being the junior ensign in his regiment to one of its senior lieutenants, though when the regiment returned home and saw no further active service, he eventually had to purchase a captaincy in another regiment.

Contrary to the impression commonly given in works of historical fiction, the purchase system was not one in which individuals simply bought and sold their commissions in transactions governed solely by market forces, with the only qualification for military rank being possession of the necessary wealth. It was controlled by a complex code of custom and practice, in which the cost of commissions was made up partly of the regulation price and partly of 'over-regulation payments'. The regulation price was a standard tariff, fixed by the State, originally to ensure that the holders of military rank were men with a stake in the country and thereby the less likely to take part in any kind of rebellion. The higher the rank, the greater the sum demanded, in effect as a bond for good behaviour. Later, it helped ensure the social prestige and exclusivity of the officer corps. For this reason, the Military Train, successor to the Land Transport Corps that had performed disastrously during the Crimean War, was made a purchase corps when it was formed in 1856.

The level of over-regulation payments varied from time to time according to changing circumstances, foremost among which was the location, or imminent relocation, of any particular regiment. If it was about to go to war, or to an unhealthy station, the over-regulation price was low, as promotions to replace the anticipated casualties were likely to become available without purchase. If the regiment had just returned home, the price would be higher, as some of its senior officers might be expected to take the chance to retire and thus create vacancies for promotion. Officers readily exchanged from one regiment to another to improve their prospects, making the appropriate over-regulation payments in each case. Although officers exchanging in this way immediately became the juniors of their rank in the new regiment, this disadvantage would soon be overcome if the new regiment offered better promotion prospects.

For all officers, promotion depended on a vacancy arising within the candidate's own regiment and on his regimental commanding officer certifying that he was capable of performing the duties of the higher rank. At least two years' commissioned service was required before lieutenants could become captains, and six before a captain could become a major. After 1850, an officer had to pass qualifying examinations for promotion, first from cornet or ensign to lieutenant, and subsequently from lieutenant to captain. Pearson (*letters 60, 26 December 1858 and 63, 30 January 1859*), refers to his studying with the other subalterns of his regiment 'for their companies', i.e. promotion to captain, the rank of company commanders at this period. Prior to the Crimean War of 1854–56, such examinations were rarely enforced, but the disasters of that campaign had clearly indicated the need for them, and they were thereafter required even for officers such as Pearson, who had by that time fought in a dozen major engagements and commanded a company on active service. Pearson (*Letter 60, 26 December 1858*) refers to Lieutenant Harry Crohan's purchase of a vacant captaincy being delayed until he passed his promotion examination, though this proved to be only a matter of weeks.

If an officer was forced to sell his commission following a court martial, the vacancy thus created was allotted to an officer from another regiment, in order to avoid any suggestion that evidence against him had been given by those who stood to gain from his conviction. A generous C-in-C such as Sir Colin Campbell, who arrived as C-in-C India in August 1857, would allow a discredited officer to sell-out without the need for a court martial that would adversely affect the prospects of his brother-officers, and Pearson's letters in June and July 1858 are full of references to the likely fate of Captain William Du Vernet of the 84th.

Commanding officers were required to submit regular returns to the Horse Guards, listing those officers who were willing and able to purchase promotion if a vacancy occurred. In the 84th at one point, Lieutenant George Blake, a wealthy young officer, was the senior of those who had indicated this willingness, and is described by Pearson (*Letter 45, 1 July 1858*) as being 'next for purchase', though later in the same letter he writes that Lieutenant Roberts Pratt (who was several places senior to Blake) had just been 'returned for purchase', implying that Pratt had subsequently decided to register his own willingness to exercise his right to buy. In fact, subsequent operational casualties allowed Pratt to obtain his captaincy without purchase, and several other officers who purchased their commissions later had them granted free, ante-dated to the time when the casualty had occurred.

No officer, however wealthy, could purchase promotion over another senior to him in his regiment if the latter was qualified for promotion and had the means and the wish to purchase the vacancy for himself. An officer was not obliged to purchase promotion when it was offered to him, and in time of war many declined to do so, as it was worth taking the chance of free promotion arising from battle casualties. Such casualties allowed the survivors, even if not immediately promoted, at least to move up the seniority ladder within their existing ranks. In December 1857 (*Letter 26, 20 December 1857*) Pearson mentions that he gained his promotion from ensign to lieutenant through the death of his best friend Henry Kenny. In peacetime it was not unknown for a very rich officer to pay officers who were senior to him not to exercise their right to buy. Though officially forbidden, this did allow poorer officers to accumulate funds that would help them purchase their own promotion in due course.

On purchasing promotion, an officer was required to pay to the State the difference in the regulation price of his new commission and his old one. For example, in the infantry of the Line, a new entrant paid the full price of £450 to become an ensign. The ensign whose promotion created that vacancy had to find another £250 to become a lieutenant, for which the regulation price was £700, and the lieutenant whose place he took had to find a further £1,100 for his captain's commission, for which the regulation price was £1,800. When an officer retired by sale of his commission (commonly referred to as 'selling out'), he realised a substantial capital sum, but it was usual for officers selling out to call upon those who stood to benefit from their departure to pay them to do so. Thus Pearson refers to Captain Willis of his regiment saying that he would be willing to sell out for £500, which Lieutenant George Oakley, the senior subaltern, then offered to pay (*Letter 61, 1 January 1859*). In theory, an officer not re-imbursed in this way was under no obligation to sell out, but as by remaining in post he would block the regimental promotion of everyone junior to him, this situation never arose.

This was one example of the officially ignored but unofficially obligatory 'over-regulation' payments that increased the cost of commissions. Pearson makes several references to his brother officers considering exchanges into other corps, and he himself had exchanged into the 84th Foot after first being commissioned in the 57th (*Letter 3, 6 March 1857*). Any financial transactions involved in such exchanges and in the sale or purchase of commissions were conducted by officially appointed Regimental Agents (in the case of the 84th, Cox & Co. and in the case of the 57th while its depot was in Ireland, Cane & Sons) who acted as bankers and accountants for the officers of their respective regiments.

Candidates wishing to obtain their first commission by purchase had to make both regulation and over-regulation payments in order to join the regiment of their choice. Wealth did not guarantee selection. More important was the test of being acceptable to their brother officers, something that, as well as being rooted in the social conventions of the time, was of real military significance, because in the stress of battle every officer has to have confidence in his fellows. Anyone who so wished could apply for a commission, but the selection of candidates was entirely in the hands of the Commander-in-Chief. After 1849, applicants had to pass an undemanding examination proving they had received 'the education of a gentleman' (either from a private tutor or one of the relatively few Public Schools).

To be selected, a candidate needed a recommendation by a patron in whose judgement the C-in-C had confidence. In practice, this meant a senior military officer or a member of the nobility or a Member of Parliament on whose support the government of the day counted. Only these, it was thought, could be relied on to ensure that the candidate came from the sort of social background in which the military virtues expected of an officer (leadership, a keen sense of personal honour, a thirst for glory, personal courage and physical robustness, etc.) were thought most likely to be found. The sons of country gentlemen or retired officers, even if they had limited means, were judged more likely to be 'officer material' than the sons of rich capitalists or the emergent bourgeoisie. This form of patronage, together with the evidence of social respectability indicated by possession of the requisite purchase money, ensured that the newly-commissioned officer would be acceptable to those already in his regiment.

Men commissioned without purchase after long service in the ranks were commonly regarded by their brother officers with some reservation, as being not of the gentleman class. Thus Pearson described the newly-commissioned Ensign George Lambert as 'a puny and undeserving snob', and added that his Victoria Cross had been awarded for no good reason, though Lambert had been the 84th's Sergeant Major, an appointment that carried much prestige. There was only one sergeant major in an infantry battalion at this period, corresponding to the present-day appointment of Regimental Sergeant Major. The appointments of company sergeant major and company quartermaster sergeant were not created until 1912, when infantry battalions were remustered with four large companies instead of eight small ones, and the rank of colour sergeant, of which there previously had been one per company, was abolished.

All new officers, regardless of how they obtained their commissions, had to pay subscriptions to various Mess funds and the regimental band (at this time maintained exclusively by the officers). In the most expensive regiments, these could amount to several months' pay, and even in ordinary regiments of the line, such as Pearson's 84th Foot, officers were required to provide their own horses and personal servants, a subject frequently mentioned in these letters. Such expenses tended to increase in line with an officer's rank, and men of modest means always found it difficult to live solely on their pay. Officers who declined to incur the costs expected of them would be ostracised by their fellows, or even obliged to leave their regiments. Pearson's letters show him taking care to live as frugally as possible and, as the cost of living in India was always lower than at home, this may account for his wish to join a regiment stationed there. He thought that one of his brother officers, Lieutenant George Oakley, was unlikely to return home, as he could not afford to live in England (*Letter 25, 16 December 1857*), and reported that a company commander, Captain Walter Snow, was so much in debt in England that he had been obliged to leave the country hidden in a cartload of straw (*Letter 45, 1 July 1858*).

Uniform & equipment

The most expensive outlay for a new officer was his uniform and personal equipment, all of which he was required to provide, to the regulation patterns, at his own expense. Pearson was fortunate in that he joined the Army just after it had gone through one of its periodic changes of uniform. In 1855, in response to criticism that the troops in the Crimea were wearing uniforms of a pattern dating back to the Napoleonic Wars, the coatee (a form of tail-coat) was replaced by a looser and longer garment, the tunic, adopted by most other European

Armies of the time in line with changes in contemporary civilian fashion. The waist-length shell jacket continued in wear as ordinary working dress. For more formal duties, when not on parade with their men, officers wore a plain, dark blue, double-breasted frock coat. Infantry officers wore a crimson silk sash over the left shoulder. In India, during the hot weather, suits of white cotton were worn. With the campaign nearly over, Pearson bought some articles of uniform belonging to an officer who was leaving the regiment, and comments that they had never been worn (*Letter 49, 26 July 1858*). This was a consequence of the new pattern of uniform having only just been introduced before the regiment went to war. As operations were initially conducted in local hot weather dress, the original owner never had the chance to wear his new uniform. Pearson mentions that, as operations continued, he obtained a jacket, trousers and cap cover in a sand colour material, "very difficult to distinguish", to which he later refers by its Hindustani name, *khaki* (*Letter 50, 6 August 1858*). During the cold weather, British troops mostly wore their home service serge uniforms (*Letter 24, 6 December 1857*), with tunics in the traditional colours of red for the infantry, heavy cavalry and engineers, green for the Rifles, and dark blue for the light cavalry, artillery and logisticians.

In the infantry of the line, the new full dress shako resembled the stylish *kepi* then worn in the French Army. For other occasions, the standard headdress for ordinary soldiers was a round cap shaped rather like a pork pie. In India, it was worn during the hot weather with a white cover, sometimes with a peak and neck flap, giving an appearance generally associated with that of the French Foreign Legion in North Africa. In some regiments, the shako was worn on active service with a fitted cloth cover. Other than with full dress, officers normally wore a peaked, low-crowned, round forage cap. The cuffs and collars of the tunic were of the regimental 'facing colour'. For infantry regiments with the distinction 'Royal' in their titles, those were blue. For the 84th, like most ordinary English regiments of the line, they were yellow. The bullion-fringed epaulettes previously worn on the coatee by officers were replaced by twisted shoulder cords referred to by Pearson variously as a 'shoulder knot' or 'shoulder strap' (*Letters 51, 11 August 1858; 56, 8–9 Oct 1858*). With the demise of the epaulette, officers' badges of rank were transferred from the shoulder to the collar. Ensigns wore one star, lieutenants a crown, and captains a crown and star. This sequence was repeated for field officers (majors, lieutenant colonels and colonels), but with two rows of lace on their cuffs and collars instead of one.

Each battalion of infantry of the line carried two large silk flags or Colours, about two metres or six feet across, marking its identity and the location of its headquarters. The first or Queen's Colour was the national or Union flag, with the regiment's number in the centre. The main body of the second or Regimental Colour was of the same hue as the regimental facings and displayed the regiment's number, badge (if any) and battle honours, with a smaller Union flag in the upper corner. They were normally carried on parade or in battle by the two senior ensigns. It was a post of danger as well as honour, though the two generally go together, and any junior officer could be called upon as the need arose. Pearson carried the regimental colour of the 84th in the attack on Bithur and thought that though the honour was great, the nuisance was greater (*Letter 20, 20–26 August 1857*).

The personal weapon of infantry officers was the 1822-pattern sword, composed of a slightly curved blade about 32 inches long, with a brass hand guard shaped in a series of ornate bars, commonly called the 'Gothic hilt'. It was a graceful weapon, but like most British military swords of its day, of questionable value for the bloody business of hand-to-hand fighting, especially as there were a number of different suppliers and not all of them produced blades that had been properly proved. Pearson's opinion of the regimental sword with which he began the war was that it was 'a mere skewer' (*Letter 24, 2 December 1857*) or 'a wretched skewer' (*Letter 37, 12 April 1858*) and, after he lost it in the fighting as he entered Lucknow, he was glad to replace it by a cavalry sabre. Swords were carried in their scabbards on two slings attached to a waist belt. The scabbard was made of wood covered with leather, and furnished with brass mounts. After Pearson's friend Lieutenant Alfred Gibaut was killed at a burning barricade, his sword was recovered from the flames but nothing of the scabbard remained (*Letter 45, 1 July 1858*).

The choice of a firearm for close-quarter combat was left to the taste of individual officers. Pearson at first preferred a double-barrelled pistol, partly because it fired a ball with greater stopping power than a revolver bullet, and partly because the working parts of the revolvers of the time were difficult to strip and clean. Like many men of his class, he enjoyed shooting for sport and for the pot, and no less than 20 of his letters refer to feats of marksmanship, mostly against small animals and wild birds, but also, in periods of static warfare, against enemy troops.

Organisation

The combatant units of the British infantry consisted of battalions with a notional establishment of about 1,000 men. When Pearson joined, most regiments of Foot consisted of only one battalion, and the terms 'battalion' and 'regiment' were in most respects interchangeable. The fact that British infantry regiments are administrative rather than operational groupings continues to baffle their allies, in whose more logically-organised armies a battalion, commanded by a major, is an integral sub-unit of a combatant regiment, commanded by a colonel with a lieutenant colonel as second in command. British infantry regiments in 1857 had five 'field officers' (a term meaning those above the rank of captain, rather than performing duty in the field) consisting of the colonel, two lieutenant colonels and two majors. For historical reasons, the regimental colonel, who was normally also a general officer, was never present with a battalion, which was commanded by one of the two lieutenant colonels. The other lieutenant colonel would be on extra-regimental duty or on leave, so that one of the majors was usually the second-in-command. Practical considerations often required a battalion to be divided into 'wings' of several companies, in which case a major would normally take command of the detached element as a wing commander. Below these were 12 captains, 24 lieutenants and 12 ensigns, though the Army Lists of the time show that in most cases about half of the ensigns' posts were vacant. When Pearson joined the 84th it had 21 lieutenants and only five ensigns actually in post.

Battalion headquarters included the adjutant (usually one of the senior subalterns), who was responsible for administration, discipline and regimental staff duties; the paymaster (an officer appointed without purchase, outside the regimental seniority list) and the quartermaster (usually commissioned from the ranks). Each regiment had one surgeon and three assistant surgeons, of whom at least two would normally be with the battalion. The rest of battalion headquarters included the sergeant-major, quartermaster-sergeant, drill-sergeant, pay sergeant, the corps of drums (who were combatant soldiers) and the band (who were not, though in the crisis of the Mutiny, when every white man who could hold a weapon was needed in the line of battle, many became so).

In theory, a battalion had ten companies each commanded by a captain and consisting of about 100 men, but as the officers and men needed for various 'regimental employments' were actually drawn from the companies, the bayonet strength of these sub-units was always less than this. When a regiment went overseas, a company cadre was left behind to act as the depot. The two prestigious 'flank companies', the grenadier and light companies respectively, were composed of picked men, the former originally trained as assault troops and the latter for reconnaissance and skirmishing, although by the time Pearson joined, these roles had increasingly been undertaken by the ordinary companies. In 1857, the attrition of experienced officers in the 84th was such that he soon found himself serving with the grenadiers. Companies were made up of two divisions, each of which had two sub-divisions, notionally of a sergeant and 25 men.

The 84th Foot had been raised in 1793, mostly in Yorkshire, where its first colonel had his family estates. In 1809 it was granted the title 'York and Lancaster' with the red and white Tudor Rose as its badge. Few regiments had any local affiliations at this time, though they were each given territorial sub-titles in an attempt to achieve an even spread of recruitment across the country. In practice, recruiting parties took men from wherever they could find them. On reaching his regiment in Rangoon, Pearson wrote that 'as usual, five-sixths of them are Irish' (*Letter 3, 6 March 1857*) though from the context he is probably referring not to the soldiers but to his fellow-officers, many of whom came from the Anglo-Irish Protestant 'squirearchy' whose sons traditionally found employment as officers in the British Army.

Just as the officers moved from regiment to regiment in order to advance their careers, so did their men whenever suitable financial inducements were offered. At this time, the British Army was its own Reserve, and whenever an under-strength regiment was ordered overseas, or needed drafts while on campaign, bounties were offered to attract men to transfer to them from regiments not being mobilised, or from those about to return home. The refusal of the Government of India to pay such bounties when its European soldiers were transferred en masse to the British Army in 1858 caused great discontent. Pearson notes that on the return of the 84th from India nearly 300 of its men volunteered to join other regiments (*Letter 63, 30 January 1859*). One effect of this system of large-scale transfers was to inhibit the growth of any local connection between regiments and the counties whose names they bore, for even if recruiting sergeants had taken men only from their allotted areas, there was nothing to stop these men volunteering for other regiments when the call came. No soldier, however, could be transferred from one regiment to another without his own consent.

The 84th, after serving creditably during the Peninsular War and thereafter in various colonial garrisons, had embarked for Rangoon, Burma (the present-day Myanmar), in April 1842. In 1845 it moved to southern India and thence returned to Rangoon in January 1854. As regiments had no permanent presence in the cities and counties allotted to them as their recruiting districts, their depots were located in any garrison town where there was accommodation available. On going overseas, the 84th left a UK depot at Chatham, Kent, where there was a garrison for the defence of the naval installations, and where the Royal Engineers had their own permanent depot. It had the added advantage of being near to the embarkation port of Gravesend, from which Pearson, with other reinforcements, in due course sailed for India (*Un-numbered letter, 12 September 1856*). Depots dealt not only with recruits but also with men due for discharge, and with the general domestic administration of the regiments to which they belonged. Overseas, base depots were established in the country where the regiments were stationed, to deal with drafts of men arriving as reinforcements and replacements, and with those departing as time-expired or invalids. When a unit mobilised for war, a rear party took care of its non-operational stores and its married families along with other personnel not sent to the front, as was the case when the 84th left Rangoon for Calcutta on the outbreak of the Mutiny in India. As is the case to this day, the wives at the base often learned more of a regiment's future movements than did its officers in the field (*Letter 54, 12–16 September 1858*).

After reporting for duty at their UK depots, new officers were taught the rudiments of their profession by garrison instructors. The most important of these, especially for infantry officers, was foot drill, beginning with the movements required of an individual soldier and progressing to the command of a squad. This was not merely for ceremonial, as the evolutions practised on the parade square were tactical manoeuvres that had a real place in combat. In the fast-moving conditions of the battle-field, when it was vital for a unit quickly to deploy its firepower to maximum effect, or when a brief delay in changing formation might leave it vulnerable to enemy attack, every man had to know what to do in response to his orders, and every officer had to know the correct orders to give. Constant repetition was needed to ensure that drills practiced on the square were followed instinctively during the noise, fear and stress of combat.

Officers did not need to practice the individual musketry drill that produced the crashing volleys at a rate of three rounds per minute which were the stock-in-trade of the British infantry. The actual procedures of loading, aiming and firing a musket could be taught in a day, though men needed more time to learn how to clean and maintain the weapon, and more still to practice these procedures so that in battle they would perform them automatically. Nevertheless, officers had to know the drill, so that they could be sure that their men did, and they had to know the weapon's characteristics, in order that it was properly employed. Accordingly, instruction in musketry as well as foot drill formed part of every officer's basic training. Pearson was still undergoing what he calls 'firelock drill' after joining his regiment in Rangoon, though he expected to be hurried through it within a few days, as the monsoon was about to break (*Letter 4, 8 March 1857*). Although the primary duty of an officer was to lead his men in battle, leadership required more than the courage involved in going forward against an enemy position or standing steady against an enemy attack. An officer was expected to maintain morale and efficiency by ensuring that his men's interests were properly looked after in barracks or on campaign, and Pearson makes several references to such domestic considerations as checking on his men's meals, making up their pay accounts, admiring their pet animals, visiting the wounded in hospital, organising sports and games and so on.

Pearson joined just as the British Army was being re-armed with a new personal weapon, the Enfield rifle. This, though still a muzzle-loader, fired by the same hammer-lock and percussion cap system of its smooth-bore predecessor, had the new feature of 'rifling', a spiral groove cut into the barrel in order to impart spin, and hence give greater range and accuracy to the projectile. When the weapon was fired, rapidly expanding gases propelled the conical-shaped lead bullet along the barrel, and the heat thus generated caused the bullet to expand, fitting into the groove and acquiring the desired element of spin. The rifle's ammunition, like that of the smooth-bore musket, came in the form of paper tubes or cartridges, each containing the bullet and standard charge of gunpowder. Loading drill required the soldier to open the cartridge with his teeth, pour the charge down the barrel, and ram the bullet and cartridge paper (serving as a wad) after it. Because the products of combustion and particles of lead from the bullet would otherwise soon fill up the rifling groove and thus turn the weapon into a smooth-bore, the cartridge paper was greased with tallow, mutton fat or similar substances to provide lubrication.

Pearson arrived at Chatham to find the current course of rifle instruction already in progress and was told that he had to wait for the next one to begin. In fact he seems to have sailed to join his regiment before this started, though he spent some of his spare time by casting rifle bullets and making up cartridges. Students were taught this as part of their background knowledge, not with the intention that any of them, even private soldiers, would actually be required to do so on service. As the new ordnance factory at Enfield Lock (from which the rifle took its name), in the north-east corner of Middlesex, had only just gone into full-scale production, not every unit, especially those serving overseas, had been re-armed by 1856. In India, the only British regiment to be fully equipped with them was the elite 60th Rifles, stationed at Meerut, a day's march from Delhi, the old capital of the defunct Mughal empire. The 84th, stationed in Rangoon, was like most other units, still entirely armed with smooth-bore muskets and Pearson's lack of formal instruction on the new rifle was therefore not a matter of great importance at this time. In August 1857, after the regiment had been operational for nearly four months, its light company was re-armed with the Enfields of casualties among 61st Foot, 78th Highlanders and 1st Madras Fusiliers (*Letter 20, 20–26 August 1857*), but it was not until a month later that the entire unit was issued with this weapon (*Letter 22, 17 September 1857*).

The military in British India

In 1856, British India was governed through the medium of the East India Company, a body that traced its existence back to a group of London merchants granted its first charter in 1600. Although it is commonly described as a kind of a multi-national trading corporation, a better comparison would be with a present-day 'quango' or nationalised industry, because since 1784 its Court of Directors had been subordinate to a Cabinet Minister, the President of the Board of Control for the affairs of India. Indeed, the Charter Act of 1833 had deprived it of the right to carry on commercial activities in India or anywhere else. Within India, the Company maintained three distinct Armies, one for each of the three great areas or Presidencies into which its dominions were divided. Originally widely separated from each other by sovereign Indian states, 'the country powers', these had by 1856 become virtually contiguous, either directly or through principalities that retained their internal independence under British protection. The three armies garrisoned the Presidencies to which they belonged (Bengal, Madras and Bombay respectively), watched the still-formidable forces of the neighbouring princely states, supported the civil power in the maintenance of law and order and the collection of revenue, and stood guard against wild tribes in the frontier regions. The Bengal Army, the largest of the three, held the mountain chain that ran from Assam in the east to the Khyber Pass and the Afghan border in the west. The Bombay Army, smallest of the three, guarded the desert frontier between Upper Sind and Baluchistan. The Madras Army supplied the frontier garrisons for British Burma, across the Bay of Bengal.

By 1856, the East India Company's troops comprised the largest European-trained army in Asia. All the cavalry, most of the infantry, and about a third of the vitally important artillery were sepoys, Indian regular soldiers dressed, trained, equipped and organised in imitation of the British troops for whom they were cheaper substitutes. Each army had three battalions of European infantry, who were recruited, like most of the artillery, from British personnel. These did not belong to the British Army, but were British subjects engaged by the Company for permanent local service in India. The remaining European troops in India came from the British Army. British regiments were normally sent to India for tours lasting up to 20 years, though there was a steady changeover of personnel as men died or were sent home and their places were taken by fresh drafts, such as that with which Pearson arrived in the country.

Each Presidency had its own fixed establishment of British Army (or 'Queen's') units, with a depot that administered them separately from the Company's troops. Thus on first reaching India, Pearson (*Letter 1, 1 January 1857*) reported with the others in his draft to the depot for British troops, 12 miles inland of Madras (the modern Chenai), and remained there for a month before re-embarking to join his regiment in Rangoon. The total British Army strength on the Indian establishment in January 1857 was some 24,000 men, in four regiments of cavalry and 22 battalions of infantry, with the Company's Europeans producing another 15,000 white troops. The sepoy establishment, including cavalry, artillery, infantry and various para-military forces, amounted to 226, 418.

At much the same time that Pearson arrived in India, alarming rumours had begun to circulate among the sepoys of the Bengal Army. To many of the men, it seemed that the times were out of joint. During the previous ten years British administrators, bringing with them British lawyers and tax collectors, had taken over the government of state after state. The most recent example had been in 1856, with the annexation of Awadh, where many Bengal sepoys had their home villages. The King, though ruling in a way that the British regarded as misgovernment, had always faithfully observed his treaty obligations. None of his subjects had sought a regime change that, though it was intended to better their lot, had actually left many of them worse off. If the British could dethrone a king in this way, it was asked, how could they be expected to keep promises made to ordinary men? New regulations required all recruits to agree to embark for service overseas, though to the high-caste Hindu sepoys who made up the bulk of the Bengal Army, this embarkation implied ritual pollution. Moreover, if a sailing troopship was becalmed, Hindus would have to eat salt beef, or Muslims would have to eat salt pork, in defiance of the dietary laws of each religion respectively. Henceforth, with returns from their land decreasing at the same time as there was a greater population pressure on it, the sturdy peasants who had since Mughal times found honourable employment as regular soldiers would be denied the service that, through its pay and pensions, had become an essential element in their communities' income.

It is commonly the case that a feeling of powerlessness fosters the spread of conspiracy theories. Men already anxious about the future found it easy to believe a rumour that the government intended to force its sepoys to turn Christian, a horrible thought to respectable Indians, who regarded Christians as low-class individuals who ate and drank indiscriminately with no religiously prescribed rituals for regular washing. The government's rationale was said to be that, because of their meat diet, Europeans were bigger and stronger than Indians, and if Indians ate beef and pork like the Europeans, they could be used in their place, with consequential financial savings, as Indians were paid less than Europeans. The vehicle for this mass conversion was said to be none other than the cartridges used with the new Enfield rifle that Pearson and others had been shown at Chatham, and on which selected sepoys were already being trained at Indian musketry depots. The story spread that the lubricant, either in or on the cartridge paper, was composed of pork fat or beef tallow, so that both Muslims (to whom pigs are unclean) and Hindus (to whom cows are sacred) would thereby be polluted. Even those who did not believe the story themselves knew that it was believed in their villages and that, when they went home, their own families, peasant-like, would refuse to have anything to do with them. The more that their officers tried to re-assure them, even to the extent of changing the drill so that the cartridge did not have to be bitten, or allowing them to lubricate the cartridges with ghee (clarified butter), beeswax, vegetable oil, or any substance they chose for themselves, the more the sepoys despaired, and feared the loss of their very place as much in this world as in the next.

The mutiny campaign

On 26 February 1857, ten days after Pearson left Madras for Rangoon, men of the 19th Bengal Native Infantry at Berhampur, a hundred miles north of Calcutta, refused to accept even the old pattern cartridges and seized their weapons in defiance of orders. The next day they returned to duty, but the episode had gone too far and the Government of India decided to make an example by disbanding the regiment. For this purpose it was ordered to Barrackpur, a day's march from Calcutta, but as only sepoy units were normally stationed there, news of the disbandment was officially withheld to allow time for the 84th Foot to be recalled from Rangoon and join the 53rd Foot at Calcutta, the only other European infantry in the area. Thus it was that Pearson, in the middle of writing home to his sister Emily (*Letter 4, 8 March 1857*), broke off to say that the order had just arrived for his regiment to embark immediately for Calcutta 'The reason is that the Bengal Native troops have all mutinied, and are in a state of insurrection, and we are now going up to quell them'.

Pearson had rather anticipated events, for at this time only the 19th Bengal NI had mutinied, and even then had returned to duty. It was indeed the arrival of the 84th and other Europeans at Chinsura, the river-port eight miles away from Barrackpur, that precipitated the next development. On 29 March 1857, at Barrackpur, Sepoy Mangal Pande of the 34th Bengal Native Infantry attacked the adjutant and European sergeant-major of his regiment and called upon his comrades to rise up and join him against those who had come to destroy their religion. Mangal Pande was arrested and the disbandment of the 19th took place under the guns of European troops the next day as planned. The 84th returned to Calcutta, expecting to go back to Rangoon, where all the married families, non-effectives and heavy stores had been left. A court-martial convicted Mangal Pande of mutiny and sentenced him to hang. A similar verdict was brought in against Jemadar Iswari Pande, the Indian officer commanding the guard, who had made no effort either to restrain Mangal Pande or to assist in his arrest. The 34th, whose men had witnessed the whole affair without going to help, was ordered to be disbanded, and the 84th Foot returned to Chinsura three more times, for the execution of Mangal Pande and Jemadar Iswari Pande and the disbandment of the 34th respectively. The Governor-General, Lord Canning, thought that the crisis had passed and the 84th were about to embark for Rangoon when news came of a serious outbreak of mutiny and disorder at Meerut on 10 May.

There, 85 skirmishers of the 3rd Bengal Light Cavalry had been given long prison sentences for refusing orders to practice the new loading drill. On the night of 10 May, sepoys of every regiment in the garrison, joined by local malefactors, attacked their officers and any other Europeans they could find. They then marched to Delhi, where the sepoy brigade stationed there joined the revolt and declared the restoration of the Mughal Empire under the last reigning prince of that dynasty (the titular King of Delhi). British authority in the area collapsed and, as at Meerut, every Christian who could not escape in time was murdered, including non-combatants, women and children. Lieutenant General George Anson, the C-in-C, India, who with most of his European troops was at this time in the Punjab, began to mobilise a force to recapture the city. British efforts were hampered for lack of logistic supplies and by an outbreak of cholera that claimed many lives, Anson's among them. During the month it took for the British to return to Delhi, new mutinies had occurred throughout the North-West Provinces (lying between Bengal and the Punjab) and Awadh. Faced with a full-scale insurgency, Canning summoned aid from Madras and Bombay, but with the few European battalions between Calcutta and Meerut fully committed to holding their existing posts, the 84th Foot, soon joined by the 1st Madras Fusiliers, were at first the only European infantry available for the threatened areas.

Travelling by a combination of railway train, river-steamers, post-chaises and bullock carts, the first two companies of the 84th reached Lucknow, the capital of Awadh, 1180 miles west of Calcutta, on 30 May. The recently-installed chief commissioner, Sir Henry Lawrence, felt strong enough to send them back to Kanpur (Cawnpore), 40 miles away, but the divisional commander there, Sir Hugh Wheeler, returned one of them to Lucknow. Thus one company, under Lieutenant Frederic Saunders, was among those lost when Wheeler and his men, after standing a 21-days siege against hopeless odds, were massacred on 27 June when he surrendered on a promise of safe conduct. The second company, two officers and 48 men under Lieutenant David O'Brien, remained at Lucknow, which came under siege a few days later while local insurgents set up a regime headed by members of the family of the deposed King of Awadh.

The rest of the 84th, with Pearson among them, formed part of the force that, first under Colonel James Neill of the 1st Madras Fusiliers ('Neill's Blue Caps') and then under Brigadier General Henry Havelock, marched to rescue besieged Kanpur. On their way, they were hampered by outbreaks of mutiny at Varanasi (Benares) and Allahabad (*Letter 14, 22 June 1857*), but pushed on during the intense heat of the north Indian summer to within 70 miles of Kanpur, when they heard of the destruction of Wheeler's command (*Letter 15, 6 July 1857*). Thereafter, Havelock's column moved even faster, fighting a series of major engagements along the way in the hope of rescuing the garrison's surviving women and children, but reached the city on 17 July only to find that all had been murdered the previous day. The column then attempted to relieve Lucknow, where the British had retreated inside the Residency, but suffered so many casualties, mostly from cholera and the effects of heat, that the entire force was soon reduced to a bayonet strength of 700 men.

Heavily outnumbered and with artillery ammunition running low, Havelock was forced to retreat to Kanpur and await reinforcements (*Letters 16–21, 19 July–4 September 1857*). Sir James Outram arrived with the additional troops on 15 September 1857 and the reinforced British fought their way into Lucknow ten days later, when Pearson lost his sword in the rush through the streets to reach the Residency (*Letter 23, 21–29 September 1857*). Although the intention had been to collect the garrison, with its women, children, sick and wounded, and return at once to Kanpur, opposition was so fierce that Lucknow was, strictly speaking, reinforced rather than relieved. The rescuers (Pearson and the 84th among them), with most of their combat supplies left in the Alam Bagh, an extensive walled park on the outskirts of the city, had to remain under siege with the original garrison until the new C-in-C, India, General Sir Colin Campbell, arrived with a larger force on 17 November. (*Letter 22, 17 September, and Letter 23, 21 November 1857*). Campbell then abandoned Lucknow and escorted the non-combatants back to Kanpur, from where they were sent down the Ganges to safety at Allahabad. He reached Kanpur just as the troops he had left there were driven inside their defences by the Gwalior Contingent, a well-trained sepoy force of all arms that had not previously taken part in the campaign. Kanpur was retaken by the British on 6–7 December, but large quantities of stores, including the cold weather items that Pearson and his regiment had left there on marching for Lucknow, were lost (*Letter 24, 2 December 1857*).

Pearson and the 84th formed part of a garrison left at the Alam Bagh under Outram to make it clear that the British intended to recover Awadh. They remained there, in touch with Kanpur and withstanding several determined assaults from the insurgent forces still holding the city, until Campbell resumed the offensive and took Lucknow on 21 March 1858 (*Letters 25–35, 16 December 1857–21 March 1858*). The 84th were then immediately sent to Azamghar, eastern Awadh, where a Rajput nobleman, Kunwar Singh, had been appointed governor by the insurgent leaders in Lucknow. The previous year he had put himself at the head of mutineers from Dinapur, besieged Ara and inflicted a significant defeat on the 10th Foot. Driven out of his ancestral stronghold at Jagdispur, he had joined the insurgent forces in Awadh, but was now forced back across the Ganges to his lands in Bihar. He died of wounds suffered during this retreat but his brother, Anwar Singh, waged a guerrilla war in the jungle-clad hills of this region until hostilities officially ended in February 1859. For a second year running, the 84th had to fight on through the monsoon and into the cold weather (*Letters 37–58, 10 April–11 November 1858*). Meanwhile, Delhi had been recaptured on 20 September 1857, and British rule was re-established in the other main areas of the insurgency well before 1 November 1858, when the dominions, obligations and servants of the East India Company were transferred to the British Crown.

The last phase of the war saw the 84th based at Baksar (Buxar) and conducting counter-insurgency operations in the surrounding districts of Bihar. From there they marched to Calcutta, where the main party embarked for home on 8 April 1859, reaching Gravesend six months later. During the war they had lost ten officers and 300 men killed by enemy action, disease, or the effects of the climate, and won six Victoria Crosses. The collection ends (*Letter 66, 17–20 March 1859*) with Pearson preparing to embark on the steamer that would take him to the Red Sea and thence on the overland route through Egypt to the Mediterranean.

The provenance of the letters

Pearson had been promoted from ensign to lieutenant without purchase on 25 August 1857. He later rose to become the senior lieutenant in his regiment after Lieutenant Oakley (who clearly did find the means to return home with them), but with a promotion block in the 84th, he purchased a captaincy in the 52nd (Oxfordshire) Light Infantry on 15 October 1861 and went back to India to join that regiment in February 1862. When the 52nd returned home in 1865, Pearson exchanged to the 12th (East Suffolk) Regiment, which had just arrived in India from the United Kingdom. In the same year he married, at Calcutta, the 20-year-old Ellen Fanny Thomas, who had been born in that city. Pearson was promoted to brevet major on 6 February 1875. The purchase system had been abolished in 1871 but substantive promotion still depended on the occurrence of a vacancy within an officer's regiment and Pearson did not become a major in the 12th until 1 April 1880. During the 2nd Afghan War (1879–81) he served on the staff as a brigade major and as Deputy Assistant Quartermaster General, corresponding to the present-day grade of SO2 G1/G4. In recognition of his services in that campaign, he was promoted to brevet lieutenant colonel on 2 March 1881. He became a regimental lieutenant colonel in the Suffolk Regiment (formed by amalgamation of the 12th Foot and the Suffolk Militia in 1881) on 1 April 1882 and commanded successively its 1st Battalion and the regimental district and depot in the UK. Pearson was promoted to colonel on 2 March 1885 and, once more in India, brigadier general in Madras in 1894, the same year that his wife died there. He retired in March 1896, having been awarded the CB, and died at Southsea in 1897.

Hugh and Ellen Pearson had ten children, six sons and four daughters, of whom one died in infancy. Emily Jane Augusta Pearson, the little sister Emmie of these letters, died unmarried at Bournemouth in 1903 at the age of 57. Assuming that she had continued to live with her parents, as single ladies often did at this time, she may well have inherited the letters after the death of her mother in 1893 or her father in 1897. Certainly they subsequently came into the possession of her niece and namesake, Emily Bryce, one of the daughters of Hugh and Ellen Pearson. She was married to the future Sir Lionel Davidson, KCIE, on whose death in 1944 the letters were inherited by Colonel Harry Pearson, her youngest sibling and only surviving brother. They later passed to his children, by whose permission they are now published for the first time.

Mutiny Letters Addressees
Extracted from the *Genealogy of the Pearson Family*

Author:
HUGH PEARCE PEARSON   =   Ellen Fanny Thomas
    b. Dinapore, India, 4 Mar 1839   b. Calcutta, 10 Jul 1845
    m. Calcutta, 7 Feb 1865   d. Madras, 23 Sep 1892
    d. Southsea, 1897

    C.B. – late Lieut Col. Comdg. 1st Suffolk Rgt.
    Lieut. Col. Comdg. 12th Rgtal. District
    Adjt.Gen. Madras Army. Col. in the Army.
    Brigr.-General

His Father ('Chaper')
HUGH PEARSON
    b. Tettenhall, Staffordshire, 7 Nov 1809
    m. Calcutta, 22 June 1837
    d. Southampton, 12 Apr 1897

    Capt. 49th Regt. Adjutant West Essex Militia
    Major, Essex Rifles Militia

His Mother ('Macher')
JANE AUGUSTA (nee Atkinson)
    b. Leeds, Yorks, 26 May 1804
    d. Portswood, Southampton, 19 Dec 1893

His Sister ('Emmie')
EMILY JANE AUGUSTA
    b. Darton, Yorks, 10 July 1846
    d. Bournemouth, 1903

'Uncle & Aunty Pearson'
THOMAS HOOKE PEARSON   =   Frances Elizabeth Ashby
    b. Tettenhall, Staffordshire,   (nee. Mettam)
    7 June 1806   b. Barwell, Leicestershire,
              27 Sep 1809

    m. Barwell, Leics, 11 Nov 1837
    d. Sandy, Bedfordshire, 9 Aug 1890   d. Sandy, Bedfordshire,
              29 Apr 1892

Lieut. General in the Army; Col. 12th Lancers; CB.

The Indian Mutiny Letters of Colonel H P Pearson

(then a Sub-Altern in the 84th Foot, The York & Lancaster Regiment)

August 1856 – March 1859

Unnumbered Letter

Chatham Barracks
August 14th 1856

My dearest Emily,

I have no doubt worried your patience completely out by not writing to you before, but I have been very much pressed for time lately, owing to my not yet being dismissed drill.

You will be sorry to hear that my poor little kitten is dead. She was killed by an officer of the 29th named "Taylor" who is (poor fellow) quite crazy, and is in fact a harmless madman. Although seen by several officers killing it, yet he immediately expressed his ignorance of the matter, and no doubt he forgot all about it.

Last night being the night of the day fixed for the opening of the new bridge at "Rochester", there was a splendid display of fireworks, which I went to see accompanied by a brother officer and friend of mine named "Kenny". The magnificent old castle and keep at "Rochester" was lent for the occasion and was filled with red lights, which, when let off exactly gave the appearance of its being on fire, and the moon behind a black cloud directly in the background greatly heightened the effect. There was a terrific explosion and myriads of rockets and shells exploded high in the air. The concluding piece was the ignition of 600 large rockets at the same time. Altogether it was well worth going to see.

I saw by the papers that Her Majesty is going to pay a visit to the "Channel Islands"; is it true?

The ship I go in sails on the 1st and not the 10th of next month. It is called the "Trafalgar", 10,250 tons, Captn. H. Taylor, commander.

I have now told you all the news, and as I have several other letters to write, I must bid you good bye. Give my best love to Chaper, Macher, Taty and Georgey Denyer and accept the same dear Emmy,

from your affectionate loving brother,
Hughey P. Pearson

Unnumbered Letter

Chatham Barracks
Tuesday Afternoon

My very dearest Father,

It is several days now since I wrote to you last, but when you hear the reason of my delay, I am sure you will say I had no time to spare.

First let me tell you what most concerns us both. Last Sunday morning the servant of an officer of the 10th came and told me that an extensive robbery had been committed in the barracks, and on my inquiring for my servant, I found he was one of the number. Naturally the first thing I did was to examine my trunks and drawers in order to discover if there was anything missing. I took an accurate list of all my clothes, money, etc. and having found my inventory in my desk I compared them, when to my horror I found that he had taken £4 in gold, also some silver, and left a £5 which was also there. He also took 20 of my best shirts, and my suit of dress black clothes, topping up with a pair of check trousers, and a few handkerchiefs, collars, etc. But the rascally thief not content with taking my things has also made off with part of Lieut. Woolhouse's parcel, which you know was entrusted to my care. This annoys me more than anything, for no doubt they will think I have carelessly left it about. But such a thing you know I would not do, for I never even opened the No.4 box in which it, as well as all the other things were, except once or twice to get out or put in my money. I only hope and trust there was no money in it. One captain of the name of "Clark" in the 24th lost £75 company money at a slap through these wretches. An officer of the name of "Bomford" in the 29th lost a valuable "revolver" and one of the 32nd named "Stabb" lost an infinite number of clothes. The brutes are both caught through the ingenuity of a cabman whom they hired and offered the pistol for sale, and who (instead of taking them where they asked) drove straight to the police station. I have recovered none of my clothes, nor do I know where they are. It is a most determined robbery, for they actually broke open the box, which was locked, and screwed up.

It is no use my taking any steps against them (viz. my servant, Maybury's and Stabb's) since if I do, I shall most likely be prevented from going out to India, as an officer was a short time since, all for a pair of old boots which his servant stole. I have now only about £2 left, and yet I have been unusually careful, and have not spent a farthing but what was absolutely necessary: the carriage of my baggage is the great item which has caused the great hole in my purse. The two servants are committed to trial at the sessions as there is very weighty evidence against them. And the fact of their being so much proof against them is another reason why I need not appear for the prosecution, as there is quite enough to convict them as it is.

Wednesday Afternoon I have now told you all about this unfortunate business, and my budget of news is as full as ever. I will now tell you what has been going on here these last 2 or 3 days. The day before yesterday the P.B.'s, Sappers and Marines all went into the trenches, and batteries (of which the Sappers and Miners have made a great number) to go through the rehearsal for the field day when the Duke was coming to inspect. Your hopeful son in command of an escalading party.

We had a telegraphic message on Tuesday to say the Duke was on his way here so we all went to the trenches. Part of the siege operation was the explosion of 2 large mines and a powder magazine. After stopping in the trenches from 10 till 1 o'clock we began to feel tired, and obtained leave to quit our companies, and go to see the mines which were about 70 yards from us in a different trench. I went by myself and when I got to the mines, seeing no one there, I walked in, and on the ground I saw a lot of wires to fire it. Most providentially I did not touch any of them, for the slightest touch would have exploded them, and in a second I should have been hundreds of feet in the air. I did not know this, and what made me leave them alone I cannot tell. A Sapper came and said for goodness sake stand still and do not touch any of the wires. I did so and got out safely. I then walked back towards my own trench, but scarcely had I got 20 yards when I heard a muffled puff and on turning round I saw nothing but dense smoke; sandbags and stones flying about and men's cries. When the smoke cleared away I discovered that the mine had exploded by accident and a good many men missing.

The Sappers get their spades and dug out 11 poor fellows yards deep in the earth. Some remained underground 20 minutes, and how they were got out alive is a perfect mystery. Two had their legs, and one his back broken; ankles dislocated, contusions and bruises were the portion of all near it. If I had been 3/4 of a minute longer there, the chances are that I should have been buried with the rest. The Duke of Cambridge then came up, and superintended the operations of digging them out. The excitement was very great, and when any muskets and shako's were dug up they all redoubled their exertions. I saw 2 poor fellows dug out, one with broken legs and the other not much hurt. None were killed. It was caused by someone kicking the wires after I left. What a providential thing it was I did not do so!

The Engineer Officers are to blame for allowing people to go over the mine. The magazine which ought to have gone off 3 seconds after the mines fortunately did not explode; if it had, a whole company with 2 officers would have met an instant death, as they were drawn up on the roof of the magazine over 240 lbs of powder. After blazing away for 3 hours after the explosion, we came home damp and famishing. However, I feel no worse.

A large draft sails to-morrow in the "Earl of Balcarras" for Bombay consisting of the depots of the following Regts.: 86th, 74th, 78th, 83rd, and 87th and I and Kenny are talking of going to see them off. I made a mistake about our ship; it is the "Agincourt" and not the "Trafalgar" and sails on the 5th instead of the 1st.

I received an answer from Cane & Co saying that the balance due to me in their hands from 28th Feby. to 8th May is £1 14s. 11d. deducting £7. 17s. 6d for band and mess and something else for In. Tax. However I shan't put up with that, seeing I never joined the 57th.

I cannot go to Rifle drill without being sent, and the Instructor has "courses", i.e. so many months in every year in which he teaches, and no officer can be taught without he commences at the very first lecture; for it would be no use attending in the middle of a series of lectures, without being thoroughly acquainted with the groundwork contained in the 1st few lessons. I came in the middle and therefore cannot go till next series.

I amuse myself in the evenings casting bullets, and making cartridges for the rifles of Kenny and myself.

I was told to get some plain clothes for my servant and some shirts, socks, and cravats, gloves, etc. which with my drill shell jacket amounted to the sum of £4.19.6.which I had put by to pay him with. This is the money my servant took and I have only £2 and a few odd shillings left.

I have written so much that if I don't stop it will come to 1s. But love to all, and the same for yourself from your affectionate and loving boy,

Hugh, Pearce, Pearson.

P.S. Address for the future "Chatham" Barracks not Brompton. I have no stamps left.

Unnumbered Letter

Main Guard Room
Chatham Dock Yard
August 28th 1856

My own precious Mother,
I received Father's letter dated August 3rd this morning with one from you enclosed. I always have your letters open before me when I answer them, so that there must have been some I have not received. I have found the list of my clothes in my desk, as I told Chaper in the letter which described the robbery.
Please tell Emmie I will write to her either to-morrow or Saturday. My appetite is perfectly frightful. I generally eat 2 eggs for breakfast, and 4 for lunch–I wish I could get a box of sardines from Jersey. The ones here are like herrings and so strong I can't eat them. I shall finish this letter before I am relieved at 11 a.m. so I cannot tell you in this letter what I have lost; but I know there is 1 collar, 1 p. handk, 1 pr. socks, and 20 shirts, also that nice pair of hair brushes in the case. I have not opened the box since I first took a list of missing clothes, and as I was very excited at the time I may have overlooked some of the things, but I will carefully go over every thing again and let you know my loss. I remember Life of Hedley Vicars was there, and also some "Leisure Hours" but I don't remember seeing a letter.
I have just received a letter from Drage; he says he cannot effect an exchange into an Indian Regt., so he has volunteered for the Cape, where his Regt. now is, having left the Mauritius. The weather here at the time you wrote that letter I have just got was just as hot as at Jersey. My thermometer stood at 123 in the sun, and 87 in the shade. There is an extraordinary cat here without tail or ears; she is most beautifully marked, and is an enormous size. She knows a great many tricks which I will tell Emmie when I write. Her name is "Twiddles".
And now dearest mother I must conclude with best love and kisses to all,

from your affectionate boy,
H. P. Pearson

Unnumbered Letter

Off coast of Cornwall out of sight of land.
Ship "Agincourt"
Septbr. 12th 1856

My own dearest Mother,
I am now fairly on my voyage and the pilot goes in less than 2 hours. Dear Father saw me off at Gravesend, and has no doubt written to you about it. Thank God I have not yet been ill and only once a little squeamish. I have just made a most terrific breakfast and yet feel all right. We shall soon now be out of the channel, having the most favourable wind that we possibly could have, dead aft; and we are slipping along at 9 miles an hour. We shall if the wind lasts get out of the channel to-morrow. I find the motion of the ship not half so disagreeable as a steamer.
It is now 9hr. 25m. and I have just left off writing to look at a magnificent man of war, 120 guns, in full sail, close to us. She is a most splendid ship. There are plenty of ladies on board and we are all comfortable. The captain's lady is on board too: she always accompanies her husband, being a good sailor. There

are also lots of little children, and a black ayah and bearer with bangles in great style. We have been most specially favored by the wind which could not be more prosperous. We passed a large Dutch man this morning and saluted her. Dear father has gone to Bourton but leaves on Saturday. The ladies are unusually well, only 2 or 3 absent. I am beginning to feel sick from sitting in the cabin so I must leave off writing or I shall be ill. Give my very best love to all and to Chaper when you see him, and believe me to be, Dearest Mother,

Your affectionate boy,
H. P. Pearson

Unnumbered Letter

Ship Agincourt, Madras
Decbr. 28th 1856

My very dear Father and Mother,

I have very little time indeed to write to you as the mail steamer leaves in one hour's time. I am quite well and happy. We arrived here to-day at 1 o'clock. We have been very unfortunate in our winds and have sighted land for the last 3 days without being able to get in. We have only had one gale of wind, on the 18th ult when we were under double reefed topsails round the Cape. We sighted Madeira, the island of Tristan d' Acunha, which you will find to the S.W. of the Cape, and Nightingale Island close to it. I will write you a long letter when I go ashore, which will be to-morrow. I cannot say much for the military arrangements of the voyage, for Mr. Saunders has certainly not increased his reputation either as a good commanding officer, or as a gentleman.

I just write these few lines in order that you may not be anxious about me, but of course I am not able to give you any of the particulars of the voyage. Tell Emmy we caught 2 sharks on the way, and also some albatross. I have just been told that it is the best plan not to pay for the letters here or you there, but each pay for the other's letters. There are a great many catamarans and masuli boats about the ship. We have had 4 drowned and 2 born. Two committed suicide. We are to go to Poonamalee I believe and are to live under tents. I will write again on the first opportunity. Best love to all. The steamer is just going and I shall be too late.

Good bye from your affectionate son,
H. P. Pearson

Send me your direction again. I have forgotten it.

Letter No. 1

Turner's Bungalow, Poonamallee
12 miles from Madras
January 1st 1857

My own very dearest Father and Mother

When the "Agincourt" anchored in Madras Roads I had not time to write what I call a letter, but only a few lines just to let you know I am alive and well. I sent it via Marseilles for once in order that you might get it earlier, and if for the future

I have anything <u>very particular</u> to say, I shall send it by that way and I hope you will do so too. Upon receiving your anxiously looked for letter (which I did just as they signalled to disembark troops immediately), I wrapped up my journal and gave it to Mr. de Carteret, who kindly undertook to deliver it. As you will see when you get it, I could not get time to finish it, but I will tell you as well as I remember what happened after.

After knocking about against adverse winds for several days we at last anchored in the roads on the 28th December. We let go our anchor at 1 hr 15 mins p.m. and stayed on board until next day at 1 o'clock p.m. when we were signalled from the Fort to land. Having dressed myself in uniform, I sat down to peruse your precious treasure of a letter, but was summoned away in the middle of it. I with some of our officers got into what they call a "masuli boat" manned by about 18 natives, and were on shore safely past the dangerous surf in 20 minutes. We then fell in and marched to the railway and went in the train 7 miles to "Avidy" and from there we marched 4 miles to Poonamallee. We reported ourselves on arrival (at 6.30 p.m.) to Colonel Impett, in command here, who treated us very kindly. He is an old Waterloo veteran and one of the nicest men I ever met. We washed our hands at his house and then went to the mess. There are only two officers here besides the Colonel, viz. Kennan and Hardy, both 84th.

We sat down to dinner very "peckish" and as for myself I can safely say I fully accounted for the whole of a mutton currie! I have often heard you speak of Indian luxury, but I could not have conceived it was as it really is. My servant Malipar waited exclusively upon me, and instinctively brought me the identical things I wanted. Oh! that heavenly currie. But I could not describe the almost intoxicating delight I was in with my plate of rice like driven snow and currie that an epicure in England would give his ears for. It was certainly beyond description, and after the vile stuff on board the "Agincourt" was all the more delicious. After the currie we had some snipe.

Livesay, Hart, Humphrey, Bateman and myself have taken a bungalow at 15 rupees each per month: it is a capital place and each has a separate airy room. I have put everything in good order and made an extremely comfortable place of it. I do not think much of the Indian fruit, at least judging by what I have tasted already, which are the plaintain and the pommello. I believe the mango is the best fruit. In the morning at 5 a.m. I had my bath and had 3 chatties of water over me. I have 3 servants: a head servant, "Malipar", then another for waiting at mess and a water-boy to fill my bath and pour chatties over me. I had my first bath the morning after I arrived. The water (kept in chatties all night) was deliciously cool and completely took away my breath. I had 3 poured over me and then got out. I have sent all my dirty clothes to the Colonel's "dobie", who has got an excellent character. I only dirtied 25 shirts but all my collars.

I go out with my gun or rifle every day. I went out and shot a bird exactly like a snipe but I found out it was only a sandpiper. I killed a squirrel with my rifle. He was clinging to a cocoa-nut tree 1 foot in diameter. I was about 40 yards off. I fired and the ball went clean through the tree taking his tail along with it. I have also shot a good many kites, parroquets and squirrels. I made a beautiful shot at a cocoa-nut to-day. I wanted some milk, and as there was no one to get me a nut I fired at the stalk of one and it came rattling down. I made a hole with my hunting knife, and enjoyed the milk exceedingly. I am sorry to say this is one of the worst places for shooting, but it is infinitely better than I ever had, and what many in England would be only too glad to get. I will prove that to you soon. I and Livesay got up at 4.30 a.m. and having engaged a "shekarri" or huntsman to show us the game, we put our guns over our shoulders and set out. We went at farthest a mile from our bungalow into some paddy fields and put up 30 couple of snipe and lots of wild duck. We returned at 8 a.m. not having shot anything but a few kites. This proves there must be game although we did not get any.

On Friday (2nd) I and Hart took 2 palanquins and went to Madras to make some purchases. On the way I saw a good many wild duck and also a heron. So I sent a coolie for my gun and told him to take it to "Avady" where I saw the game and to wait there till my return from Madras. I went to Madras, and went on board the "Agincourt" to see my chums there. I then went to the Clarendon and had some lunch. At 30 minutes past 3 we started from Madras in the train to Avadi 8 miles off and arrived at 4.15 when I found my servant waiting with my gun. I saw a heron in the tauk but it was too hot to go and shoot him and I could not wait till sundown for fear of being late at mess, so I just loaded and got into my palanquin. The sun soon set, and as the bearers stopped to rest I sauntered into a small clump of bushes about 50 yards square, the palkee bearers acting as beaters. I had not taken 6 steps when up got two splendid snipe. I fired and missed. Went on a bit and another rose. Fired, and knocked my first snipe over. Flushed several more out of shot, and put up a hare but did not get a shot at it. I thought it was no use taking one snipe home, so I went into a place exactly like the first. I only saw one there however. I fired and he fell. I saw him on the ground with his leg broken and went to pick him up. To my astonishment he rose and flew off. I up with my gun and let drive at 60 yards and dropped him as dead as a whistle. They were both capital shots. I only fired 4 shots, and considering it was the first time I ever fired at snipe in my life, it was not so bad. I sent them with my complements to Mrs Hely.

I have had a shocking bad account of Rangoon from those who have just come from it. You are always obliged to sleep with a revolver and dagger by you, for the Burmese are both murderers and robbers. They come boldly in at night and first put a sentry over you with a drawn sword, while they rob you of every mortal thing. This man stands by your bed with uplifted knife and if you do not wake it is all right, but if you happen to shew any symptoms of waking, down comes the knife, and you are a dead man in a moment. An officer of ours named "Madigan" was recently murdered in this manner. The only plan is to keep a lot of dogs in your room. That is what I shall do. My servant keeps all my guns etc. in capital order and is a very good man. I pay him 8 rupees a month. I have just got a silk white hat for 2 rupees, and 12 prs. white trousers for 18 Rs. the lot. I am on duty to-day Saturday (3rd) and must leave off for the present. I like India very much, at least what little I have seen of it. I also hear from our officers there that an ensign cannot live on his pay in Burmah, and that it is hard work for a lieutenant to do so. It is also an extremely unhealthy country, so much so that out of our regiment there are only 250 effective men, and the day before we arrived, a detachment of our invalids 100 strong marched in here en route for Europe. Our two officers named Kennan and Hardy are going to Europe next month on 2 years' leave, the former in charge of invalids.

I am going to draw different views about here. There are some very pretty views indeed. It is nothing near as hot as I expected, not so much as on board ship. I am very little troubled with mosquitos and only have about a dozen bites every night. I sleep without curtains. As you will see on Mr. De Carteret's arrival, I did keep a journal and diligently every day I put down what was worth noticing. I am as you say a very long distance from you, but that circumstance (if such a thing is possible) increases my love and affection for all of your dear selves, and what keeps my spirits up is the anxious looking forward to the time when we shall meet again. Every one in the "Agincourt" said often that I could not do without smoking in India, and that before I had been a month there

I should begin, however to this moment I feel just as little inclination as ever. They told Kenny the same and the poor fool suffered himself to be persuaded into it, and had an idea that he was a man when he smoked. On Monday morning next I intend going for some more snipe. I wish I could give you a couple. I read in the papers the other day that a Major and Mrs Pearson with a female servant had gone to Malta. Hart's regiment 29th is under orders for Persia.

To-day I was going round the men's dinners and I saw a man carrying a dish of meat across the compound, when a Brahminee kite pounced down and carried off about a lb. of it. I am now going to sketch a Hindoo's tomb near here.

Sunday 4th. Went to church at 11 a.m. and had a very nice sermon from the clergyman. There was a nice ball at the Governor's Lord Harris on Thursday last and we were invited to go but no one out of our bungalow went as we did not care about it. A mosquito got up my leg to-day, and when I looked I counted 65 bites below the knee. Tomorrow I and Hart are going out for snipe; we have 2 dozen marked down for us. We have no parades or drill here, only orderly officer once a week. I have just powdered all my bites, and it cools them very much. Colonel Impett an old Waterloo veteran commands here; he is an extremely nice old fellow, and we all like him very much. I am getting quite as cunning as those rascally natives, and they have not cheated me yet. Kenny is on leave with his uncle at Palavarum, but as no official notice was sent he will lose his pay for the month. How disgusted he will be at hearing it.

5th. I went out shooting this morning to some groves about a mile from here. I started at daybreak, and arrived there just as it was light enough to begin. I heard a partridge crowing and kicked him out of a bush. I pulled the trigger but the cap was wet and hung fire, however I shot the mate, an old cock, just after. I fired when he was too near, for it carried his leg clean away. I afterwards shot a couple of snipe, and should have shot more but the caps got damp with the dew and would not explode.

Whilst walking I ran a thorn into the muscle of my foot, which gave me great pain. I put a poultice on and I hope it will cure it. We are going to get up a cricket match between the 43rd. and 84th. officers and men. I have put my name down to play. I saw a hare this morning but could not get a shot at it. I am about to mention a thing whilst I remember it. Do you know anything of that beautiful "Shakespeare" of mine? I have my "Scott" and "Milton" but no "Shakespeare".

Bateman is being taught Hindoostannee by a native Moonshee, but he pays 10 rupees an hour for it, viz. £1!!!!

I have been a good deal bitten by mosquitos, but if you do not scratch the bites they will not be felt after a minute or so. I have good fun shooting at kites out of my window with my rifle. I saw one just now but he flew before I could get an aim at him. I hear them firing a volley over a soldier of ours who died last night–2 died within 12 minutes of each other. The Heathens held their feast to their god, named Ram-Sammee, this morning while I was out shooting. I saw them carrying the idol in a large frame on men's shoulders, and beating tom-toms and firing guns in quick succession. They passed close to a grove I was shooting in and frightened all the birds.

I have just had a pair of pyjamas made for 4 annas. The colonel say he thinks we shall go to Rangoon in about a week or 10 days, but still you had better direct to Poonamallee, and when we go I will write and tell you.

I was talking to Colonel Impett at mess last night and I found he knew Uncle Key well, also Uncle Pearson, and Stewart Northey! I am going to send my letter of introduction to W. Cochrane Esq., as soon as possible.

And now my own dearly beloved father, may God protect and bless you and dear mother, and also those dear ones with you, and may he grant that we may all live to meet again and spend many happy years here below, that I may have an opportunity of trying to repay in a slight degree your kindness which has been great and unvaried to me ever since I was born. God bless you all, dearest creatures, and that he may take us all to him when we leave this world is the earnest prayer

of your most affectionate and loving son,
H. P. Pearson

Unnumbered Letter

Turner's Bungalow, Poonamallee
January 9th 1856

My own dear little Emmy,

I received your nice little letter enclosed in Papa's and was much delighted to find you had not forgotten me. I shot a little squirrel the other day, and I have got the skin dried ready for you, not a red skin, but a pretty grey one with yellow and black stripes. You may depend upon it I shall not forget "Juzzif": I often think of him now. Tell that to dear Papa as I had no room in my note to him. On Tuesday last Colonel Impett took me to a place called "Tripassore" 30 miles away, shooting. We went out on Wednesday morning and also in the evening, and bagged 4 couple of snipe, of which 1½ couple fell to my share. We returned on Thursday morning. We slept the 2 nights we were there in a public bungalow built by government for the accommodation of travellers, as there are no hotels yet. In a village called Trivallore (on our way home) I saw a great number of monkeys on the roofs of the houses. I threw a line at one of them and the people were very angry for they hold those animals sacred. I enjoyed myself very much indeed and Colonel Impett was exceedingly kind to me all this time.

I went out shooting yesterday morning to a place about 6 miles from here, and started at 3.30 a.m. so as to arrive there by daylight. We shot till breakfast time, and shot 4 couple of snipe, and a mongoose, which, with 3½ couple of snipe I shot – Livesay shooting the other bird. I have a bath every morning of course. A man has just come to my bungalow to tell me I must post my letters before 4 o'clock or they will be too late for the steamer; it is now past 2 and I am on duty, so I must wish you good bye. Give very best love to dearest Tuty and accept the same,

Dearest Emmy,
from your affectionate brother,
H. P. Pearson

P.S. I will sit down to write you a regular long one after this is gone.

Letter No.2

Turner's Bungalow, Poonamallee
January 15th 1857

My own very dearest Father and Mother,

I am greatly afraid I shall not be able to fill up this sheet like I did the last, for, living in such a remote and out-of-the-way place as Poonamallee there is nothing important happens from one month's end to the other. We have just received an order from the Adjutant General to hold ourselves in readiness to embark for Burmah on the shortest notice, so that when this reaches you, we shall in all probability be settled in Rangoon.

I have received but one letter from you, dated 19 Oct. which I got on board ship, but the last mail which came in brought me none. Now I am quite convinced that you will write by every mail, and I therefore imagine that the last letter has gone across to Rangoon.

I have had lots of shooting here, my best morning's work being 7 couple of snipe, and a partridge. I start on my shooting excursions at 3 in the morning so as to arrive at the ground by daylight. I then shoot till the sun begins to get hot, and then walk home under an umbrella. I have had one of the "Agincourt's" midshipmen to spend a few days with me. I frequently mention him in my journal. His name is Brett, brother of the W.E.M fellow. He is a magnificent chap, and was, always a chum of mine. The "Agincourt" sailed for Rangoon on the 16th inst with sepoys on board. Mrs Crawford has gone overland to England. I am afraid you will have to wait sometime for my journal, for it has taken a trip to Rangoon in the "A" with De Carteret.

I find the Brahmninee Kites annoy me greatly out shooting. They go with you, and when you shoot a bird they pounce down and walk off with it. The other day I was out and had a snipe carried off by one; I followed him and knocked him over. I recovered the snipe, but it was much torn. The detachment of the 43rd which came over with us marched to Bangalore this morning. It is a 16 days march. The 12th Lancers are coming here in a day or two from Trichinopoly. My dear little gun is admired by every one here; and many is the wonderfully long shot I have made with it. I am really quite astonished at the good shooting I have made. Just fancy, I never saw a snipe fly before I came here and yet before I am here 3 weeks, I bag 7 couple before breakfast. I shot a quail, but it was just like a very young partridge.

I bought a "Pariar" dog the other day for 2 rupees: he keeps people away from the house very well. In the evenings I go and play rackets and fives and then go to mess at 7. I shot a mongoose the other day, and I have saved the skin for Miss P. The Indian fruit is in my opinion the most rotten stuff that I ever tasted, and there is not a single description of fruit to compare with the worst English fruit. I have shot about 32½ couple of snipe, a brace of partridges, and a quail since I came here, and I am now going out with our Colonel to try my luck again. The Colonel has been very kind to me indeed, and has taken me shooting several times. He once took me to a place called "Tripassore" with him, but we were unfortunately taken to bad ground, and did not get anything but 5 or 6 couple.

Janry.29th. I have just come back from Tripassore where I have been for 3 days with Hart. I shot during my stay 26½ couple of snipe, 1 quail, and a "Florican" (a bird very rare, and greatly sought after in this country). They are as lazy as a hen, with a long neck, and of a delicious game flavour, frequently fetching as much as 25 rupees each. I was extremely fortunate in coming across one, and presented him to the mess. I am afraid I shall be late for this mail, and must wish you good bye with best love to all,

Your affectionate boy,
H.P. Pearson

Letter No. 2A

Queen's Depot, Poonamallee
February 12th 1857

My own dearest Father,

You see I am scrupulously careful not to miss a single sail without writing; but I am nevertheless in much anxiety till I receive all your letters beginning with No.2 up to the present date: however, the Fates have decreed that I must wait till I get to Burmah to receive my long expected letters, and so wait I must. I hope, dearest Father, that when this reaches you it will find you all in good health, for that is the chief consideration. I am very well indeed and as happy as I can be separated from those who are dearest to me. However, I hope soon to return, and oh what a happy day it will be when we meet again!!

We have nothing to do here except orderly duty once a week, and I occupy my mornings and evenings in my favourite pursuit–"shooting". I have been calculating what has fallen to my gun since my arrival, and as I know it will interest you I will enumerate the slain: 1st. 74½ couple of snipe–2½ brace of quail–1 brace of partridges–1 couple of wild ducks–and lastly (thought worth more than all the rest put together) 1 brace of "Florrican"!!! Yes, dear Chaper, your own boy Hughey with that splendid gun you gave him actually slew ? Florrican before 2 months of Indian life is over his head. But in case you do not know what a Florrican is, I will tell you. It is a bird larger than an English hen pheasant, and something like that bird with its tail cut off. You expect to meet with it about as often as you would a red-deer or hippopotamus in Jersey, and everybody says "What a lucky fellow that is to get them!!". Hardy, one of ours who has been 11 years in India, and the Sportsman of the Regt, never had the luck to come across one yet. I do not think I have done badly considering I never saw a snipe fly before I arrived here.

I have bought a pellet bow for 3 annas and can shoot pretty tolerably with it. It is like a common bow with 2 strings, and shoots small clay pellets with great force. I hear we are to sail on Saturday next, 14th inst., but I do not think it is at all likely. How is dear Emmy getting on with her music and lessons? Please tell her I will write a nice letter to her by next mail, and should do this mail but have only just time for this. I hope dear Mamma, Aunty and Emmy are well and also your dear self. Please tell Emmy to send my love to Aunty Micklethwaite, and all cousins when she writes next. I went to Madras the other day and went into some of the 12th Lancers tents; they are all jolly fellows, and one of them named Captain Harford knows Uncle Key very well indeed.

Have you got my Shakespeare all right? Our monthly pay as Ensign, including Company's allowances, tentage etc. amounts to 182 rups. 13 annas, about £18 4. 11. or perhaps a little more. The climate agrees very well with me and I take plenty of exercise. I found my notes very difficult to change and at last got rid of one to Kennan of ours who is going home in the "Gloriana" in charge of invalids.

I hear there is magnificent shooting at and near "Rangoon", but it is dangerous to penetrate into the interior except in bodies of 5 or 6, for the Burmans are so treacherous that they will murder one for the sake of his gun. Bison and deer (both red and spotted) abound in great quantities (I should say "numbers") and one often meets tigers and elephants. Kenny is still on leave at his uncle's. I am thinking of going shooting soon to "Poody hitterum" 8 miles off. There are partridges in abundance there. I shall be late, I am afraid, if I do not bring this to an end. Give my very best love to dearest mother, aunty and sister, and accept the same my own dear Chaper,

from your most affectionate boy,
Hughey

P.S. I am sorry I cannot answer your questions (which doubtless you have put to me) because I have only had one of your letters. Bye, bye. Love to "Joevelly"!
P.P.S. I have just re-opened this to tell you that we have received the order to sail in the "Salamanca" for Rangoon on the 16th. inst

Letter No.3

Doctor Le Presle's Bungalow
Rangoon
March 6th 1857

My own dear Chaper,

The ship "Salamanca" arrived with our detachment on board at Rangoon on my birthday, and we landed that same afternoon. I got your letter No.2 yesterday, also 2 official letters (1 of them from the Horse Guards granting my claim for exemption from the Income duty on my pay, and the other from the Commander in Chief's office relieving me from the payment of Mess and Band subscriptions while in the 57th Foot; stating also that the necessary instructions have been issued to the Regimental Agents. (The first letter is dated 10th Septbr., the other 11th Septbr.)

And first dear Chaper let me congratulate you heartily upon the legacy you have been bequeathed, and express my regret that the old lady did not take it into her head to leave 10 times the amount. However, it is better than nothing.

I am living in a bungalow belonging to Doctor La Presle and Woolhouse for a few days till I can get a mat house built. I enclose this in a letter I wrote to Miss P. on board ship and which of course I could not send till I got here. I have written several letters to you, directed "Rouge Bouillion".

In Emmie's letter I told her my pay was 182r.1a.11p. but I find as this is a full battah station we get 202r.3a. 10p. or more than £20 per month. I find I can get a "tat" or pony for 30 to 50 rupees but a Pegu pony will cost 80 to 250, so I intend to get one for about 40 rupees (£4).

I have got a letter from the Agents of 57th Regt. stating that "they have to account to the Public for the stamp on commission in the 57th Regt, and that it must be for my commission in the 84th that Messrs. Cox & Co. have charged me a similar sum". The letter goes on to say that "they will be most happy to place to my credit at Cox's the amount they have deducted for my Band and Mess Subscriptions (not only on appointment but the annual) and Income duty, as soon as they receive the authority from Horse Guards," which of course they have already had as their letter is dated 9th Septr.

Oh! Chaper, there is most magnificent shooting here of all sorts. About a mile from here there is elk, deer, and spotted deer, also teal, widgeon, snipe, jungle fowl, and pea-fowl, and about 4 miles in the jungle there is tiger, elephant, pig, cheetar, pannther, and bear. There is any quantity of deer and wild fowl. As soon as I am dismissed drill I am going up country for a fortnight with Penton, a capital fellow, and the most beautiful shot in Burmah. He has taken a liking for me, and I for him. He has offered to take me under his protection up country, and this "he can easily do, being both old enough and experienced. He is extremely cool in danger which is a great thing out tiger shooting. I forgot to mention buffaloes in my list of game near here. It is a great saving of money to get leave, for when up country you spend little or nothing. From my window I can see dense jungle extending much farther than the eye can reach, and plenty of game there.

The fellows of our Regt. are not such nice fellows as I expected, and I am disappointed much in "Woolhouse". However, there is Penton and La Presle who are capital fellows, and so is Hardy, but he has gone home. As usual 5/6ths of them are Irish.

I have been this morning to see the wonderful Pagoda here; it is a truly magnificent place. It is 400 feet high, and covered with gilt from top to bottom. I will describe it another time. I have nothing to pay for your letters; the stamp carries them through. I am going to collect curiosities of which there are a great many here.

Thank you dear Chaper for your kind advice, and rest assured I will follow it. Now dearest Chaper good bye: give my very best love to Macher, Taty, and Emmie, and dearest Father, that God will bless you and those dear ones at home will ever be the prayer of

Your grateful and affectionate boy,
Hugh P. Pearson

Letter No.4

Rangoon
March 8th 1857

My very dear Emmie,

I sent a letter to you by the mail steamer "Oriental" yesterday, which I began on board the ship "Salamanca", and as I had not sufficient room in it to answer your questions I determined to sit down and write you a good long one. I shall answer all your questions most scrupulously, and very glad I am to have the opportunity of doing so. I should very much like to have seen your pretty birthday presents; I hope you wore your nice bracelets on my birthday. How fortunate we are to have such good and kind parents and Taty. I hope you behave well to Taty, for she has been very very kind to us both ever since we can recollect. Many little boys and girls as you well know have neither papa, mamma or aunty to teach and take care of them, and as we are blessed with them, it is our duty to shew our gratefulness to God by behaving well to them always. You, dearest little one, do not yet know (as I do) what invaluable friends you have in them, but, when you (as you some day will be) are separated from Ihem for a time, then you will know what an enormous share of your happiness is gone till you are again restored to them. Some people, I believe, say that from long separation children are liable to forget their best friends, but what monsters they must be; were I to live 5000 years, I should never for one moment forget, or would my love be lessened for, that dear Papa, Mamma, and Aunty that God has given us. Now my dear Emmie I will answer your questions first, and then fill up these sheets by questions for you to answer, and a description of every thing I think will please you.

Firstly, there is a small volley of questions in the middle of your letter that I will now answer in the order you put them. Answers–I have no kidmutgar or bearer, these servants being peculiar to the Bengal Presidency, but I have an excellent "butler" and "mehtee-boy", and when my pony comes I shall get a "horse-keeper". I do not find the heat oppressive yet, although we have had it 114° Fahrenheit, but all the other officers do. This inclines me to believe the country will agree with me, and the fact of my being the only one of my brother officers who has not been ill confirms it. The heat of the sun where a person exposes himself is of course more or less injurious, particularly on the line, where the rays of the sun descend upon the top of the head. I have not heard a word about my ayah, and indeed have not asked because, if she is not dead, she is (or at least her presidency is) as distinct, and has as little to do with Madras as China has. I have taken one or two sketches, but none at Rangoon yet, nor shall I be able till I am dismissed drill, for the morning and evening are taken up with drill and if I would entertain any hopes of seeing you again, I must not go out in the middle of the day. I have seen frogs as large as squirrels, but none so large as those you speak of: they make a dreadful noise all night long. I have never yet ridden on an elephant, and in all probability never will, for elephants are not used in that quantity here that they are in Bengal and it is only occasionally that you see them. I saw one this morning (8th), this making only the third since my landing in India. There are plenty of wild ones within 2 miles of this.

I saw plenty of splendid men-of-war and other ships of all sizes on my voyage out, but these you will see I have taken notice of in my journal which I sent home by Mr De Carteret. Our voyage was not a very quick or particularly pleasant one, for, unfortunately, the passengers were not the most agreeable people in the world, and there was no getting away from their society. We were 110 days inclusive of the days we sailed and arrived. We only had one mild gale of wind and no severe squalls. We did not touch at the Cape of Good Hope although we went within 250 miles of it, driven by contrary winds. We sighted the islands of "Madeira" and "Tristan d' Acunha" or "Tristan da Cunha" on our way to Madras, and the island of "Preparis", inhabited by cannibals, from Madras to Rangoon.

I have seen plenty of monkeys, and there is one in the house I now live in exactly like Jacko. There are thousands upon thousands of monkeys and alligators in the Irrawaddy up to Rangoon. I am shortly going to get a monkey: I have not seen any baboons or ourang-outangs–I am going to build a mat-house and live with Kenny in it, and when I am settled I shall get 5 or 6 dogs, a monkey, 1 or 2 cats, and a pony.

I like Burmah better than India, for many reasons; the nights are now so cold that I have a blanket on and in the afternoon there is a delicious sea breeze. The Burmese manufacture an enormous quantity of curiosities of all sorts, and when I can afford it I shall get some. There are an immense number of pagodas about here, and, lately, most of them have been destroyed by order of Government. An officer of ours named "Sandwith" was superintending the destruction of a pagoda, and he found upwards of 3 lacs of rupees under it. This amounts in English money to £30,000. There were magnificent golden-bowls, and enormous pagodas made of solid gold 10 feet high, but the most beautiful and costly thing was a whole suit of chain armour made of gold, and covered thickly with the largest rubys [sic] and diamonds ever found here. The cost was estimated to be about 2 lacs of rupees or £20,000. If he had only reported the finding of treasure he might have had a large share, but unfortunately he gave it to Government and now he bitterly regrets it. Frequently little gold and silver "Samees" or idols are dug up in the gardens. The Burmese do not use knives but only a weapon called a "dar": with this they cut down trees, split the finest peas, eat their food, fight their enemies, and in short do everything with it. Every Burman carries one with him wherever he goes.

I am glad to hear "Juzzif" is well; dear "Joevelly" give him plenty of kisses from me, and tell him how much I should like to see him. If he were here he should have a little monkey servant to attend him and catch "flebeas". Every one who keeps dogs keeps a monkey for this purpose, and they all submit to be pulled about with great docility. The houses here are invariably built on piles and raised 5 or 6 feet from the ground, for when monsoon sets in there is sometimes 3 feet of water. Some of the houses are built of mat, and all are thatched with leaves. I found my couch a great luxury indeed, and always sleep on it. There are scarcely any mosquitoes here now, but in 2 months time when the monsoon sets in, no one can sit outside the door without a rug wrapped round his legs, a great coat on, and his hands in his pockets. When at mess they sting through your chair, and also through the thickest pair of boots. I saw hundreds of whales coming out, and several sharks, and on the voyage from Madras here we saw a great many "melaugers" or "sea-serpants", and a great deal of floating seaweed.

Friday March 12th. The mail which arrived here the beginning of this week brought me No.3 of your letters: it then proceeded to "Moulmein", and on Sunday, it returns here from that place, carrying with it my letter to you, so I must get it finished.

First, I must tell you that I have bought a bay pony with black points, remarkably handsome, and one which belonged to a Mr Penton of ours. I gave 90 rupees for it and am very much pleased with it. I rode him out the other day, accompanied by Kenny on his pony; we went into the jungle and saw five elephants, and a herd of buffaloes from which last we ran as hard as we could go as they are very dangerous, and almost invariably run at Europeans. I began my drill 3 days ago, and now am in firelock-drill. We shall soon be dismissed, for they are anxious to get it over before the 15th of May, on which day the monsoon sets in. Last Thursday we all went to see the Madras Artillery reviewed by General Bell; all went off well: the 84th is going to be reviewed on the 16th inst. I left Doctor Le Presle's house yesterday (12th) and am now living with Blake, paying 20 rupees per month.

11 0' clock. I must now conclude suddenly as the order for our embarkation for Calcutta has just arrived. We are to go on board the "Bentinck" this afternoon at 5 o'clock, and proceed immediately to Calcutta and from thence to Barrackpore. The reason is that the Bengal Native troops have all mutinied, and are in a state of insurrection, and we are now going up to quell them.

I remain in haste, dear Emmie,
Your dearest brodie,
H.P. Pearson

P.S. Best love to all. It will, I think, be best to direct your letters as usual, for when the 84th have quelled the insurrection at Barrackpore, they will in all probability return. Do not be alarmed if you do not hear for some time.

Letter No.5 missing

Letter No.6 (7)

In the Camp, Barrackpore
April 20th 1857

My dearest Emily,

In my last letter home I said that I would write to you next, and just now the thought entered my head that I must write to-day or I should be late for the mail leaving Calcutta on the 22nd. Father told me always to number all my letters that I send home but unfortunately I forget the number of the last I sent and shall therefore call this No.6. The mail is not yet in, so I shall not send this off till I hear by it. The last letter I had from you is No.4 dated Jan. 11th and I could not make out why I had not heard by the last mail.

We are now in Barrackpore for the third time and arrived here last Friday. We have come to see a native officer [Isre Pande] shot, or hanged, and to disband the 34th N.I. which are in a mutinous state. You must excuse this bad writing as I am sitting on my bed with my pillow for a table and of course can neither write straight or well. I went last Saturday to see the condemned man; he is in a tent and beside him stand 4 loaded sentries with fixed bayonets, always looking at him, and having orders to shoot him if he escapes. The other night he did try to get away but was immediately bayonetted in the shoulder. His crime is for ordering the guard under his command not to assist the adjutant and serjt. major of the 34th when they were shot by the sepoy [Mangal Pandy] whom we hung not long ago. He is a magnificently well-made man, about 6 feet 1 inch in height, and a fine broad chest, also very handsome. I think he will be executed to-morrow.

Yesterday I took a walk in the Governor General's Park to see his collection of wild animals. I saw 2 bears (one of which was mad and spit at every body that came near him), a giraffe, a tiger, a cheetah, a black leopard, a tortoise, 5 or 6 ostriches, a porcupine, an emu, 2 monkeys, and plenty of birds. I went to look at the place where all the elephants in Barrackpore are kept. There were about 82 when I went, from the size of a dog to an enormous large beast you had to look up in the air at. One of them made salaam to me when the mahout told him; he knelt down, raised his trunk in the air, and trumpeted to me. One of the officers in the 53rd has a dog named "Buckkas" which sings in accompaniment to his master . . . a very curious fellow but not half the sense that dear Joevelly gehoume has, or even that Juzzif frebbend has, a little man!! One day at Chinsurah I got a venomous snake, and put in a bottle for you. The sepoys here are all very mutinous, and we have always the artillery loaded where a sudden rush could be made. I will now answer your questions, and then I will leave a space for telling you anything you may wish to know in the letter I am now expecting.

Tuesday 21st April. Ah! here are the long expected and therefore doubly welcome letters from you. I knew you would not disappoint me for a disappointment in not hearing from you is, I am sure, equal to that which you would feel if I missed writing. I at first intended only writing this sheet full to you, but now that I have had two such nice letters from you the least I can do is to endeavour to repay you by writing 3 or 4 sheets to different members of our happy little family. I received No.6 (the birthday letter) before No.5. The drum-major put No.6 into my hand just as I was taking a walk to the Governor General's Park, and when I got it I was on thorns till I could separate myself from my comrades and retire by myself under some shady tree in that lovely park to devour, as it were, each individual word and syllable of that most precious letter which is dearer to me than all the wealth of India. And not till I had read it 5 or 6 times over did I rejoin them all. Your dear letters are of priceless worth to me, but this one more than all, for in it each word written by each dear one is kindness and love, and anxiety for my health and welfare. And another delightful thought was that No.5 was yet to come. As I was reading the letter in the park I saw one of our officers named Hely thrown from a Pegu pony of our adjutant's, but fortunately he was unhurt.

I dined at the mess of the 70th N.I last night, and in the middle of dinner a most tremendous storm came on, and for 2 hours the rain poured in torrents unceasingly: I went after dinner to the camp which was one unbroken sheet of water in some places (for instance in my tent) a foot deep. I immediately sent all my things to a bungalow occupied by Colonel Reed and 2 of our Captains, where I spent a comfortable night. This morning I came down to my tent and struck it, and pitched it on a higher spot of ground. It was while I was busy pulling my tent down that I received No.5, which I have just read. There is a parade ordered for 5.30 this evening to see the execution of the unfortunate criminal. To-morrow we are going, I hear, to Dinapore, but whether true or not, I do not know.

We have just received the intelligence of the destruction of Rangoon by fire. I bought the other day at Chinsurah 2 large volumes of the "Illustrated London News" for 1849. It contains all the history of Her Majesty's visit to Ireland, the Sikh war, the great murders of Rush and the Mannings, and many other interesting things. I am keeping them for you. Tell dearest Macher that I always sleep with mosquito curtains now, I should have been eaten up before this if I had not. My bed in camp consists of my railway rug to lie upon, the shawl Aunty gave me to cover me, and my cloak for a pillow.

There is to be a ball here to-night for all who wish to attend, but of course I shall not go. Not long ago I went into Calcutta to get some clothes and boots, and when in the train I was invited to breakfast at Fort William by three officers of the 53rd who were in the carriage with me: I accepted it, and stayed with them the best part of the day; they were very kind to me. I saw Government House and the adjutants on the maidaun in front of it. When I saw the extensive maidaun, it reminded me of the great display of fireworks that Chaper once told me of, which began by the simultaneous ignition of so many blue lights, the smoke of which prevented any thing more being seen.

The other day I wrote to Cousin Jane at Bourton, and also to my friend Drage telling him to write and let Chaper know when he heard from me. What do you think Emmie? I found out that my servant (not Malliapah) was once servant to "Stewart Northey". I asked him how he liked him. He said "I no like him, sahib, he too much plenty bobbery make". I think Macher will laugh when she sees how admirably his character was portrayed by the few words of his former servant. I am sorry to say that the description of Burmah that I heard at Poonamallee and wrote to you is true, at least as regards the savage natives of its inhabitants; they did kill an officer of ours named "Madigan" for the sake of money. I will just put down the usual monthly expenses for Father to see.

Mess bill	about	70Rs	Food being expensive	
Wine bill		10		
Servants' wages		15		
Syce		10		
Grass cut		3		Rs
Keep of pony		15	Pay per month	202
Share of rent		20	Expenditure	158
Pauckallies		5		44
Dobie		5	Balance 44Rs.=£4.8.0	
Sundries, mending etc		5		
		158		

The chief cause of expense is food, which is always dear. My mess bill was as you see, Maybury's 3 rupees less, Kenny's about the same, and all the rest much more. The lowest share of house rent is 15 Rs. and where I was living it was 20 Rs. this is a correct account of the scale of living in Burmah, which is a dreadfully expensive place.

Tell Chaper always to direct his letters as he has done—it is the safest way. I shall be very delighted to hear you play your tunes. I am remarkably fond of the "Last Rose of Summer"; it is a sweet tune. I like the others too. I am glad to hear the good account dear Chaper gives of you. I knew you would apply yourself to your studies, and when you think how much dear Papa, Mamma and Aunty spend upon your education, it proves that it is a duty you owe to them as well as to yourself to improve and take pains with your lessons. I have a few Indian sketches but not many for we have travelled so constantly and had so much to do that there is scarcely any time even to write. If I had been in Jersey I should have taken you to see the launch of the "Chieftain". Remember me to Mr Le Nouray when you take your next lesson from him and tell him how much I should like to see him again.

I should very much like to see "Jiny". An officer of the 53rd has a creature about as large as a rat which he names Tiny. How does dear Papa like his walks in the country? How I should like to be with him. I would have helped him and Juzzif against the big dog. I have not yet, dear Emmie, had any adventures to amuse you with but when I get back to Burmah I shall most probably have plenty. I never before heard about the great comet, but it is very unlikely. The cockroaches were certainly awful; few ships were as bad, because, the voyage before, the "Agincourt" was laden with sugar and molasses which you know soon collect them.

Ah! missie, I hear the warning bugle for the execution parade, and I must get dressed. I must also close this letter for to-morrow (22nd) is the last day we can post letters. This letter is not as long as I wished but it will not do to be late. Bless you all, dear ones. Give my best love and many kisses to Chaper, Macher, and Taty, and accept the same dear Emmie,

from your loving affectionate brother,
H.P. Pearson

Love to gehoume gehoume and his frebbends.

Letter No.8

Chinsurah, near Calcutta
April 28th 1857

My own dearest Father and Mother,

I have since the last letter I sent discovered that I ought to have numbered it 7 instead of 6, so now you will have 2 number 6s and no 7. I wrote my last to Emily, and when we left Barrackpore I found out that I was a day late for the mail, and ordered my servant to lock the letter up, but the stupid fellow I am afraid sent it off without being sealed, as I have no recollection of sealing it myself.

We are going again to Barrackpore for the 4th time to disband the 34th Bengal N.I who have been in a mutinous state for some time. I left off in dear Emmie's letter by saying that we were just going to see a native lieutenant hanged. There was, it appeared, some hope of a reprieve for the unfortunate man, but it proved to be mere rumour, for he was executed that same afternoon at 5hr. 30min. p.m. Whilst being escorted to the gallows he addressed his fellow sepoys, saying that he had eaten the company's salt for 31 years and had proved a traitor after all, that he fully deserved his ignominious death, and was quite prepared for it. He certainly died game to the last, and even though he richly deserved his fate, yet I heartily felt for the poor creature. We hear that all the native troops are in a high state of mutiny, and, that in all probability we shall not go back to Burmah for some time. This I am very sorry for: I like Burmah very much, and dislike Bengal as much.

I have been obliged to get 2 prs of blue regimental trousers, having grown out of those I brought out. They cost 26 Rs. a pair. I have also got a forage cap of the new pattern, the order having come out to do so. I have had both my shell jackets turned, and they are as good as new.

There has been a game of quoits here between O'Brien and Penton of ours. The terms were, that O'Brien was to win every rubber he played with Penton one day out of seven for 3 bottles of brandy. They began yesterday, and O'Brien won, beating Penton every rubber in the day. O'Brien is a magnificent player, and his adversary a very fair one. I am getting a bit of a dab at it, as I play nearly every day. This and cricket are our only amusements.

We have had many violent storms here accompanied with thunder and the most beautiful lightning I ever saw. I still keep my resolutions, and am as little inclined to break them as ever.

Having told Miss P. all the news, there is none left for me to tell, so I must conclude by saying I am, and have been, in the best of health all along. Best of love to Emmie and Aunty, and the same to both your dear selves, and now good bye,

from your most loving and affectionate boy,
H. P. Pearson

P.S. I hope you are all well and happy.

Letter No.9

Chinsurah, nr Calcutta
May 8th 1857

My very dearest Emmie,
I am now going to write to you and Aunty as it is your turn. We are still, as you see, in Chinsurah, and heartily sick of it we all are. For my part I am exceedingly anxious to hear of the arrival of the order directing us to embark for Rangoon, but so many reports are circulated daily about our return, that I have almost given up the idea of our going back at all. I have just bought a table for 4 rupees, and now I need not go into the mess room when I want to write.

I must tell you while I remember it that we went to Barrackpore for the 4th time last Tuesday and encamped in the same old place: next day a parade was ordered at 4 a.m. and we all turned out at the specified time, native troops and all. About 8.30 a.m. we performed the duty for which we were ordered to Barrackpore, viz. to disband the 34th Bengal Native Infantry. Everything was conducted on the same principle as when the 19th were disbanded, and the 34th were no more inclined to resist than their predecessors the 19th. As soon as they had been disarmed and paid, our Grenadiers and No.1 Company (to the former of which I was attached) received orders to march them to a place called Pultah Ghaut about 3 miles distant and see them cross the river there. We accordingly marched them off, arriving at Pultah Ghaut about 12 noon. I then had something to eat for the first time since leaving Chinsurah 26 hours before. We remained there for 2 hours and were picked up by the steamer and conveyed to this place. I fervently hope this may be our last expedition to that place, and that the next time we are afloat it may be on our way to Burmah.

I have not had a letter from you for a long time. No.6 is the last in which the latest date is 4th March. I think it is odd I have not had a letter, but it must be some fault in the Post, for I know you would, one of you, write every mail. However, I must hope to hear soon.

I am getting an expert shot with a weapon they call a pellet-bow, and yesterday I killed a little squirrel with it. It is like an English bow in shape but made of bamboo, and having 2 strings which are kept apart with a bit of stick. It shoots little balls (about the size of a large marble) made of mud and dried in the sun, to a very great distance and the natives can most of them make sure of hitting an egg at 20 yards distance.

I yesterday wrote a letter to Uncle Pearson, but of course I had nothing to tell him except what you already know. We received accounts of an enormous fire in Rangoon on the 19th ult. which destroyed the entire native town. The 35th (H. Majesty's) gave assistance at the fire, but, much to their disgrace, they pillaged right and left, and have been nicknamed "The Royal European Decoits"; now the people there begin to feel the want of the old 84th.

I still continue in good health, and though the weather is very hot (sometimes as high as 108° in the house) yet I am very comfortable and never, or very seldom, inconveniently hot. You would be surprised at the quantity of ice we consume. The average daily consumption is 1 maund and a half or 120 lbs weight

Saturday 9th. Two of our officers came in last night from a dinner with the "Governor General", and he told them that we should return to Rangoon in the course of a week or 10 days in the P.& O. Company's steamer "Oriental", which is hourly expected. I am delighted with the news. All our officers are invited to a ball at Government House on the 25th inst. but I trust we shall be in Rangoon before then. I hit another squirrel with my pellet-bow just now but did not kill him. I killed a snake about 15 inches long yesterday in a drain at the back of our barracks. I have put him in spirits for you. Our assistant-surgeon "Hanbury" is going to England on sick certificate for "liver" complaint: he starts about 20th. inst.

I shall not write to Aunty till 2 or 3 days, when the post will come from England, in order to answer questions; however, her letter will go by the same mail as this. Give my very best love to Chaper, Macher and Taty, and accept the same, dearest Miss P.,

from your affectionate brother,
Hughey

Letter No. 13

Barrackpore
May 16th 1857

My own dearest Father and Mother,
I have not long ago finished a letter to Miss P. but I prefer putting this in a separate envelope and paying for another stamp in order that if one goes astray the other will reach you. I told Emmie all the news up to that date and therefore you must not expect much in this.

The 1st Madras Fusiliers arrived some days ago and have been sent to Allahabad and Benares, and two steamers have been sent to Ceylon to bring H.M.'s 37th and one steamer to Burmah to fetch the 35th. No news has arrived from Delhi owing to the telegraph wires having been cut and, as you may suppose, everyone is in a great state of excitement about the proceedings which must, ere now, have taken place there against the mutiniers. To-night is the time fixed by the seers for the murder of all the Europeans, but no one seems to pay much attention to their reports.

Penton is going away soon, and I am going to take the Caboul horse off him. Blake went into Calcutta yesterday and bought a very pretty horse but he did not mention the price he paid. Revolvers are at a high premium just now, those you get in England for 70 rupees being sold for 120 and sometimes more. We go to drill here every morning, and are in battalion drill now. What do you think we pay for beer at our mess? 10 annas (14½d English) per bottle!! Is not this enormous? I drink iced water, and soda water. We pay 10 rupees each a month for ice. There is no mess established yet so we have all our meals at home. I took a walk into the park last night and heard the band of the 2nd Grenadiers (niggers) play a few tunes.

You had, I think, better address my letters for the future to "Calcutta", for I see no chance of our going to "Rangoon" again; our next step I expect will be to Madras, and then home, but there is a possibility of our being transferred to Bengal, then we shall embark from Calcutta. The Governor General's ball took place last night, only 2 of our officers went. Humphrey talks about getting an exchange into the 39th or 42nd; indeed he has already written home to make arrangements about it. What do you think, dear Chaper, would be my best plan? I will tell you what my ideas are, and you can think it over. The 84th will be on their way home most probably some time next year, and I should like to go with them to see you, and stop a year or so in England, but I like this country very much indeed, and would like to come out again, or at any rate to exchange out of this regiment When I get my lieutenancy (which most probably will be either before our return home, or at any rate in the first year after our arrival) would be the time to exchange, for then I should lose nothing by it. However I leave it all to you who know so much more in these matters than I do.

The day before yesterday I killed 2 squirrels with my pellet-bow; very good shots! We never hear any news from China. How is it I wonder? I am sorry to say we have not the most remote chance of going there. I have just heard from an officer who was at the ball last night that nearly all the men there danced with revolvers secreted under their tunics, and that there was a great scarcity of ladies there, all being afraid of being attacked. I just heard too that all the provisions and stores which were to have been sent to our regiments up country dare not be dispatched. Yesterday another steamer was sent to Ceylon to fetch the "Ceylon Rifles". This leaves the island without troops. I shall now leave off for to-day, and leave the rest of this sheet for any news that may come between now and the departure of the next mail, and also for answering the letter I expect by the mail which is expected on the 28th instant.

29th inst. No signs of the mail yet so I must fill up some more of this with a few incidents which happened since I left off writing last. I have bought Penton's mare for 60 rupees. She is aged about 11 or 12, colour flea-bitten grey, and a pure Arab. She has the stud mark on her ears, which is only allowed to be put on Arabs: plenty of fire in her although not vicious, and goes capitally. The reasons for her going so cheap are, first, her age, and secondly, the fact of her being undersized for a buggy. Kenny has just got a chestnut horse for 80 Rs. but I do not like him as well as my mare. Blake has got a splendid Arab mare and gave about 560 for her, but he is a man with 300 a month beside his pay, and as much more as he likes. He is the best judge of a horse in the regiment, and would do your heart good to see the lovely shaped creature he has got. It is rising 4, and a prettier animal I never saw. However I am very well satisfied with my old "os". I went to hear the band in the park on her last evening, and "ossed" it about to my entire satisfaction.

Yesterday morning at 3.30 a.m. we turned out, and at 4 marched to the general parade ground, where all the "nigger regiments" were drawn up; after standing at open order for 2 hours Lord Canning came on the ground, and was saluted by the artillery with 20 or 19 guns (I do not know which) and by all the regiments with colours dropped. He rode down the line, and then went away, and soon after we did the same. The parade was ordered for the purpose of publikly thanking the 70th N.I. for their loyalty in volunteering to march against the mutinous regiments at Delhi. The Governor General is a common looking man, not a bit like what you would expect.

Yesterday afternoon about 4 p.m. a tremendous "nor-wester" came on, and we were standing under our verandah to take shelter, when "Popplewell" suddenly said "There is a dingy swamped". We looked and sure enough there was a boat upside down in the middle of the river with 5 men sitting on the bottom of it and about 40 yards distance from it in various directions were 4 more natives in the water. We rushed to the bottom of our garden which is not 10 yards from the edge of the river, and called out loudly to some dingys which were close to the bank, pointing at the same time to the "swamped boat". They looked and coolly said "atcha sahib". We did our best to make them go to the rescue, even offering money, but not one would go. The boat bottom upwards, floated down with the 5 individuals calmly sitting on it, and the 4 men in the water swam about for upwards of ¾ of an hour when the wind fell, and dingys then put off, rowing as if they were very anxious not to get into a perspiration. In about 5 minutes they picked up one out of the water, who, as soon as he was in the boat, took an oar and helped to pick up another, who did the same in his turn, till they were all saved. None of them appeared the least exhausted from their long submersion. I have sent my boy into Calcutta to get some stuffing put into my saddle: if he comes out by the early train I shall ride out in the evening.

Were either of you, Chaper or Macher, ever in Barrackpore, or Serampore, which is just the other side of the river? All our fellows are providing themselves with horses and when the 70th N.I. go up country (which they will do on the 1st or 2nd of next month) there will be very few without some sort of a nag.

Blake of ours has got a pretty little jackal which one of the men caught the first time we came to Barrackpore. The men of the Grenadier Compy. take care of him, and carry him about in the havre-sacks on the march, and when in barracks he is tied to a peg in front of their rooms. He is a very pretty little animal, with a sharp, funny little nose like a fox, and is very fond of a puppy which is in the barracks. A day or two ago its mother came boldly in the middle of the day to where it was and would not go till driven away by the men, who were afraid she would rescue it. The young-un knew its Macher and tried hard to get away to her. Is not it extra-ordinary how the mother found her offspring after a lapse of 6 or 7 weeks, and in a place at least a mile distant from where it was taken? And still more wonderful is it when one thinks how boldly and cunningly she must have behaved to enter in the middle of the day into the very heart of the cantonment. This is all I have to tell you at present, so "more anon".

30th inst. Saturday. I went out riding in the park with Kenny this morning, and on our return we found that the Regt. was ordered up country, and it is perfectly true. We go by a company at a time, the first going to-morrow morning. We are to go to Lucknow, passing through Benares and Allahabad, and the mode of transit is bullock and horse dawk from Raneegunge, first going there by train.

Sunday 31st inst. I had intended taking my poor old mare up country but I find that probably we shall go much higher than Cawnpore, perhaps to Delhi, and even above that, so I must e'en part with her, much as I regret it. I think I shall send her in to Calcutta either to-day or to-morrow to be sold at Cooks' by auction. I really am very unfortunate in buying horses, and although you perhaps may think I was in a hurry to buy, yet I can assure you I waited till nearly every one had got theirs, and there was every probability of our remaining here at any rate till after the monsoon. It was just the same at Rangoon; I had only bought my pony 3 days when we were ordered away.

I go on Thursday next with the Light Company, and band, and ours will be the last party to leave. I am very anxious for the "Oriental" to arrive before our departure in order to get my gun and rifle with me; she is expected to-day. There is a very good chance of my seeing the Himalaya mountains that I always was so anxious to visit, and shoot over. I shall take my saddle and bridle, brushes, curry comb, etc. with me. There is no signs of the mail yet, and I am very anxious to hear from you. You must not be uneasy if you do not hear from me for perhaps months together now, for the communication is entirely cut off between the upper provinces and Calcutta, but I know you will rely upon my writing at every opportunity, and, dearest ones, you may depend I will not disappoint you. I will put in a slip of paper with the directions, which in my opinion will be best, and most likely to reach me. I think it will be better to write it here for a bit of paper might fall out.

> H. P. Pearson Esq.,
>   H.M. 84th Regiment,
>   Cawnpore, or elsewhere, Bengal

This is my idea, but do what you think best. The mail does not leave till the 4th proximo, but the post closes on the 2nd. However I shall not seal this till the last moment, in case there should be anything else to tell you. Whatever else there may be I will put it in a postscript. Please give my best love to my own dear Taty and accept the same,

> Dearest Chaper and Macher,
>   From your truly affectionate boy,
>   Hugh Pearce Pearson

Letter No. 14

> Quartered in the "Ameer of Scinde's House", Allahabad
> June 22nd 1857

My own very dear Mother,

It is now a long time since I wrote you a letter, so it is fairly your turn now to have one all to yourself. My last letter I believe was to dearest Chaper, and I hope it sufficiently prepared you all for any disappointment you might have in not hearing from me by every mail. However, as circumstances are at present, I am afraid I shall find but few opportunitys (sic) for sending any correspondence to you, and, as my letters necessarily, must be few and far between, the least amends I can make for the disappointment will be to assure you that the few you get shall be "uncommon long".

It would have rather amazed you to have seen me at breakfast this morning; my plate was my left hand and the forefinger and thumb of my right acted as a knife and fork. But this is anticipating. I will tell you what occurred (or at least part) for were I to attempt to tell you all I should fill a ream of this paper, and, as I have kept a journal since my departure from Barrackpore, it will help me materially in remembering everything that occurred by the way: of course what I do not put in my letter you will read in my journal. I intend to give you no news about this mutiny except the very latest because you will read the true account in the paper I have ordered to be sent you,viz. "The Friend of India". I am glad to be able to say that you may rely upon all that is in that paper being correct.

First, however, I will tell you that "Maybury" whom Papa remembers at Chatham is dead. He killed himself by starvation and in the extreme desire to save money denied himself, or rather, denied Nature the support she needed. On the journey from "Raneegunge" to "Benares", which takes 10 days, he ate but one dinner and lived the remainder on biscuits and tea begged from the men's rations. In this country where food, and good food, is needed more than any other he neglected to take it, and the consequence was that on reaching "Benares" he stretched himself upon a bed of sickness from which he never rose.

I will not enter into the details of each day's journey (for you will see everything entered minutely in my journal) but will just mention a few events that happened during the time it occupied.

I started from Barrackpore on the 4th June with a detachment of 88 men under Lieut. Gibaut, went by train to "Raneegunge" and from there by bullock train. We usually started at 4 p.m., travelled all night and arrived at our halting place at about 8 or 9 a.m. The usual length of the march was 27 miles, but we have done as much as 56 without a halt. The men were put 4 in a bandy, then there was one for the cooks, one for us two, one for provisions and one for the sergt.-major and apothecary, making a total of 26 bandys, each with 2 bullocks. It was very slow travelling, and having no springs the bandys jolted awfully. It is no use mentioning every little place we halted at because you do not know them, but we halted at 2 large places where you may possibly have been, namely "Shergotty" and "Sahessram". We went within 40 miles of my birthplace [Dinapore], and within 20 of "Hazaareebaugh". We went over the Rajmahal hills, and through the Dunwah Pass where 3 bears and a tiger crossed our path, and where a deer stood in the road 150 yards from me, giving a good chance if I had had my rifle. I also saw plenty of duck. Living on the march is very cheap. I need not spend more than 8 annas (1s.) everything included.

After 10 days journey we got to Benares, the holy city, and were sent to the mint, as there was no room in the church for us. There were some of H.M.'s 64th there, and a day or two after we arrived the 78th Highlanders came in. Blake of ours has been rescuing Europeans from villages some way off, and one night brought in 15 men, women and children, including one poor old man of 86 and 2 little orphans who had seen both parents cruelly murdered before their eyes.

About 4 p.m. every day about 20 or 30 carriages drove into the compound of the mint, and as many as 80 or 90 ladies and gentlemen with little children slept in the verandah for safety. At daybreak they drove away again.

I left Benares in the steamer "Calcutta" with the head quarters of the regiment on the 19th June and arrived at "Allahabad" on the night of the 22nd. I amused myself during my journey by firing ball at alligators, adjutants, etc. and one day I shot at a native whom I saw robbing a native boat. The ball struck the ground a little to his left, and I never saw any man run as fast as he did.

We were not allowed to go into the fort, because cholera was raging so bad amongst the Madras Fusiliers that they lost 50 men in 3 days and buried 19 in one evening. Our troops are burning all the villages about "Allahabad", and every day 10 or a dozen niggers are hanged. Champagne is selling here at 8 annas a bottle by the natives: this is what has been stolen out of the houses burnt by the insurgents.

The 6th N.I. murdered 16 of their own officers the other night They sounded the "alarm and assembly" and when the officers came out they shot them all, seized 2 or 3 lakhs of treasure and went off with it to the King of Delhi. Every bungalow with a thatched roof is burnt to the ground, and all the valuables taken out, but when the Madras Fusiliers came up and drove them out of the place they could not take all with them and many of them buried what they had "looted". Some of our men have found silver mugs, others horses, some have found wine and beer, and all have found something. I have got a book of music for Emily and many nice well bound books that had escaped the notice of the rebels. Many of the officers who were here when the row broke out have lost their wives and children and all have lost their property. One gentleman was telling me he had seen his wife murdered whilst he was bound and in addition to that had lost 25,000 rupees worth of personal property.

A day or so before we arrived 150 of the Madras Fusiliers attacked 7000 mutineers and had it not been for a regiment of Seikh Horse that covered the retreat of the Fusiliers, they would have been cut off to a man, and the fort taken; as it was, they got a good licking and lost a lot of men.

News came from Delhi yesterday (27th) that the King of Delhi was hanged, and that 30,000 men, women, and children had been slain at Delhi, also that the city was razed to the ground. The general told the mutineers that he would give them 12 hours to clear out of the place, but they said, "Oh! we know the English will not fire on defenceless women and children". However, at the expiration of the time the batteries opened, and 30,000 of them were killed. About 53 regiments have mutinied altogether, and are all collected at "Lucknow".

I am going up to Cawnpore to-morrow or next day with a force consisting of 200 of the 85th, 200 of the Madras Fusiliers, 150 Seikh cavalry, and 4 guns to join the main army under General Wheeler: there is no more bullock train travelling, we shall have to march all the way, 150 miles. I suffer dreadfully from prickly heat, but I believe it is a healthy sign so I grin and bear it Thank goodness that is the only discomfort I have felt as regards anything being the matter with me. Parties of the 64th and 78th Highlanders are daily arriving in "Allahabad", and I should hardly think it will be left without European troops again. As there is no grub to be got here we draw our rations with the men and we live upon that and a few pigeons I occasionally shoot with an old sepoy musket I got, and cartridge powder with slugs made out of bullets serve me for ammunition.

We have been twice turned out in the night by a false alarm, and one night whilst I was patrolling with a corporal and file of men, I heard a couple of shots fired, and the bullet from one went rather too close to be pleasant to my nerves. It was only some fool firing at a horse, and if I had my way I would have brought him in prisoner and had him severely punished—as if we had not enough to do without turning out at midnight because some young gentleman thought fit to practise with his revolver!!

In all probability you will have to pay the postage of this, for stamps cannot be procured here, but I dare say you will not mind for once or twice. The last letter I got was No.9 but I cannot expect to get any up in these uncivilized parts. Tell me if you or Chaper have ever been to "Allahabad", "Cawnpore" or "Lucknow". Father mentions "Sitteghur" and the "Hive" in one of his letters. I am sorry I did not know I was so near places that would interest me so much, for I could any day have gone to see them, and must have passed the "Hive" dozens of times, but never knew it.

Kenny bought a horse the other day for 100 rupees, and I think he has made rather a mess of it. I should very much like a horse to ride going on this march of 15 miles a day, but still I never should think of giving 100 rupees for one.

The mail leaves this in an hour's time so I must disappoint you with a short letter now. I am quite well and always have been, and sincerely hope you all are so too. Give my best, very best love to darling Chaper and Miss P. and accept the same, dearest of mothers,

from your most affectionate, loving, son,
Hugh, Pearce, Pearson

P.S. Still direct "Calcutta, to be forwarded", in the corner.

Letter No.15

Camp at "Kitoohin",
75 miles from Cawnpoor
July 6th 1857

My own very dearest Father,

The last letter I sent you was from "Allahabad" and the number of it was 14 on the letter, and 15 on the envelope; this mistake was in consequence of my having lost the list of letters sent and received, but I have since found it and find that the letter before it was No. 13 written from Barrackpore, and dispatched on the 31st of May. However, you must call my last No. 14, and this No. 15.

We have received dreadful news within the last 4 days from Cawnpore. The European force there consisted of 2 companies of H.M. 32nd, 100 of our men under either Saunders and Magrath or O'Brien (I do not know which, and am not certain of the number of men belonging to us who were there, but know there were some) and 15 men and a serjeant of the 1st Madras Fusiliers. This with 2 guns completed the gallant little band. They have been entrenched in earthworks for several weeks surrounded by 8000 rebels, 2000 cavalry, and 19 guns, and kept sending secret messengers conjuring us to come with the greatest haste if we would save them. This we did, marching 16 and 17 miles daily, with 60 rounds of ball ammunition a man. But unfortunately, we were too late; we marched from Allahabad on the 30th June and on the 3rd we received the dreadful news that not a single European was alive in Cawnpore. We at first disbelieved it altogether but messenger after messenger came and all told the same sad tale. At last one wealthy native met us and confirmed all that the others had said; he was a man who was known to be a friend to the Europeans and had a chit to that effect from General Wheeler who commanded the force at Cawnpore. To crown all, a letter came from Sir H. Lawrence at Lucknow saying that he knew it was true, and every day brings in fresh confirmations of the news. This "baboo" or wealthy native who came in said he was eye witness of the massacre, and said it happened as follows.

Their provisions being exhausted, and no signs of instant succour being seen, General Wheeler was obliged to surrender. The "Nana", who is a Mahratta and who commands the rebel force, said that he did not wish to hurt the Europeans and that all they (the rebels) wanted was to have possession of Cawnpore; if the European troops would evacuate that, he would provide boats for them across the river to enable them to go to Calcutta. They, conquered not by the mutineers but by hunger, were induced to yield on these terms and embarked in boats provided by the "Nana", but, when they reached the middle of the river the boatmen jumped out and swam to shore and at the same time a tremendous fire from both sides of the stream was opened upon them; cavalry were ready to cut down all who should be able to reach the shore, and every man was killed. One boat contrived to slip away down the river for 18 or 20 miles when they landed, but the unfortunate creatures were cut down to a man by 1000 cavalry sent for the purpose.

"Khaga" July 9th. I quite forget whether I mentioned poor Maybury's death, at any [missing] now tell you that he died on the 15th June [missing] arrived in Benares. General Havelock is coming 1200 men and 6 guns and is 3 marches from us. Two companies of ours went up country when we went the last time to Barrackpore, one commanded by O'Brien, the other by Saunders with Magrath for his subaltern. Now one of these companies was in Cawnpore when the massacre took place but whether O'Brien, or the other two were with it is uncertain.

I have just been told that the dawk for Allahabad leaves in 10 minutes and as I shall not have another opportunity of writing for some time I must leave off if I would be in time. Give my very best love to Mother, Aunty and Emmy, and accept the same,

dear Chaper,
from your affectionate son,
Hugh P. Pearson

P.S. Still address to Calcutta.

Letter No. 16

[sent unfinished]

Camp Cawnpore
July 19th 1857

My own dearest Father and Mother,

My last letter No.15 was sent from a village called "Khaga" where we encamped, and in it was a little slip of paper which was only intended for Chaper to see, as it said we expected an action. We have now had 4 hard fought battles with an overwhelming enemy, and although the odds were no less then 7 to 1 against us, yet British pluck has always won the day.

Your dear son was within an ace of being sent to eternity, and it was through the interposition of the Almighty alone that he escaped. I am but slightly wounded, so insignificant indeed is it that I did not think worth while to have it dressed, and the only effect was a rattling headache for 2 days, which has now entirely gone away. I was struck by a rifle ball on the right temple, and it just grazed a little flesh from it; if it had struck a quarter of an inch more to the left I must have been killed, for it would have passed through my right eye, and then my chance would have been indeed a poor one. This is not the only escape I had for a grape shot passed through the two legs of my trousers and actually did not hit me. I was standing with my side to the enemy who were firing grape from a large 24-pounder, and a ball just passed clean through both legs of my trousers just below the knee, tearing them almost in two pieces. The ball that struck me on the temple knocked me down senseless for a few seconds, but I soon got up, and should not have known it had not some flies settled on the place, which caused me to knock them off with my hand, and then I saw the blood.

Poor Capt. Currie, who was commanding us, was struck by a 24-pound shot behind: it carried away the fleshy part of the inside of both thighs, exposing all the entrails, and then struck a poor private of ours in the chest, killing him on the spot.

The whole of the Cawnpore force was against us, and it consisted of 11,000 infantry, 700 cavalry and 8 guns of which 4 were 24-pounders. Our little force was only 1500 infantry, 20 volunteer cavalry, and 10 guns. We fought from 3 p.m. till 7.30 p.m. against this enormous force and took all their guns but two 9 pounders which they took away with horses. All the damage was done by the artillery and rifles, for neither dare they cross bayonets with us nor even charge our little squares with their clouds of cavalry. They had most magnificent gunners, and not a shot was fired by them that did not tell a fearful tale. I saw 6 men of the 64th knocked over by a 24-pound shot: 4 of them were killed on the spot and the other 2 had their legs taken off at the hip. Our brave general told us he had been in 26 actions, and had never once seen a heavier or a better directed fire; so hot was their fire that we laid down under a bank for shelter and even then their shell and musketry did fearful execution amongst us. Our artillery was stuck in a field all the time we were exposed to that awful fire, and but one resource remained. The general came up whilst we were lying down and called out, "The 64th and 84th will rise and charge".

At this time the enemy had got so impudent that they sounded "the advance", and their whole force did advance with tom-toms and bands playing and flanked by cavalry. Then it was that our general uttered the above words, and our 2 regiments rose and advanced steadily with sloped arms: when we rose we gave a British cheer which must have gone to the inmost soul of the enemy, for they stopped their band, and retired on the big 24 and immediately commenced firing round shot. We were about 1000 yards from them when they began firing, but when we had gone about 200 yards and were about 800 from them they began firing grape shot.

I do not know, my dearest Chaper, whether you were ever under fire of grape, but in all my life I never saw anything to equal it. They fired with fatal precision, and as the gun was directed at us and the left company of the 64th you may imagine how awful it was. For the first 400 yards of our advance, if we threw ourselves down directly we heard the report we were in time to let most of it go over us, but as we approached the gun of course the shot reached us sooner, and if we were not on our faces as the gunner applied the match we were too late. It was in the last discharge but one that the grape shot went through my trousers and the last round was fired when we were only 100 yards from the gun!! Of course, we all fell down on the instant we saw the gunner raise his hand to apply the match, and when the grape was well over us we rose to a man, gave them a well directed volley from our whole line: then our general cried "Charge", and with a truly British cheer we rushed upon the brutes who, as you may suppose, ran like fiends. I never heard such a cheer as our men gave: it was not a cheer of victory, but a yell of revenge. The 84th gave this awful yell, screeched out the word "Cawnpore" and rushed like madmen at the gun. If the enemy had but stopped there, our men who were murdered at Cawnpore would indeed have been revenged or else not a man of the 84th would have left the field alive, but fortunately for them they ran or few would have remained to tell the tale. Major Bingham of the 64th first touched the gun, then Ayton of ours, and then Kenny. I have only given........ [missing].

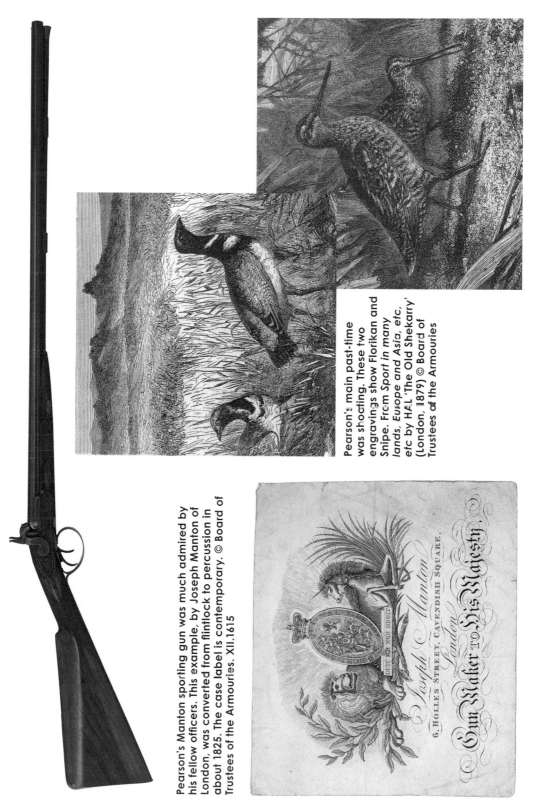

Pearson's main past-time was shooting. These two engravings show Florikan and Snipe. From *Sport in many lands, Europe and Asia, etc, etc* by HAL 'The Old Shekarry' (London, 1879) © Board of Trustees of the Armouries

Pearson's Manton sporting gun was much admired by his fellow officers. This example, by Joseph Manton of London, was converted from flintlock to percussion in about 1825. The case label is contemporary. © Board of Trustees of the Armouries. XII.1615

Pearson described his regimental sword, the 1822/45 pattern infantry officer's sword (right), as a wretched skewer, and quickly replaced it with a more serviceable 1853 pattern cavalry trooper's sword and scabbard (left). © Board of Trustees of the Armouries. IX.6594 and IX.2861

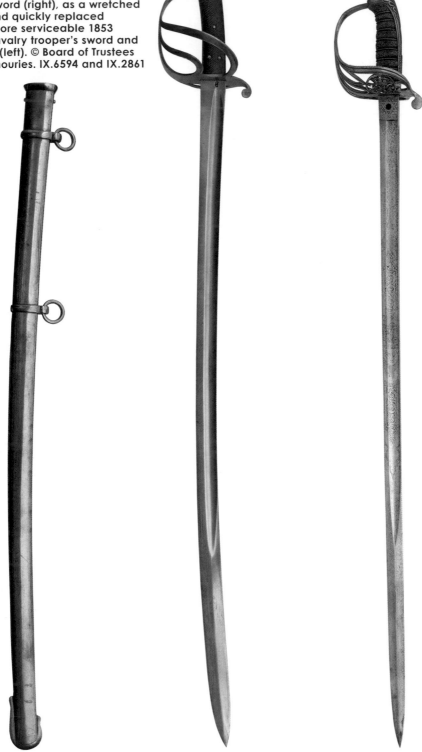

Pearson purchased for himself a double-barrelled percussion pistol, probably similar to this example by John Manton of London (top left). He would have preferred a Witton and Daw six shot percussion revolver (bottom left), or a self cocking revolver, such as this Model 1851 Deane, Adams and Deane six shot percussion revolver (right, top and bottom). His aunt later bought him a modern English revolver. © Board of Trustees of the Armouries. XII.1389, XII.4163 and Pattern Room Collection 3597

Contemporary photographs of the river Ghat at Cawnpore, and the well into which the remains of those massacred where thrown © York and Lancaster Regimental Museum (1998.83)

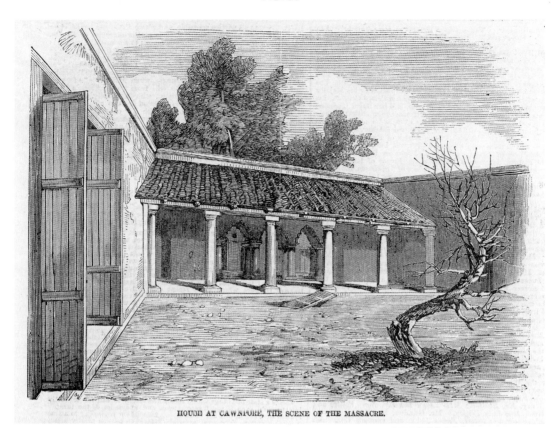

HOUSE AT CAWNPORE, THE SCENE OF THE MASSACRE.

Many officers passed through Cawnpore once it was recaptured on the way to front and visited the scene of the massacre of the women and children. This engraving is from the *Illustrated London News* (23 January 1858) © Board of Trustees of the Armouries

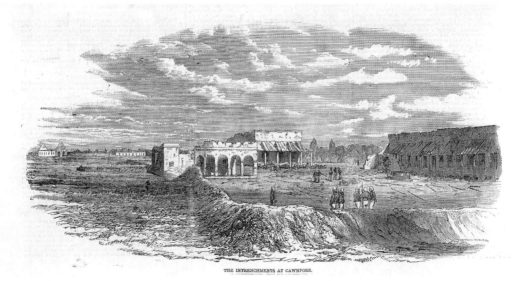

THE INTRENCHMENTS AT CAWNPORE.

Pearson noted the accuracy of the engraving of Wheeler's entrenchments at Cawnpore that was reproduced in the *Illustrated London News* (24 October 1857) © Board of Trustees of the Armouries

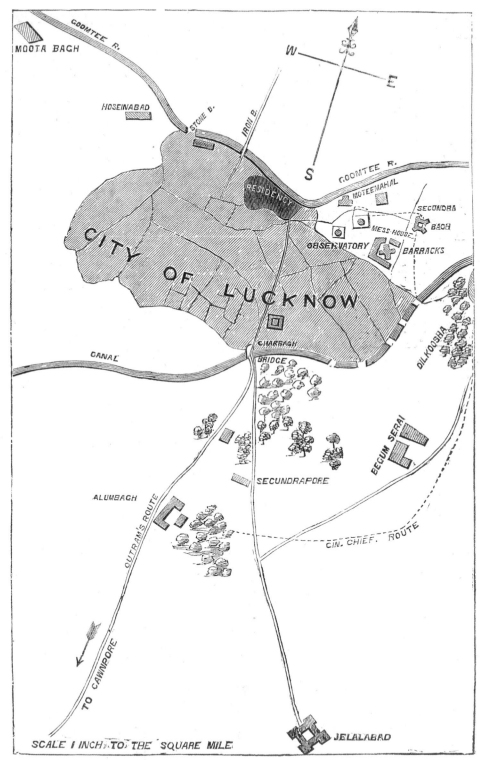

A contemporary map of the City of Lucknow. From the *Illustrated London News* (16 January 1858).

A dramatic engraving of The Residency at Lucknow after the siege.

Pearson's describes how the rebels tried to under mine the defences at Lucknow, and how the British would often lie in wait for the miners.
From *Sketches and incidents of the siege of Lucknow / from drawings made during the siege by Clifford Henry Mecham* (London, 1858). © Board of Trustees of the Armouries.

An engraving of Havelock's grave at Alum Bagh.

An engraving of Fort Jellalabad.
From *Sketches and incidents of the siege of Lucknow / from drawings made during the siege by Clifford Henry Mecham* (London, 1858). © Board of Trustees of the Armouries

Letter No.17

Mugrawar–left bank of Ganges
August 1st 1857

My own very dearest Father and Mother,

Seldom is it that I have time to write, and still more seldom is it that an opportunity occurs of sending letters when they are written, but now fortunately I can both write and post letters, and you well know your boy would not allow an opportunity to slip of letting you know he is well in times of peace, much less now that he is fighting against the enemy, and when false reports are sure to be circulated at home which might make you miserable as to my safety.

I have now been in six separate actions and in every one but the first, under a heavy fire. I have seen men of my own company killed and wounded by me and in this last action on the 29th ult. my right hand man was shot through the head whilst talking to me, yet God has been merciful and has preserved me not only from the dangers of battle but also through all the hardships and fatigue, the exposure to the sun by day and to the dew and rain by night, which, as you well know, are always consequent upon a campaign in an enemy's territory.

We have had hard fighting, very hard indeed; most of the fighting on this side of the river has been village fighting, and when those wretches are surrounded in their loopholed houses and their village is set on fire you may easily imagine how desperate they become, for, knowing they are sure to be killed sooner or later their only object is to sell their lives as dearly as possible.

In these last two actions (both on this side of the river) we have had this sort of fighting and as they were both fortified towns we took you can imagine what a fire we were under. After we had licked them well in the field they took to their towns, and after shelling them for some time, we set the place on fire and laid down outside exposed to a murderous fire of musketry and gingals. More men were killed and wounded outside this town than in any action in the field; our adjutant (Browne) was shot through the leg and put in a palanquin; the bearers ran away and left him, and immediately the brutes in the town fired at him, hitting him through the arm, and in the hip. He has 3 wounds but none dangerous. An officer of the 1st Madras Fusiliers was shot dead on the spot; another of the same corps (the adjutant) was shot in the lower jaw, smashing it to bits; an officer of the 78th Highlanders was severely wounded and these are all the casualties amongst the officers.

Our list amongst the men is large. I had 1 killed and 3 wounded in my own company. We took 20 guns from the enemy on this side of the river, and 49 on the other. After utterly routing the Nana's army between "Allahabad" and Cawnpore, we crossed over here into Oudh to relieve Lucknow which is at present held by 50 of the 84th and 150 of the 32nd (Queen's) against 75,000 of the enemy.

We fought our way for more than half the way to Lucknow losing at the rate of 100 men every action, and our General then decided upon retreating 10 miles. Nobody knows why he has done this, but there was a report that the rebels had crossed a bridge 5 miles ahead of us, had blown up the bridge and placed 70 guns in position the other side. If this is true no wonder he does not go on.

Another report said that Lucknow had fallen: this is not at all improbable and if it is the case, of course there is no use in going on, for the only reason we crossed over was to relieve Lucknow and come back. At any rate here we are 10 miles in rear of where we fought the two actions and we are going still farther towards the river into an entrenched camp which is to be made by the soldiers of the column. Lieutenant Dangerfield is to have the Victoria Cross for leading the way into (as the order expresses it) "a loopholed house filled with desperate fanatics". He is a lucky fellow indeed. He belongs to the 1st Madras Fusiliers. I expect we shall all have a medal. I am sure we deserve one.

It would rather astonish dear mother to see the things I am obliged to do; for instance, it is not by any means uncommon for me to walk for a whole day under a hot sun, wet up above the knees, and then after the action to sleep on the damp ground all night without ever thinking of changing my wet socks, boots and trousers. As to sleeping under cover, it is a thing I have not done since I crossed the river into Oude, and what is more, I am not likely to do so for some time. You will perhaps say "Why did he not change his socks and sleep under cover?" but you must remember that we had to cross a wide and swelling river, and were not allowed to bring anything but what your servant could carry and you know that would not be much. The men brought nothing but 1 blanket and a pair of socks, and have had neither tents nor beds.

My scratch which I got at Maharajhpore is gone and has left nothing but a small scar to show the place. I have kept the trousers which were shot through to shew you how narrow an escape I had.

We are losing many men from sun-stroke, but I, fortunately, or I should say providentially, have not yet felt anything beyond having all the skin peeled off and my face being as red as a turkey cock's comb. We took two sepoys prisoner the other day, and they were blown away from the guns: the stink of fresh flesh was sickening in the extreme, but I have seen so many disgusting sights and so much bloodshed that I have grown quite callous, and the day of the action I held the leg of a man in my company whilst it was being amputated: he was close to me when the ball hit his leg just above the ankle breaking the bone to atoms. What a crunch a ball makes when it hits a bone! A subdivision of our light company under Captain Willis captured a 9-pr.gun from the enemy and fired it at them as they retired.

I will tell you as well as I am able the date of all the actions, the name of the place, and the number of guns captured at each. Futtehpore fought on 12th July, 11 guns taken; Aoung 15th July, 5 guns; Poundoa bridge, same day, 5 guns; Maharajhpore and taking of Cawnpore 16th July, 11 guns; Bitthoor 19th July, 18 guns (this last was not an action but merely the destruction of the Nana's palace), then in Oude; the action before, and subsequent capture of the fortified towns of Unao and Busseeratgunge, 20 guns, fought on the 29th of July.

I, Kenny and Ayton were the only 3 of our regiment who were in every action. Barry was in all but Maharajhpore (when he was on the baggage guard). The rest have only been in two—viz. those on the 29th ult. We have lost the following officers since our coming from Rangoon to Bengal: Maybury, Saunders, Currie, and perhaps O'Brien and Magrath if Lucknow has fallen.

I received your letter No. 10 on the 19th of last month when I had crossed the Ganges into Oude, and wrote one in such a hurry that I had no time to finish it, on the 22nd (I think). I am glad dear Juzzif has had his likeness taken, and should very much like to see it. Dear Macher and Emmie you say have had their likeness taken and also your dear self. I should so much like to see them. I am very pleased to hear you talk of visiting Guernsey: it will be a nice change for all of you, and a great point is that it is a step nearer to that precious little isle in which I so much want to see you once more "England" .

I sincerely hope you receive the "Friend of India" regularly, 2 papers by each mail. It is a paper you can rely upon as containing the "puckah" news, and is the "Times" of India.

I have just been looking at Browne's wound in the leg: the wound much resembles yours with the exception that it has gone right through his leg. It is in exactly the same place on the same leg. As regards money matters, dear Chaper you may safely trust me, for so far am I from wanting money that I have some the other side the river as well as a month's pay not yet drawn.

You mention how slow the promotion in the 84th is. You will now change your opinion: I gave you our list of casualties, and according to that I should be either senior ensign or junior lieutenant. If again, Lucknow has fallen O'Brien and Magrath are certain to have been killed, but one must not be in a hurry to say it has fallen, for report is our only guide. Old Reed, our Lt. Colonel, went home in the "Nubia" on sick certificate for 15 months and in all probability he will leave the regiment for he cannot last long. Our senior captain, McCarthy, has 42 years service and can never stand this work, so there will be an awful run soon. But dearest Father I do not intend, if possible, to stop in this regiment and when I can get an opportunity I should like to exchange; however, I will return home with it, and we can then talk it over. I still am as firm as ever as regards drinking and smoking, and notwithstanding the earnest entreaties "just to smoke a weed for company" I am as little inclined as ever to begin. I think my temptation to play billiards is so limited here that I need hardly name it. I am very delighted to hear you are all well, and if you in half as good spirits as I am you must be really happy.

Oh! dearest Father and Mother, what a proud day for us all that will be when (if I escape) I shall embrace you with a medal on my breast! How opportunely I sent Nos 5 and 6 for, as you tell me, they reached you on dear mother's birthday.

I did, as mother says, go to see the wild animals in the park and one bear was mad and spit at every one who came near him. It was a very amusing thing to see the elephants swimming across the river when we crossed: they only kept the tip of their trunk and the mahout's head above water, and the trumpeting was dreadful.

Our sick and wounded are going to be sent across the river this evening for we actually have not enough carriage for them, so you may imagine how little we could bring across of our own things. I sent a little while ago to see poor Lloyd of my company whose leg was amputated. He looks quite well and will no doubt get over it. Poor Captain Beatson our Adjutant General died from sun stroke just after the battle before Cawnpore. I went to his sale and bought all his potted meats and jams, etc, and although I gave a heavy price yet I never repented it. Kenny found in Cawnpore a bag containing 1000 rupees and some gold and silver bangles etc. He took them to Ayton of ours who then commanded the detachment of the 84th in Cawnpore, and he took 300 rupees out to give it to the men; the remaining 700 he divided amongst the five of us who were there: we each got 140 rupees and afterwards I boned 36 more on my own hook out of a hole in a wall. I have also some bangles of silver. I found a nice little rifle by "Egg" London and took it in. We raffled for it, and Kenny won it. I also boned a splendid milch goat, and many other things which I do not remember just now.

I hope dear Uncle, Aunt and all my cousins at Bourton are well. I must write to them when I can get another opportunity and tell them all the news here. Now dearest ones, I think I have told you all that has happened and must wish you good bye. Give my very best love to dear Aunty Kate and Emily, and to all at Bourton when you write, and accept the same, my very dearest Father and Mother

From your most affectionate boy,
Hugh, Pearce, Pearson

P.S. I am quite ignorant as to how the postage is paid of these letters, but as we of course cannot get stamps, I know you will not object to pay a little for the letter, especially in these anxious times. H.P.P.

Letter No.18

Mugrawar, in Oude,
left bank of Ganges
August 4th 1857

My very dearest Emmie,

The last letter I wrote (No.17) was posted here on the 1st of this month, and will I hope catch the mail leaving Calcutta on the 9th. In it I told dear Father that I would write to you next, and although I have but little to tell you owing to my having written so recently, yet I must write now or never, for we advance again tomorrow and I shall not have another chance for perhaps a fortnight.

The best news I have, or I should say what interests me most, is that we have just received a very considerable addition to our force in the shape of 4 24-pounder guns, and also our light company which marched in about 80 strong last night. I think tomorrow or the next day we shall have a chance of trying their abilities against our friends in front.

Cholera is very severe amongst the troops, and that, together with the killed and wounded, has reduced our little army considerably. The 64th regt. took the field 520 strong, and their return of effective men is now only 108.

I mounted the right outlying picquet on the night of the 2nd inst. and was relieved yesterday afternoon at 6 p.m. I was posted under a tree about 50 yards from a small tope in which there were 7 or 800 monkeys of all sizes. I am sure you would have been greatly amused to watch their antics, I know I was, and spent several hours under the tope watching them. They were uncommonly tame, and when I held up biscuit, they came and took it out of my hand. One old lady with a little wee baby in her arms was really surprisingly docile and came 3 times to take biscuit from my hand. Their little babies in arms were the oddest of the whole community: when their mothers came to get biscuit they got extremely alarmed and tried to prevent their mammas from going any further, but the old ones were much too sensible to lose a bit of biscuit by not fetching it, and so whenever the youngsters began to show signs of fear, the mamma gave it a slap on the face and I dare say told it not to be so stupid. One old fellow came onto a branch just over my head, and caught hold of the turban on my forage cap; if it had not been stitched on, it would in all probability have now been in his possession.

A herd of about 60 elephants came down to bathe in a tank close to the tope, and after they had done washing, the drivers were going home by a short cut through the tope, but when the leading elephant saw the monkeys chattering and shaking the branches above his head he stopped and could not be induced to go on. The other elephants came up one by one and every one refused to go into the tope, and all the 60 elephants drew themselves up in a line outside. The mahouts beat them, and struck them with their iron hook for some time to no purpose, but at last the whole 60 set up a hideous roar and trumpeting and rushed like mad things through the tope, upon which all the monkeys young or old, rich or poor, set up such a screaming, chattering and shaking of branches that it entirely frightened the poor deluded elephants, who tore away as if certain destruction was close behind them. I never saw so ridiculous a sight, and what made it more so was that directly the elephants ran out of the tope the monkeys ran after them throwing stones. All my picquet burst into a roar of laughter and I joined most heartily. Indeed I doubt if the most sedate and grave person could have kept a serious countenance at this absurd spectacle.

About midnight a party of the enemy came to within 200 yards of one of my sentries, but whether their courage failed them or what I do not know but they went away again very soon. I heard a good deal of firing on my right but saw nothing more than a few of the enemy's cavalry about 2 miles off. The enemy are now 18 miles off us in our front, in a strong entrenched position on the opposite bank of a river, the bridge over which they have blown up. They have 19 guns in position ready for us, so you see we have plenty of work cut out for us. It is something like this:

(See page 64 for map)

or at least this cannot be far wrong.

6th August. Thursday. Whilst I was in the act of finishing the above sketch or plan, we received an order to march in an hour to attack the enemy, who had again taken up a position in the village of "Busseerethgunge" 12 miles in our front. I hastily packed up my few things and was ready in a few minutes. As soon as we were on parade it began to rain very hard and the natural consequence was we all got soaked through in about 5 minutes. It soon ceased, and we marched on to the road where the remainder of the force was. Our General then came out to the front and said, "Soldiers, you have now defeated the enemy in 7 different engagements. You have driven them each time from the field and captured their cannon, and here in my hand I hold the thanks of the Government for your heroic deeds. Soldiers, the enemy are again in your front. I knew they would be when I retreated to this place; they number 30,000 fighting men and a score of guns, but numbers are no object to you. Men, I do not ask you, but I command you to defeat them, and you shall do so. Tomorrow morning (if I am alive) I will send a report to the Commander-in-Chief of the action and of your behaviour in it. It is for you to decide what the contents of that letter shall be."

The men gave the old fellow a hearty cheer, and the column moved on. We marched for 2 or 3 hours, a great part of the time in a heavy rain, and about 6 p.m. halted in sight of the enemy's position. I went to bed wet and tired, and when the "rouse" went at 3.30 next morning, I felt sick and ill. However, it went very much against my ideas to fall out sick at such a time and so I went on as well as I could. We soon came in sight of them, and could distinctly see and hear them. We opened fire with our 2 24-pounders and also with shell from a howitzer. I never saw such magnificent shots as our artillery made, and as we were on a high eminence we could distinctly see the effect of our shot. Before we fired we heard them shouting and tom-toming to keep their courage up, and saw them beckon to us to come on, but the result will show that they might just as well have saved themselves the trouble of doing the latter.

The first shot we fired was a shell from our 24 pr. howitzer; it burst over their battery, and had the effect of shutting up their mouths. The 2 next were round shot from our long 24 prs. which (as I said in the first part of this letter) only arrived a day or two ago. These 2 shots went through their village from one end to the other, down the road which was straight, killing 7 or 8 each ball. As soon as they felt the effect of these 3 pills they left their battery and ran into the houses, from which they opened fire with matchlocks and gingals. We advanced to the village, and the General gave it up to the tender mercies of the 84th, as he said, "to do as they liked with". They did clear it with a vengeance for in 5 minutes there was not one live nigger in the village. They then (the enemy) got into a

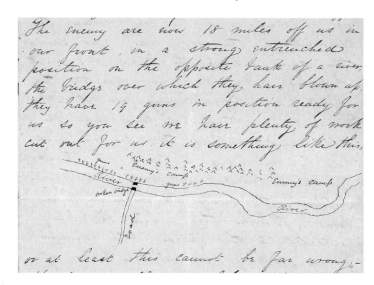

Pearson's sketch of the enemies position on the right bank of the river.

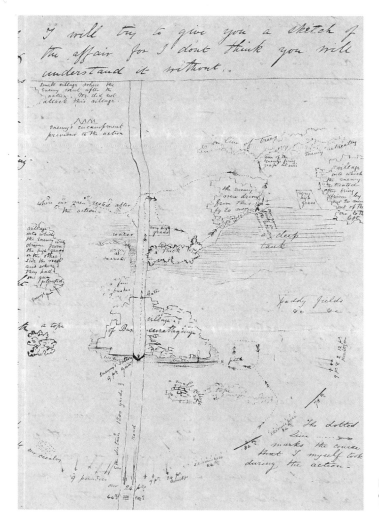

Pearson's sketch of the attack at Busseerethgunge on 6 August 1857.

very thick cover the other side of "Busseerethgunge" and there they stood firing at us, and we at them, for 2½ hours. We then saw that they must either be turned out or else we must stand up to be shot at, so we charged bang at them, turned them out of that, and then they went right and left to two villages on each side of the road. Well this was awful work, especially as they were pegging away at us with grape from one of these villages, our guns being in the rear. We laid down under a bank, the grape coming in showers over us, but not hitting any of us, till at last our guns arrived, and set to work at the village where their gun was. In the meantime, as we did not like to be idle, we (i.e. a subdivision of about 20 men with Ayton, Woolhouse, Gibaut, and myself) went to the village on the right, and scoured it out: our little band was then going to the right to another village, when we found ourselves in the presence of about 300 of the enemy and a gun. There was nothing left but to go at ' em, and at ' em we went at the charge: they gave us the volley and then (would you believe it!) they positively thrashed their gun horses into a gallop, and gun, enemy and all were out of sight in 2 minutes! The idea of 300 men and a gun running from 20 men with only their muskets is so preposterous that it makes one laugh, and had it not happened when one has something else to do, I really should have given vent to my feelings in a good fit of laughter. After this we went back to the road just in time to see the enemy flying from the field. I will try to give you a sketch of the affair, for I don't think you will understand it without.

(Sketch see page 64)

This sketch I know is correct, and so I hope you will keep it, as I may one day wish to copy it. I intend making a sketch of each action I have been in, so that I can explain it to you when I come home. I thought it would interest you to know which way I went, so I have marked it by a dotted line and arrows.

I think we were opposed by 6000 infantry and lots of cavalry. When we drove them out of the places marked "villages where they retreated after being driven from the road" they went clean away to their strong position on the opposite bank of the river, and we rested in the place I have marked as "where our men rested after the action" after 3 hours continual fighting.

Only one man of the column killed (he was smashed to a mummy by a round shot) but about 25 wounded. We made great havoc amongst the enemy and their dead and wounded were lying in all directions. The grape came hurtling along from one of their guns at us, and we must have suffered severely had there not been a cover under some houses. After resting for about 5 hours we marched back again to this place, for we have expended a ¼ of our ammunition and have only 850 fighting men left. The General came up and told the 84th he felt proud of them and was glad to see Captn. Willis at their head. He said it would be folly for him to attempt to cross the river with such a handful of men in the face of 30,000 enemy and 19 guns in a strong position, and that we must retire to the village we had marched from to wait for reinforcements. He was sorry to be obliged to leave our friends at Lucknow to their fate but he could not risk the lives of his men to save even them. The column then marched back to "Mugrawar" where our men are and where I dated this letter from just before we went to attack the enemy. A magistrate named Willock who is attached to the force found 6 gold mohurs in a box in Basseerethgunge. He kindly gave me one, and indeed he parted with all but 2. It was very kind of him to remember me and 16 rupees are not to be found everywhere. I see by the papers that Lieut. Greville R.N. is appointed Admiralty Agent at Southampton: is that Stapleton? I suppose you all saw that Wallace has retired from the Essex Rifles and a Captn. Whitehead late 42nd appointed to the Majority. I must not forget to tell you that I received a letter by last mail from Aunt Micklethwaite dated June 3rd, in which she mentions cousin Edith's marriage. I cannot make out the name of their residence in Montgomeryshire–is it Frontfraith? I was extremely disappointed at not hearing from you, for I fully expected to have received No. 11 long before this.

We have taken 5 prisoners: 2 are to be blown away from the guns and the remaining 3 hanged. The force is likely to remain here for 2 or 3 months as they are not going to send reinforcements from Calcutta for 2 months and it is utterly impossible to advance without. Poor Maud, an artillery officer, unfortunately broke his leg after the action: he was sitting on a gun carriage and by some means or other his leg caught in the spokes of the wheel. Cholera is our worst enemy: 6 men of our light company were taken ill with it before we had been back half an hour and the General ordered us to move out of the village we now occupy and go to the extreme right of the entrenchment.

Friday 7th. At 5.30 p.m. the 84th marched out of the village on the left and went to one on the extreme right about a mile distant. Of course we soon got there and the men piled arms for a while and then got into the houses. About 8.30 the "alarm and assembly" went, and the men were out in less than 2 minutes. Our picquets fired at some of the enemy's cavalry that were hovering about, and as soon as they saw we were prepared they wisely went away. We have 2 guns on our right ready for them.

I am glad you have some bathing now. Oh! if it was a quarter as hot in Jersey as it is here how you would enjoy a bath! What a luxury I should think it here! I am obliged to get a leathern bag full thrown over me and even that refreshes me wonderfully. How far superior would a nice sea bath be! Dear Joevelly! I do not think he would like the big guns: they would frighten him very much poor fellow. I hope he is all webbel. I should so much like to see your likenesses. I am very glad you play "Annie Laurie"; it is in my opinion one of the most beautiful pieces of Scotch music and I do not know [a] Scotch piece that is not pretty. How does little Madame Bichette get on? I should like to make her acquaintance and that of her son Bichot. I have not got a monkey yet, but when I do I shall call him Jacko. As to Pariahs, I have none and do not mean to get one. Flies are the plague of one's life here and it is impossible to do anything between 5 in the morn and 8 at night without a coolie fanning you.

Aunt Micklethwaite says she wishes you would go and spend some time at Ardsley, and says that you are going to Guernsey on the 18th June. If so you will (by the time this reaches you) be able to describe all the sights there. I am now so near the bottom of the paper that I must not say anything else except that I leave you to give my very best love to my precious Chaper, Macher, and Taty, and dear little Emmie accept the same from your own loving brodie,

                    Hughey

Letter No.19

CampCawnpore
August 15th 1857

My dearest Father and Mother,

I wrote a long letter, No.18, to Miss P and sent it off on the 7th inst. via Calcutta, and so you may suppose I have not very much news to tell you. I intend to send this via Bombay by way of a change.

We have had another action since I last wrote and of course totally routed the enemy. It took place on the 12th inst. near "Busseerethgunge" and lasted about 2 hours. The 78th Highlanders made a very brilliant charge, capturing 2 guns in a battery at the point of the bayonet. They were met with 4 showers of grape and suffered considerably, having 7 killed and about 20 wounded out of 100 men. The enemy fired very well and for the first time used shells; these they fired with great precision, but it is the opinion of our artillery officers that it is more luck than skill with them, for the firing of shells and the cutting of fuses is much too scientific for them to comprehend.

One of their shells stuck an ammunition tumbril of ours, killing 3 men and 3 bullocks besides smashing the shaft to shivers. We had no time to stop for it, yet as there was plenty of ammunition in it the General would not leave it for the enemy and Gibaut of ours was sent with 14 men to guard it until fresh bullocks could be procured. He had not been long there before the enemy's cavalry was observed charging down upon him in hundreds, and I was immediately sent with 12 more men to reinforce him. The column had by this time gone nearly half a mile away and could not see what was going on. I doubled my men as hard as they could go towards Gibaut's party and it appeared to me just a toss-up whether I or the enemy would reach him first. When he observed me coming it cheered up his spirits, and waiting till the cavalry (about 700 in number) came within 200 yards of him, he gave them a volley and then stood ready for them.

I soon reached him and having formed our little party round the tumbril, we waited for whatever might happen. They did not go away but kept about 200 yards off, firing with their carbines at us. We were now in a very critical position, and if they had been Russians or French cavalry against us I would not have given much for our chance, but they were only "niggers" and their hundreds dare not charge our little handful. We are just wondering what the end of it would be when we saw them gradually retire towards a tope of trees, and we soon saw the reason of this, for 2 of our 9 pounder guns were coming to our aid. Gibaut ordered them to unlimber and give them a round or two, and they soon did so. The first shot knocked over 2 men and horses and the second went no one knows where, we could not see the strike. They all scuttled off, and we limbered up and rejoined the column as soon as possible.

We marched on to "Busseerethgunge", more to say we had occupied it than anything else, for there was not a soul to be seen. We then marched back to our old position at "Mugrawar", 12 miles, and reached it about 6 p.m. having marched 25 miles and fought a battle between 2 p.m. on the 11th and 6 p.m. on the 12th inst The 84th had only one wounded, yet they had been under a fire of musketry from a village about 150 yards off, and shot and shell from other directions for 1 hour and a half. The enemy's cavalry annoyed us for some time during our retreat and we had to stop twice to speak to them with our 24 pdrs. At last a shell of ours burst in the middle of a lot of them and they did not bother us after. It was a very fortunate thing that we (the 84th) escaped so well: 3 shells burst exactly over us and I heard the bullets from them spattering all round, and expected every moment to feel something nasty in my back, but they did not hurt a soul. Again, a well directed round shot came disagreeably straight for the centre of my company. The men saw it coming and I and they went down on our stomachs "uncommon sharp": and it is just as well we did for it whistled over us and struck some yards in our rear.

We marched from "Mugrawar" in the morning of the 13th at 4 o'clock and reached the river about 6. By 4 p.m. every body and every thing was safely landed at Cawnpore and the last party that left Oude broke up the bridge by which we had crossed the marsh. The enemy appeared just as they had broken it up, and of course could not cross.

I went yesterday to see the bungalow where those poor women and children were foully murdered on the night of our victory at Cawnpore, and I picked up some hair which was torn from some poor creature's head. I send it to you in this letter. Every man who is discovered to have had a hand in the massacre is first made to lick with his tongue a square foot of the clotted blood and then is hanged on a gallows erected in the compound of the bungalow.

I also went to see the place where General Wheeler held out for 23 days; it is a range of barracks on an open plain. I never saw such a scene. There is not a single square foot in any part that is not riddled with shot and shell, and how they could have held out at all is beyond everyone's comprehension. There is no roof and the floor is a mass of bricks and timbers. What a terrible retribution is at hand!! The cowardly murderers dared not in thousands attack the brave 200 in that place!

I wrote a long letter to Uncle Pearson a day or two ago and told him all the news. I have not yet received No. 11 and am extremely anxious to hear from you. I shall send this via Madras.

Good bye, dearest ones. Give my best love to darling Emmie and Aunty, and accept the same from your most affectionate, loving son,

                    Hugh Pearce Pearson

P.S. How is Joevelly?

Letter No. 20

                    Camp at Cawnpore
                    August 20th 1857

My very dear Father and Mother,

I yesterday was delighted to receive your No.11 dated 30th June containing the account of your expedition to Guernsey etc. The letter was given to me when on picquet, and you well know that I could not have got it at a more suitable time, for nothing is more devoid of interest than an outlying picquet. The last letter I sent was No.19 dated August 15th and posted somewhere about that time, but as the dawks are very uncertain, and are frequently stopped by the rebels it is quite possible that you may receive this before it.

I have been in another action since I last wrote, and as hitherto came off scatheless. We fought 3 regiments of native infantry, 1 of cavalry and 4 guns. They held their ground with more pluck than ever they have shewed before and actually stood to be charged and bayonnetted by us. Owing to their determined resistance they suffered great loss, and more than 400 are said to have fallen on the field, and our spies say that few escaped without a wound. Although the old 84th was in a very hot fire of musketry, yet only 1 man was hit, and that slightly: 1 man was missing for a time but was afterwards found with his throat cut from ear to ear and minus his musket and ammunition. It is conjectured that he fell from the effects of a sun stroke and was subsequently cut up by the enemy's cavalry.

Our Light Company was armed with the Enfield rifles belonging to the killed, wounded and sick of the 78th, 64th and Fusiliers, and did good execution with them. The engagement took place at Bitthoor, a town 12 miles from Cawnpore and the place where the palace of the "Nana" is. Owing to their having horse artillery we only captured 2 of their guns, both 6 pdrs, 1 native made, the other most likely taken from the arsenal here when Cawnpore was in their hands. Our worst enemy was the sun, and no less than 6 of the 84th were buried that evening from its effects.

I carried the regimental color *(sic)* in the action, and however great the honor may be, I know the nuisance is greater. In a thick garden where we went it was with the greatest difficulty that I could get through at all; as it was, the top of the color was torn off by the branches of trees, and to make matters worse the bullets were cutting through the trees in all directions, and no enemy could be seen on account of the surrounding brushwood. Once, I went behind a mud house roofed with straw to tie up the top of the color, when ping, ping came a brace of bullets through the roof. These were of course random shots for it was impossible that anyone could be seen in such thick cover.

Our men actually got within 30 yards of them but the 12-mile march, the sun, and their empty stomachs had so weakened them that not only were they unable to charge them, but could not even load their muskets: the Fusiliers on our left got within the same distance of them but they had had their breakfasts and grog and went in at them with a will, killing a great number. We had our baggage attacked and 2 camels taken, but the Fusiliers came up and retook the greater part of what was lost. Had they not arrived at this critical moment all our baggage would have been taken. Three servants who started 2 hours after the column with their master's grub were caught by the cavalry and their heads cut off. "Bitthoor" was fought on the 16th inst exactly a month from the battle of "Cawnpore".

Major McCarthy has got 15 months sick leave to England and I don't think he will ever come out again. No news has come in from Lucknow and there is but little doubt that poor O'Brien and Magrath of ours and all the Europeans there have met with the same fate as the poor fellows here with General Wheeler. However, no news has come that Lucknow is fallen, so we must hope for the best.

The enemy are now entrenching themselves in a battery on the Oude side of the river, exactly opposite our entrenched camp, and have brought a heavy gun down and put it in position. The old General is going to abandon the entrenched camp after going to the trouble of making it almost impregnable. The enemy will of course march in, and fine work we shall have to retake it The whole of the Gwalior troops, 7000 in number, are now marching against us; they are a complete army, infantry, cavalry, and horse artillery, and have more courage and skill than any other natives in India. Their artillery is in every respect equal to ours, and they understand elevating principles and everything about shells. The only reinforcement that we shall have is a paltry 60 men, which will hardly replace our casualties of the last action. To complete our predicament, all our big gun ammunition with the exception of 1200 rounds has been expended!!!

August 22nd. I have just received a letter from my cousin Jane dated June 23rd acknowledging mine of April last. There is no news in it except as regards the members of uncle P's family. Neither is there any news of importance here within the last few days. The 78th Highlanders have buried 25 men and 1 officer in the last 5 days from cholera. We bury about 2 per day, and every other regiment loses more than we do. The Fusiliers lost 1 officer yesterday, and the cavalry 2 officers last night, all of cholera. The old General put us into tents pitched in a swamp, and with only a single instead of a double roof. The rains came through the roof of every tent by night, and the sun by day, and this is the sole cause of the mortality which is now raging amongst the men. I was up to my ankles in water for more than an hour whilst it rained, but I took the precaution to change my clothes, socks, and boots as soon as it left off. Others said "Oh! it will rain again in a few minutes and it is no use changing," but it did not.

Thank God I have been in the best of health ever since I left you, and I and Kenny are the only two who have not been sick a single day. Nine actions have been fought, and I have been in all. Kenny has been in eight. But Ayton is the only one in the regiment beside myself who has been in all. I forgot to mention in the proper place that Ayton's horse was shot through the heart in the engagement of the 16th inst. at "Bitthoor". All our sick and wounded are going to "Allahabad" immediately, under a strong guard. Sir Colin Campbell has arrived in India and taken the command.

I laughed very much at that part of Emmie's letter where she says that she is unable to go out in the heat of the sun which she is sure must be nearly as hot as it is in Bengal. Tell her I have seen as many as 7 and 8 strong men lying insensible by the road side at one time from sun strokes, and this as early as 10 in the morning. This happened on the way to Bitthoor on the 16th inst.

The hire of country hackories to carry our baggage is enormous, being 30 rupees a month. I suppose you get the "Friend of India" regularly. How do you like the paper? I wonder if I should be sick now in crossing from Southampton to Jersey. I wish I had the chance of trying.

25th. How uncertain life is! Poor Kenny, my friend, my chum, is now no more. At 7 p.m. on the 23rd inst. he dined with us in good health, at 9 that night he was seized with cholera, and at noon next day (24th) he was a corpse. We buried him this morning at 6 o'clock, and so much was he liked that he was followed by nearly all the officers of the force, and a very complimentary order was inserted relative to his being more than once conspicuous for his coolness and gallantry under fire. Poor Kenny was my best friend and no two fellows could be more suited to each other than we were, and I am sure I shall never in this regiment meet anyone half as good as he was. This is the second son Colonel Kenny has lost in this regiment within 18 months.

All the regiments here behave very kindly to me and I need never dine at home unless I like. Tonight I dine with the 78th. I received a very kind letter from Colonel Impett at Poonamallee inquiring after the welfare of myself and the old 84th. After I have done this letter I will write to him.

How fortunate Uncle P. is in selling the colt for so much as £270. This is exactly the sum that an officer of the Bengal Artillery has won at cards during the last fortnight. I saw the order issued by the Duke of Cambridge relative to officers messing in the papers and was, as you may suppose, much delighted at it.

I think I have managed to make a nice long letter in a small space this time, don't you think so? I shall look forward to the time when I shall hear Emily play her music with great delight. I can very well imagine that she plays uncommonly well and as she grows older of course her progress will be in proportion. You mustn't part with "Juzzif' Oh no!! Joseph Denyer is too good for that! Oh yes he is. I cannot say I like mangoes, but as to mango and fish, they are truly delicious. Poor Kenny's effects are not to be sold, as he expressed a wish that they should be sent to his uncle at Madras.

26th Wednesday. Yesterday, we had foot races and racing in sacks for the men's amusement. It was confined to the 84th yesterday but to-morrow a grand day comes off: every kind of amusement is got up, open to the garrison, Seikhs included. There will be mile and half-mile races, jumping in sacks, and hurdle races, bobbing in treacle, putting a 24 lb shot, running after the pig with the greasy tail, and in short every amusement that the present circumstances will allow.

I have just come from the sale of my old chum's things which, contrary to my expectations, took place at 11 a.m. I bought a nice rifle he had for 40 rupees.

Smithett of the artillery has a very nice pony (flea-bitten grey) which he is going to let me have for 80 rupees if I like it. My pony in Burmah has just been sold for 80 and that will just balance it. A grey mare I had at Barrackpore Hely bought for 60 rupees, and the "tat" I now have and which I gave 30 rupees for is yet unsold.

What a rascally set of cheats Government are! When we were coming from Allahabad the Commissariat supplied the officers with 1 bullock hackory between two to carry their tent and traps. Every one supposed that they would pay for them, but a day or two ago they sent to say we were to settle with the hackory drivers, and told us the rate of wages was 5 annas per bullock per day when moving, and 2 annas per day per bullock when halted. Now they have 4 bullocks and this amounts to 20 annas or 2s. 6d. a day when moving, and 8 annas or 1s. a day when halted. In addition to this we are to pay them 5 annas a day for half their journey back to Allahabad. This altogether amounts to about 50 rupees a month!!

I am now going to close this epistle or I shall miss the post. Give my very best love to dearest Aunty and Emmy,
and accept the same, dearest Father and Mother,
from your affectionate and loving boy
H. P. Pearson

Letter No. 21

Camp Cawnpore
September 4th 1857

My own darling Emmie,

I received your letter enclosed in Chaper's No. 11 as I always do with unmingled satisfaction and delight, and as I have not written to you since August 7th I think it is again your turn to get one. My last letter home was No.20 dated the 26th ult; the last received by me was No.11 dated June 30th.

There is little or nothing to tell you, for since the battle at "Bitthoor" we have been living peacefully in camp, but yet I must not on that account diminish my supply of letters to you, for if I did I should get a good scolding from Chaper, Macher and everybody else and "that would nebber do. Oh no!" [sic] But I think if I look in all my pockets I may find a thing or two to tell you which will, I am sure, amuse you. Ah! Now I remember something.

After the fight at "Bitthoor" a great deal of plunder and booty fell into our hands, the most part of which was the property of "Nana Sahib", the leader of the mutineers: there were horses and carriages, elephants and camels, furniture, books and nearly every thing you could name, and amongst other things was a monkey, yes a fine, grey bearded, patriarchal-looking old chap which was the favourite of the "Nana". Well! This old fellow was "boned" by a very nice man named "Willock", a magistrate sent with the force, and a great friend of mine. He was named "Nana" after her old master and had a nice pole erected for him to climb up. One day last week some officers including myself went to see "Willock", and we amused ourselves by playing tricks upon the "Nana": we tied a little puppy to his chain by a string and then put a piece of cake just so that the monkey could not reach it, but the puppy on account of the length of his string could; how do you think "Nana Sahib" got the cake? I know you cannot guess it, so I will tell you. He waited till the puppy got a bit in its mouth, and then pulled him by the string round his neck till he could reach him; he then deliberately opened the puppy's mouth and took the cake out, I need not tell you he ate it. After he got the cake he let the string loose till the pup got another piece, and then pulled him in again. When the puppy would not open its mouth he beat him till he did. This monkey is so tame as to let anyone shake his hand and stroke his soft fur.

I find the English mail is just in and some few of the officers have got letters but I have not got one yet. I shall not post this till to-morrow for I greatly expect No. 12.

I see the English government has only [just] heard of the revolt at "Benares" and the massacre at "Jhansi" and are sending an immense number of troops out to India. I wonder what they will do when they hear of the massacre of 210 women and children at Cawnpore and of 100 European troops in boats at the same place. What will they do when they hear of General Wheeler's heroic and unparalleled defence for 23 days of an old building in an open plain against 15,000 of the enemy with endless resources?

Tell dear Father that the 84th is, by a General Order, transferred from the Madras to the Bengal Presidency from the date of their arrival in Bengal on the 19th March last. Perhaps however he may know it. Ask Chaper if he remembers the "Baileys" who used to live in a large house close to the gate of "Bedford Grammar School". One of his sons is in the "Madras Fusiliers" here and directly I saw him I recognised him. Ask him too if he remembers "Gregory Way", the son of old "Way" of "Boreham" and the brother of a schoolfellow of mine at "Felstead". He got an ensigncy in the "West Essex" and afterwards came out here with a commission in one of the Native Regiments: he had his head cut off by the mutineers at "Allahabad" on the 6th of last June. It was his uncle who was a captain in the W.E.M.

Sunday 6th. The day's letters are in but no welcome epistle from you has come. So I must e'en finish this without waiting any longer. The latest news is that General Outram left "Allahabad" for Cawnpore on the 5th inst. with a reinforcement of 1500 men (H.M. 90th and 5th Regt.). If this is true he will be here in 4 days and we shall again cross into Oude.

An officer of the Seikhs has a very curious little dog, a native of Central China, and it has the head of a bulldog although not above 6 inches in height It has an odd way of always keeping the end of its little tongue protruded from its mouth and the name of the animal is "Chumpo" but his master calls him "Tsumpsa". He is a remarkably well conducted specimen of the canine species, and is a most particular friend of mine, so much so indeed that I generally visit him at least once a day. I should very much like you to see him for he would amuse you as much as "Juzzif's little frebbend" "a nice little man". Do you know, Emmie, I seriously intend getting a nice monkey to amuse me. Don't you think it would be a good plan? I will wait to see whether you approve of the scheme.

Yesterday afternoon I went with some other officers to see the field where we fought the battle of Cawnpore: it is certainly very interesting to revisit places fraught with so much interest, especially as I recollect every part of the field. I had not time to go to the spot where poor Captn. Currie of ours received his mortal wound, but tomorrow afternoon I intend going on purpose to see this spot.

Cholera has not quite disappeared from the column: this morning Captn. Sheehy, H.M. 81st at present serving with the Volunteer Cavalry fell a victim to that disease, and is to be buried this afternoon at 5.30 o'clock.

The camp is now very jolly, and all last week has been spent in getting up amusements for the officers and men. We have had foot races of every description for the men, besides jumping in sacks, putting a 24-pounder shot, pig with a greasy tail, etc etc, and for the officers horses and pony racing, hurdle racing etc, etc.

I bought a pony (flea-bitten grey) last week from Smithett of the Artillery for 80 rupees. It is a very nice pony and exceedingly fast but in wretched condition; however, I hope soon to make him look a little better. I sent away my servant "Malliapah" the other day for getting drunk and taking some of my beer. He was very penitent, so I got him another situation, with Oakley of my regiment.

I am very sorry to hear of poor Flora's death: is Joevelly sorry too? I am delighted to hear what good accounts I get of your progress in music and often wish I were in the parlour of No. 5 Plaisance Terrace listening to you playing "Annie Laurie", but I dare say I soon shall be. How I envy you your walk on Noirment Point! You were quite right in supposing that I should have expressed a wish to shoot the rabbits there for I most certainly should have done so. I am astonished at pussy not liking my Joevelly; it only shows what bad taste she must have. Naughty puss! had you scratched my dear "Juzzif' how angry I should have been! You don't mention that you gave the "marshter's man" yash his own man any lemonade. This is not right. Oh! no it is not! You must have given him some I think. Did you not? Once yash! I know you did. And what did Josephine think of the old hog-backed horse? Pray tell me.

You must in your next letter give a long account of Guernsey, and I shall be on thorns till I get No. 12, so tell dearest Chaper to write by every mail.

Now dearest sister good bye for the present. Give my very very best love to dearest Chaper, Macher, and Gaty, and accept the same,

darling Emmie,
from your most affectionate brodie,
Hugh P. Pearson.

P.S. Do write soon. I shall write next to Macher.

Letter No. 22

Camp Cawnpore
September 17th 1857

My own darling Mother,

I have just received the long looked for No.12 and as we are going to cross the river to-morrow into Oude I must write now or not till we come back. I have a great deal of news to tell you, and will therefore begin at once to open my budget.

General Outram's force, consisting of Her Majesty's 5th Fusiliers and 90th Light Infantry with Major Eyre's battery and 2 8-inch howitzers, joined us here yesterday. He brought up 1500 men, and we are now in a position to defeat the greatest force that the rebels can bring against us. On the way up from

"Allahabad" General Outram heard that a party of the enemy 300 strong with 2 guns had crossed the river from Oude and did not know of his being so close to them; he accordingly sent 100 men and 2 guns to lick them, and they did so with a vengeance. They came across the rebels close on the bank of the river (they having just come from Oude on a plundering expedition), and when they saw the Europeans coming they made a precipitate retreat into 3 boats (which had just brought them over) and pushed out into the river. Our 2 guns then unlimbered and opened on the boats with grape shot. 2 boats were sunk instantly and all on board either shot or drowned, but the third managed to get some distance before it was observed and was not sunk, but very few lived to tell the tale. As they swam to the bank they were shot and bayonetted by our men and not more than 8 or 9 escaped out of about 200.

In about a week more I hope to have the pleasure of writing to tell you that we have relieved Lucknow; it will not take us more than that to get there. How delighted I shall be to shake the hand of poor old David O'Brien of ours who is there! The niggers are in a most delightful state of fright, and the other day 2 regiments sent 6 men each to Gen. Havelock to say that they would lay down their arms on condition of a free pardon, or if we wished it they would help us against the mutineers. He told them that we did not want any assistance from them and that he would not listen to them, but that if they really wished to prove their good will towards us the best way to do so would be to pitch into those who would not lay down their arms when we crossed over. They are collecting in great numbers on the opposite bank of the river, and actually come to bathe in the sacred stream every morning within range of our 24 pdrs. But the other day they came down in numbers to bathe and our artillery officer could not resist the temptation of sending a "pill to be taken immediately" into them, which pill did "with malice intent" kill and destroy 4 of the rascally murderers. They also erected a battery on a sand bank just opposite, so when it was finished we sent a party of the Fusiliers (Madras) in the steamer across the river and they destroyed it quite unmolested.

I enclose an interesting account of the defence and massacre at this place written by a Lieut. Delaforce who with 3 others were the only ones who escaped. The force is formed into 2 brigades: 1st Madras Fusiliers, 5th Fusiliers and 84th right brigade, 78th Highlanders, 90th L.I and Seikhs left brigade. The 64th are to be left behind to garrison Cawnpore.

On our return from Lucknow we shall in all probability go to Delhi. I wrote to Uncle on the 12th inst. and told him all the news up to that date. I received a letter from Cousin Jane on the 19th August. I, Ayton and Barry are the only officers of the 84th who have been in all the 9 actions, and I hope I may be preserved through as many more. I have now told you all the news, and will finish this letter by answering No. 12, which as I received it from Chaper must be answered to him.

Dearest Chaper,
I have indeed as you say undergone great hardships, but still I am, if possible, in better health when knocking about than when in quarters. I think dear Mother would be astonished to know that I was on picquet for 24 hours in heavy rain without any shelter, and when I came off had not the means of changing, all my baggage having been sent to Cawnpore by order of the General who did not allow us to keep even a servant behind. I have not sold my saddle and bridle,

and have got 2 mounts. My mare has strained her back sinew in a jump and is very lame, but my grey galloway is all right. We had a great paper hunt the other day and went at a great pace. I got 3 spills but was not hurt. I am afraid my little mare is hardly up to my weight, for though she is extremely fast and jumps beautifully, yet she is very slight and requires a light weight.

One of my falls was a very odd one. We were going at full tilt across a large maidaun where some bullocks were grazing. One was standing still and I was going in front of him when just as I reached him he moved on; the mare's chest struck him full in the ribs and sent him flying about 5 yards, and the shock sent her rolling too and I could not help following her example. She is a very willing little creature.

My traps are all right at Dumdum. I packed them up before leaving Rangoon. You advise me to note what things are dear in India. The answer is "everything". A shilling in England will get as much if not more than a rupee here. Fancy a pair of thin blue cloth regimental trousers 28 rupees at Harmans!

You say, dear Chaper, that what you say is very true, viz. that we shall have good shooting at Lucknow. I am afraid we shall but it will be "street shooting" rather dangerous now-a-days.

I wrote to the editor to alter the direction of the paper but will counter order it. The "Friend" costs me little or nothing dear Chaper, so I must keep it on. We shall be at the fall of Delhi yet.

Tell Emmie I have got a lady monkey who is very loving and takes great care of a little dog who occasionally visits it. I must now leave off, having exhausted my budget of news. One thing I forgot to tell you, viz. that the 84th have all got the Enfield rifle now.

Best love to dear Emmie, Taty, Mother and yourself. Hoping you are all in the best of health.

I remain, Dear Macher and Chaper,
Ever your most affectionate son,
H. P. Pearson

Letter No. 23

"The Heron Khana", Lucknow
November 21st 1857

My own very dearest Father and Mother,

What would I not give to be able to send word to you by telegraph that I am alive and unhurt! What dreadful anxiety you must have suffered at not hearing from me for so long! But yet one thing comforts me, and that is, that in your dearly prized letters Nos.13 and 14 received a few hours ago you trust in your boy's writing to you whenever it is possible. I am so delighted you say this because it will prove such a comfort to you during the long time that has elapsed since my last letter. Always, dear ones, think this, and know that whilst I am alive and have my right hand to write with I will never omit any opportunity of writing something, however short it may be.

The reason of my not writing will be easily explained when you hear the account of the troubles, hardships, and privations which have befallen me and every one else in General Havelock's force since the date of our departure on the 19th Septr. last from Cawnpore to the relief of the beleaguered garrison of Lucknow. Thanks to the unutterable mercy of Almighty God I have been preserved in health and safety whilst my brother soldiers have fallen by my side both from sickness and the sword. May he ever preserve me as he has done, and soon grant that I may return to all those I so love!

Since the 23rd of Septr. I have never for one minute been out of fire, and whilst I write our heavy guns and mortars are breaching the walls of the "Kaisah Bagh" or King's Palace, raising a deafening din, and (from necessity) sending their shells whizzing over our heads a little nearer than is agreeable. In this I think you will agree with me when I tell you that one of our mortars sent an 8-inch shell into the house where I am on picquet, which burst in the lower room, but fortunately did no damage with the exception of smashing a Seikh's pouch to atoms: and yesterday one of our own 18's coolly sent a round shot slick through our house (mistaking it for the lower buildings of the "Kaisah bagh" from which we are not more than 80 yards distant). All this time your son was watching the proceeding of pointing the gun from an upper story of the self same house! This shot also hurt no one, but it might have done so, and for my part I think if a man is to be killed it is much more satisfactory to suffer from an enemy's shot than from that of his own side. What think you?

I will tell you the casualties in my regiment before I go farther (this is since our arrival in Bengal). Killed and died: Captns Currie, Pakenham, Lieuts Saunders, Poole, Gibaut, Maybury, Ensign Kenny. Wounded: Captns Willis, Lightfoot, Anson, Brigadier Russell (all slightly) Lieuts O'Brien (sev.), Ayton (sev. right arm amputated at socket), Browne (sev.), Barry (slightly), Oakley (sev.) Woolhouse (sev. right arm amputated above elbow). Poor Poole's death was very melancholy; he was shot dead by a sentry of the 5th Fusiliers, but he alone was to blame, as he did not answer the twice repeated challenge of the sentry. It was a dark night, and he wore a large turban round his cap. He was visiting the sentries, and to do so, had to expose himself to the enemy's fire; in his anxiety to escape their observation by running along a hedge he neglected to answer the challenge and consequently was shot. He just lived long enough to free the sentry from all blame.

The force met with the most desperate resistance, as the undermentioned list will show: out of 2500 men and officers who entered Lucknow on the 25th September, 615 men and 47 officers fell before 8 o'clock the same night!! I hope I may never see such a frightful scene again as I did that day! Many officers who were at all those hard fought actions in the Punjaub say that they were nothing to that day.

The advance to the [Charbagh] bridge defies all description, but to give you a faint idea of it I will tell you that there were 7 guns pouring grape on our column as we advanced in sections along a narrow road, and that there were clouds of the enemy's riflemen in the thick elephant grass which grew on both sides of the road firing without intermission, and from the bridge to the residency was a succession of streets, loopholed and lined with men, through every inch of which we had to fight our way. We got to our fellows about 7 p.m. Ever since then we have been besieged by the enemy, who surrounded us and cut off our retreat

We have been on half rations all the time, and if we had not had bullocks for our guns instead of horses we should have had no meat. Our allowance has been 8 oz. meat and 10 oz. of otta (a sort of coarse oatmeal). I never once had enough to eat as you may suppose. We were allowed to bring no servant and no clothes except what we stood in, so I had to wash my own clothes myself, clean my own boots etc etc. Soap sold at 15 rupees a cake, brandy 50 rupees a bottle, a shirt cost 30 rs, a pair of socks 10 rs, tobacco 50 rs. a pound–these were our market prices.

We all expected to walk into Lucknow, drive the sepoys out, and then go back to Cawnpore ourselves with all the ladies and garrison. Under this impression we left all our baggage, servants, ponys etc at a place called "Allum-baugh" (a large garden outside the city) and never saw them again till the 17th Novr. Fancy being for 8 weeks in the same shirt, socks, trowsers and coat, without soap and on rations hardly enough to feed a canary bird! It certainly is a great blessing to have a good appetite, but not in such a time as this. The men got vast amounts of money in the city and did not care what they gave for an extra pound of otta; the consequence was that the cooks robbed the officers and men of half their rations and sold it back to them at exorbitant prices. I have seen men give 15 and 20 rupees for a lb. of otta!

The many escapes I have had are beyond number: I will some day relate them for your amusement I have now been in 13 general actions besides skirmishes, sorties etc, and have got through all unhurt. When we (Genl Outram's force) came into Lucknow we rushed madly through all the streets, and got in in one day, but Sir Colin's force took 6 days coming the same distance and occupied all the principal houses as they went, so that now we can go to "Allumbaugh" in safety.

One piece of news you will be glad to hear. Sir Colin's force surrounded a lot of niggers in a garden [Secundra Baugh] so that escape was impossible. Our fellows then rushed in and had a terrible revenge. Sir C ordered the bodies to be counted and it was found that more than 1700 had been slain in that one spot; not a single man escaped. They generally manage to get out of the way, but they were fairly outdone there.

Sunday 29th. Since I finished writing the above there has been another casualty in our Regt: poor Sandwith was killed on the 22nd inst. whilst leading a party of the 84th against a bungalow occupied by the enemy. He was the only European hurt, but more than 70 of the enemy were slain. You will see the casualties of this force mentioned in the papers: what it amounts to I do not know.

On the 20th and 7th of November I kept dear Emily's and Father's birthday as well as I was able. On the 7th I drank dear Chaper's health in a glass of "aqua pura", having nothing else, but on Emmy's birthday I managed to get some beer and performed the ceremony in due state. I hear Lieuts are to get 1500 Rs. prize money and hope it is the case. I know we shall get something high, for upwards of 26 lakhs of treasure were found the first day in Lucknow, and nearly 3 times as much afterwards.

It is useless for me to try and tell you all that occurred since I last wrote, for if I did you would be kept another mail, and I would not like anything to delay this. I will just tell you one of my many narrow escapes, and then I must leave off, for the letters all go to-night. I was one day washing my shirt at a well in the middle of the yard where the 84th stopped, when a man rushed across, crying "Look out for that shell". I looked up and saw it coming whish-oo, whish-oo, whish-oo into the square and pitch about 4 yards from me. Down I went like a shot behind a large log of timber, and as I did so, bang it went! A few bits whizzed over my head but did no harm.

You will be sorry to hear of poor Major (or, I believe, Colonel) Biddulph's death. You very likely remember him at dear Uncle Pearson's at Bourton.

I had some lovely rifle shooting with the Enfield in Lucknow and used frequently to astonish the natives. Penton and I have played the mischief with them and have bagged 16 between us besides those we wounded. Many an hour have I passed at a loophole and generally with effect.

Do not trouble yourself, dear Chaper, about my wanting money. I am now 3 months pay in arrears, and lots more in hand. And now my own dear ones, good bye for the present, and look out for a "long one" by next mail. May the vessel

that carries this letter be swift and the wind that wafts that vessel fair, and then many anxious hearts will be relieved! Tell dear Uncle, Aunt, cousins and all at Bourton that I am safe, and constantly think of them. Give my very best love to dearest Aunty and Emmy, and accept the same, dearest Father and Mother,
From your most affectionate boy,
Hugh, Pearce, Pearson

P.S. I have a nice birthday present for Miss P. but cannot send it. It is a "gold mohur" but keep that a secret and I will send it when I can register the letter. I know you won't mind bad spelling for I never even wrote my name for 2 months. Woolhouse is gone down and the stump is quite well but he is wretchedly thin.

Letter No. 24

Allumbaugh, Lucknow
December 2nd 1857

My own dearest Father and Mother,
    I sent off No.23 on the 29th ultimo just to set you all at rest as to my safety, but I intend in this letter to tell you the principal occurrences of the last two months. Whilst I remember it I will tell you that I yesterday bought a very new double-barrelled pistol from La Presle for 60 Rs. I have long felt the want of a pistol but could get nothing except revolvers, which kind of weapon I do not at all like, for two reasons, the first because they are always getting out of order, the second because the ball is too small (in my opinion) to take effect instantly on penetrating and I always am an advocate for a light pistol and a heavy ball. I never had much opinion of revolvers and now, since the mutiny commenced, I have had many opportunities of judging, and must say that the only pistols (revolvers) that stood the work were "Deane and Adams'" improved revolver with lever ramrod (which could be cocked or not at option) and "Whitton and Daws" revolver; as for Colt's they were always out of order.
    I am now on outlying picquet in rear of the camp, and, thank goodness, once more in the open country and out of range! You cannot imagine what a curious sensation it was for the first two or three days after leaving Lucknow! I could scarcely bring myself to believe that I was once more free, and no captive after a long imprisonment was more glad at being released than I was! We left Lucknow on the 23rd ultimo at 3a.m. and the whole force marched in silence and undiscovered to the "Martiniere College". The retreat was so beautifully planned and executed that the enemy had no idea till next morning about 10 a.m. that we were gone, and long after we had left we could hear the boom of a gun or the crack of a rifle fired at the place which we once occupied.
    In this happy state of ignorance did our friends remain till about 10 a.m. and when they discovered how they had been duped their fury knew no bounds. In the course of the day they fired a "Royal Salute", and issued proclamations to the effect that it was all up with the sahibs, that the sahibs had been "driven out of Lucknow, and that as soon as the sepoy regiments had had a little rest they would follow them (the sahibs) with all their force and drive them neck and heels out of India". The "old guard" (as we are called) have been left behind to keep Allum-baugh and the adjacent villages till the return of the rest of the force who have gone with the "chief" to thrash the Gwalior contingent at Cawnpore. The "old guard" is that brigade which has held Lucknow so long, and consists of the following regiments: 5th Fusiliers, 32nd, 84th, 90th L.I., 1st Madras Fusiliers, 78th

Highlanders, Seikhs, Volunteer Cavalry, Captn. Maude's battery of Royal Artillery, and Captn. Olphert's battery of Bengal Artillery. Those are the "old soldiers"! the "Fighting Brigade"!! the "Old Guard"!!! But they are also divided into two parts, viz. "Havelock's heroic little band" and the others who came up afterwards. Barry and I are the only officers of the 84th who belonged to the "little band" (which consisted of 200 of the 78th, 200 of the 84th, 200 of the 1st Madras Fusiliers, 100 Seikhs and Maude's Battery) and, I have no little satisfaction in telling you that I am the only officer of the 84th who has been in every action from "Futtehpore" to the present time. You will be sorry to hear that poor old General Havelock died of dysentery on the morning of the 15th ult. just as he was about to enjoy the honours that awaited him, and reap the reward of his labours.

I will now tell you why the force went back: it appears that the "Gwalior Contingent" (the finest body of native troops in India) had advanced on Cawnpore during the absence of the force and closely invested it. It is said that for 2 days and nights they kept up a fire that has rarely been equalled in rapidity and constancy, and that Sir Colin arrived, most opportunely, engaged them, defeated them, and was going to pursue them to the death. This has yet to be confirmed. The "old guard" grumbled greatly at being left behind, and certainly it did seem unfair to leave us here after such hard work in Lucknow, but when one comes to think it over it is not so bad as it would seem. The report is now that we shall remain here until the return of Sir C with 20,000 men, and that then we shall be sent as an escort for the women and sick to Calcutta and then home. It is not at all improbable, and I only hope it may be so; at any rate we can't have any more fighting, as the whole brigade would hardly form one regiment, so shattered is it! The strength of the 84th is now 414 all told!! The 78th is nearly 500 strong.

I will now just copy a few principal events that occurred (with their dates) out of a brief diary I kept. (I commence on Saturday 19th Sept., all the occurrences previous to that date being related in No.22 date 17th Sept.)

Sept.	19th	Crossed the river into Oude. Skirmish with the enemy–drive them from the sandhills, and occupy them.
"	21st	Action at Mungrawarra, and advance on Busseerethgunge.
"	22nd	Halt at Busseerethgunge
"	23rd	Action at Allum-baugh
"	25th	Advance on Lucknow. Relieve garrison. Gen. Neill killed. Loss of the force on this day 47 officers, 615 men. Casualties in the 84th 1 officer killed, 4 wounded
"	28th	Lieut. Poole 84th killed by a sentry of the 5th Fusiliers.
"	29th	Grand sorties on different parts of the enemy's position. Officers of the 84th sent with the party, Lieuts. Penton, Gibaut, Blake, and Ens. Pearson
Oct.	6th	Lieut. Gibaut 84th killed in the trenches while endeavouring to extinguish some woolsacks which the enemy had fired. Attack by the enemy on our position. Am sent in Lieut. Gibaut's place.
		(Nothing unusual occurs till)
Nov.	16th	The 84th take the "Heron Khana" and capture one gun. Lieut Ayton sev. wounded (right arm amp. at socket). Sir C's force take the "Secundra-baugh" and kill 1700 of the enemy there
"	18th	Servants arrive with baggage. First grog issued. Am sent on picquet.
Nov.	21st	Received letters Nos 13 and 14 from home

"   22nd   Lieut. Sandwith 84th Regt killed. Am sent on picket to 32nd Mess house

"   23rd   The force leaves Lucknow at 3 a.m. and marches to the Martiniere. Detachment of the 84th under Captn. Rolleston (to wh. I am attached) marches to the Dil Koosha and bivouacs for the night on the plain

"   24th   Detachments of Regt. sent to join their corps

"   25th   The force marches to the Allum-baugh and arrives at 2 p.m. I am taken ill and travel in a doolie

"   26th   Browne (adj.) and Crohan rejoin the regiment

"   27th   The sick and wounded women and children return to Cawnpore escorted by the whole of the force, except one brigade which is left to hold the plain around Allum-baugh. I am sent on picquet to extreme right.

"   28th   The Camp is moved to a new position

Dec.   1st   Purchase a double-barrelled pistol for 60 Rs

"   2nd   An escort of infantry (90th) and cavalry are sent to Bunney Bridge to bring the mail etc. I am sent on outlying picquet to the rear of the camp and
HERE I AM!

Friday 4th. We are very hard worked now. I was on picquet on the 2nd inst. came off yesterday morning, to-day I am on orderly duty and to-morrow I shall be on picquet again. The road between Cawnpore and this is not open, and the letter I sent the other day is now at "Bunney Bridge" half way between this and Cawnpore. Sir C. came across the "Gwalior Contingent" at Cawnpore, and as his leading brigade entered our entrenchments the niggers retreated from them. The Cawnpore garrison then made a sortie and captured 2 8-inch howitsers, 2 24-pr guns, and 1 light field gun: 17 officers were killed during the bombardment, amongst whom was Colonel Wilson, H.M's 78th Highlanders, who was in command. All the officers' baggage was put in the assembly rooms before we marched up here, and has all been looted by the sepoys. Of course everything I had there is gone, and amongst other things my tunic, new shell jacket, shako etc etc. The 84th was at the recapture of Cawnpore and our first fight was at Futtypore (Futtehpoor) on the 12th July.

Sunday 6th. We had divine service this morning at ¼ to 8 but only prayers were read. There has been a great deal of firing all this morning between our guns at the Allum-baugh and a gun of the niggers who our men call "Nancy Dawson". They are very fond of playing at long bowls and know better than to bring their guns out in the open. To-morrow the 84th send 2 captains, 4 subalterns and 200 men to relieve the party now at Allum-baugh. I am happy to say I do not go. There is lots of game here, I mean in the wild fowl line: geese, ducks, teal, widgeon and snipe are to be met with in the neighbouring 'jheels", but unless one is well armed and mounted it is dangerous work. Penton shot a wild duck last night, and 3 couple of snipe a few days ago. Pigeons are very plentiful, but ammunition is very scarce, and what little there is kept for game.

It is very distressing not hearing from Cawnpore: I have no doubt that No.15 is lying there waiting to be read. I am very much annoyed at losing my desk (wh. was left at Cawnpore); it contained my journal of the journey up from Barrackpore to Cawnpore, with some sketches of the actions who took place, and observations on them. It also contained a gold mohur and all my letters from home.

The nights here are cold and sometimes frosty, and generally speaking the weather is very cool and comfortable. There is a scarcity of food for the horses, and we have only 9 days provisions; however, a large convoy is daily expected. My monkey "Jacko" was in Allum-baugh all the time I was in Lucknow, and was taken great care of by Donelan our Quarter Master. The consequence is that he has grown fat and saucy like "Joevelly": he is now outside my little tent, and has a little basket house of his own into which he retires at night and when the sun gets too oppressive for his delicate constitution. He also has a piece of green baize for a counterpane and it is truly ridiculous to see him wrap himself up in it like a man. Oh yash it is!

In looking over my pocket book a day or two ago, I came across the enclosed piece of paper marked "Georgey Denyer's Hebber, 7/20/56" and on looking into it I found a lock of the brown pet's curly hair. Give it to Miss P. to look at, and when she has looked well at it she must send it back to me in the first letter she writes, for I could not do without a remembrance of dear "Juzzif'. Oh no!

In one of the actions we fought since my letter of September 17th (viz. "Mungrawarra" on Sept. 21st) our cavalry alone cut up more than 120 sepoys; it was the first action in which we had cavalry enough to use. The regiments (Queen's) in Sir C's force were: 5th, 8th, 23rd, 32nd*, 42nd, 53rd, 64th, 75th, 78th, 82nd, 84th*, 88th, 90th, 93rd*. and 1 squadron of the 9th Lancers, Peel's Naval Brigade, Rocket Battery and a lot of artillery: besides these he had some 3 or 4 Regiments of Madras N.I., Seikhs etc etc etc. Of these regiments only those I have marked with a (*) star saw any work coming in; some regiments, for instance the 8th, 42nd, 88th, never saw a shot fired, but were left to keep the road open. I ought to have said "the regiments and detachments of regiments in Sir C.'s force were etc. etc" for what I have put above would lead you to think that the 78th, for instance, had no work to do; that part of the 78th who were in Lucknow with Sir J. Outram's force of course saw as much as we did, but the detachment of the 78th that came up with Sir Colin saw nothing. The 93rd are a splendid regiment, and their bonnets and petticoats have "established a funk" with the niggers. All the regiments here are in full dress and fight in it too.

One day before we went into Lucknow, about 20 of the enemy's cavalry came towards our baggage on the road, and as they rode quietly along Captn. Nunn of the 90th L.I., who commanded, thought they were our own cavalry, and would not allow the men to fire. As soon as they got on the road they charged down on our men who were straggling about, cut down Captn. Nunn and 15 men and then cleared off, leaving about 20 of our people killed and wounded. A few men who were unhurt made excellent practice at the enemy retiring and pulled down about half of them. On this day I lost my bedding.

Tuesday 8th. Yesterday a party of the 84th went to Allum-baugh to relieve some of the 1st Madras Fusiliers; the officers were Captns. Rolleston, O'Brien, Lts. Penton, Peate, Barry, Blake. A foraging party went out to a village called "Bijanoor" 5 miles off to get gramm and wheat. It consisted of 200 men of different corps, 2 guns, and 30 cavalry. I do not think I mentioned that "Hardy" joined us on the 23rd ult. He had only been at home a short time when he was ordered out again.

How very fortunate I have been in getting my promotion so soon! I expect soon to see myself gazetted vice Kenny, deceased. I shall be out of the break, or at any rate very nearly so. The run in the 84th is not yet finished; old Reed has gone home to have his name scratched out, and Major McCarthy cannot stay. Those two are certain to go and very likely Major West also. Is it not very unfortunate losing all my uniform and desk etc at Cawnpore? I suppose Govt.

will give us compensation for it. If they give us 750 Rs. (as I hear they will), it will do very nicely but I had many things there that no sum of money could replace.

I have been obliged to buy warm clothing at officers' sales on account of the extreme coldness of the nights and early mornings. The best things I bought were 2 flannel shirts (like those I bought at Chatham when you were there), for which I gave 20 Rs. and 2 prs. flannel trousers 6 Rs. I also bought a flannel coat and some warm socks. Every body wanted warm things and consequently anything of that description sold for much more than cost price, but I was determined to get some warm clothing, and was prepared to give almost any sum for them. (I think you will say I was right.) I saw one flannel shirt sell for 26 Rs. and bid up to 20 Rs. for it myself, and prepared as I was for high bids, yet must say this rather astounded me!

In the skrimmage going into Lucknow I lost my regimental sword, and picked up a cavalry one wh. I use now. I afterwards found it belonged to poor Pakenham, and before he had it, to Kenny: it was dyed with its last owner's blood when I picked it up. The next regimental sword I get shall be one I can trust my life to, not a mere skewer (like my last) which one blow wd. cut in half.

The latest news is that the chief has surrounded the Gwaliors in Cawnpore and is teaching them a lesson they won't forget, but I don't believe it. I once (in Lucknow) took it into my head to go up a mine of ours to see what it was like. A miner was sitting at the end of it with a pistol in his hand waiting for the niggers to break in, and I could distinctly hear them picking away a few feet off: as I had no particular wish to have a personal combat under ground, I scuttled out faster than I went in, and soon after the nigger who broke in was shot by the miner. We killed a great many that way, and one civilian name Kavanagh settled 4 by himself.

By the way, talking about Kavanagh reminds me that I must tell you of a thing he did wh. has never, I am sure, been surpassed in daring. Before the C-in-C entered Lucknow, Gen. Outram wanted to send a plan of the city in order to direct him, and also directions as to how he should advance and what places ought to be taken. Gen. Outram dared not entrust so important a thing on paper for fear the cassid who took it should be caught, and of course he could not send a verbal message by a nigger, because the least mistake wd. ruin all; in this dilemma, Kavanagh (who is the head clerk in a Govt. office) stepped out and volunteered to go disguised as a native to Sir Colin and carry any instructions. At first Sir J. Outram wd. not hear of it, but on Kavanagh pressing the point, he reluctantly consented. (This was at a time when the enemy kept the sharpest look out, and they had captured the last three of our spies who went out.) Kavanagh was dressed as a native with shield, tulwar and pistols, his skin was dyed, and a Seikh's beard stuck on; thus accoutred he went one night through the heart of the city and after 14 hour' trudge he reached Sir Colin's force and delivered his message! Being a civilian, he could not by the rules receive the "Victoria Cross" but Sir J. Outram promised to exert all his influence to procure it for him as a special favour. I am very anxious he shd. get it, for it never was better won.

In Lucknow, everybody was covered with lice and I, as well as every one else, had my hair all cut off. It was the only plan to get rid of them.

I forgot to say Kavanagh was a married man with 5 children, all in Lucknow when he went out.

I have just had a polka jacket, pair of trousers, and cap cover dyed sand colour. It is a splendid dress and is very difficult to distinguish. I should say it was nearly time for the "Agincourt" to arrive in England, and if so you will soon get my journal. I suppose Woolhouse will soon be on his way home and then you will be able to get all particulars from him.

I think I must now shut up shop and get this letter off. Give my dearest Taty and Emmie my very best love and tell them that No. 25 shall be sent to them. Tell Miss P. that I am delighted to hear she is getting on well and will bring her lots of nice presents. And now my own best-beloved and dearest of parents, about whom (together with Taty and Emmie) I am thinking day and night, accept the unbounded love and gratitude of your dearest and only boy,

Hughey

P.S. Don't be alarmed if you do not hear from me for weeks together, for sometimes circumstances will occur who preclude every possibility of writing. Rest assured I will always write when I can. I had two splendid Cashmere shawls for you and Taty worth about 400 Rs. each, but when a prize agent was appointed I was compelled to give them up. A Colonel Palmer who did not give up his loot was cashiered.
Good bye

Letter No. 25

Allum-baugh, nr Lucknow
December 9th 1857

My dearest Emmie,
I only sent off No. 24 yesterday and so I have no fresh news to tell you. However, I will amuse myself by answering all the questions you put to me in Nos. 13 and 14, and then I will wait a few days till I have something new to relate.

I read your account about your school with great interest and was very sorry that Mary French is not a good girl: I have no doubt she will reform her behaviour and take example by you. I am very sorry I cannot send you the pretty blotting book I bought, as were I to attempt sending it from here you would never get it. When the times are a little more settled, I will see what I can do to send it and a few other little presents. I had a little birthday present ready for you, but I was shut up in Lucknow without any possibility of writing, and of course could not send it; when I get to a safe place I will do my best to get it conveyed to you.

I am delighted to hear you have given up printing and now you have done so you will soon write nicely. Miss Dodd must be a very nice person, and certainly she has hit upon the proper way of teaching little girls how to be thoroughly conversant with the French language. If I had been made to converse during school hours in French, I should soon have been able to talk fluently. It would be a capital thing if all boys were taught to write with their left hand, especially those who are intended for the army. Poor Woolhouse and Ayton in my regiment have both lost their right arm and will have to learn writing with their left hand.

Our regiment was present at the disbanding of the 34th N.I. and 3 companies of that regiment were on detachment, so probably Miss Sullivan was correct in saying that those companies had not revolted. You say that you think I must be somewhere near the mutineers. I am about 2500 yards from them now and when you were writing I was 15 miles from them (that was before Futtehpore). You ask if Delhi has fallen: it fell somewhere about the 19th September, I think. You write on 16th Aug. and say you wonder where I am then; most probably fighting at Bitthoor, for it was fought on that day. (I made a mistake in saying that I was 15 miles from them the day you wrote. I was confounding 9 Aug. with 9 July on which latter day I was 15 miles from them. On 9th Aug. I was at Mungrawarra in Oude). You must not allow Georgy Denyer to be so dainty, oh no you must not! You ought to get on fast with botany for you used to take great interest in it, and had several books on the subject.

The Kaisar-Baugh or King's Palace in Lucknow is nearly the only building of any consequence that we had not got possession of, and the enemy had (and have now if they did not kill them) 1 gentleman, 5 ladies, and a little child prisoners in it. They allowed these unfortunate people to write to their friends in the Residency, no doubt imagining that we could never get in to rescue them, and that therefore there was no harm in one knowing they were there, but when Sir Colin comes back they will find to their cost that British soldiers when avenging their slaughtered countrywomen are not to be deterred by anything niggers can do from exerting their strength to the utmost, and that the British Lion when roused is no plaything, and more than a match for half a dozen Bengal tigers. They had a taste of what awaits them, at the "Secundra-baugh", when 1700 of them were slain, and if they swear again to conquer or die, they may as well leave out the word "conquer", for the other is pretty sure to be their fate.

Friday 11th. An officer went with 6 troopers the night before last to Cawnpore, and took the mails with him. He arrived there in safety and returned this morning with some newspapers and letters. He brought news of poor Ayton's death from the wound received at the taking of the Heron Khana on 16th November. He was one of our senior lieutenants.

All the sick and wounded, women and children have gone to Allahabad under a strong escort. Sir Colin came up with the Gwalior Contingent on the 7th inst. and took 37 guns from them. He also captured the whole of their ammunition, treasure, camp equipage, and stores and followed them up to the 14th mile stone from Cawnpore where the pursuit was given up. I yesterday amused myself by shooting pariahs with Hardy's rifle: they are a great nuisance at night, howling all about the camp.

Monday 14th. Last Friday, after I had done writing, a convoy consisting of 20 cavalry and 200 infantry left for Cawnpore to bring back provisions and the mails: they are expected back about the 19th inst. It was found that the post master at Cawnpore had sent us 2 bags of dead letters, by the officer and 6 men who went down, instead of sending the new ones. He has had a severe reprimand from Sir J. Outram for his neglect. The weather is dreadfully cold, with a piercing northerly wind, and poor little "Jacko" lies huddled up in his basket all day long with his green baize rug wrapped round him. This morning, an escort of 200 men with cavalry and guns went out to some village 10 miles off to bring in grain. They have not yet returned.

Wednesday 16th. I am once more on picquet and have the whole day to write to you in. The escort which went out the other day came back late at night and had succeeded in getting a fair quantity of grain. Not having any fresh news to tell you, I will answer your questions in No. 14. Oh! what a mistake I have made! When I look in Chaper's letter to find yours, I see written, "Emmie will write next time, but cannot now as it would be overweight". Wasn't that a mistake, to say "I will answer your questions in No.14" when you did not write in that letter at all. I must now write to dear good aunty and must bid you good bye for the present. Give my best love, and kisses without end to dearest Papa, Mamma, and Taty, and with the same to your dear little self,

believe me to be, darling Emmie,
your most affectionate and loving brother,
Hugh Pearce Pearson

Best love to Joevelly and his "frebbend".

Letter No. 25 (sic)

Allum-baugh, nr. Lucknow
December 16th 1857

My own kind and good aunty,

I do not think you have had a letter all to yourself since No.11, so I determined to send this to you as it is fairly your turn. I told all the news to Emmie, but still there is plenty left to tell you, and amongst others, many things that would not interest Emmie.

I am getting on very fast in the regiment, and my gazette must have been in the papers long ago. Since my last letter (No.24) I have gained one more step through poor Ayton's death, which occurred on the 28th of last month. I shall also have two more steps soon, for both Humphrey and Oakley have applied for their exchange. Oakley's father is dead, and his mother and sisters are living in Madras, and it is for this reason he wants to exchange. However, he could not live in England as he has not the means to do it. Humphrey is disgusted with the regiment and has made up his mind to retire if he cannot get his exchange. Besides this, old Reed and Macarthy must go; they have no alternative.

I have been spending money on weapons of self defence lately, and have bought a very pretty brace of "Egg's" pistols in case complete. I am now well set up, and I think the money I spent on them is well laid out. Instead of prize money, we are to have 6 months' batta; this will be very nice. I shall also get about 750 Rs. for the loss of my kit at Cawnpore; this, with my pay for September, October, November and December, will be something exceedingly good.

It is very kind of Aunt Micklethwaite and cousins to take such interest in me. I am, as you say, in the midst of friends, though at the same time far away from them. I have lately been amusing myself by shooting with Hardy's rifle, and have even astonished myself sometimes.

Friday 18th. I will now tell you what we get to eat, at least what I get. For breakfast, beef roast, boiled, minced, stewed or hashed, bread, tea sugar and milk, salt. For dinner, beef (cooked in different ways) sometimes a chicken currie, and always a pudding of some kind. Once I had pancakes, yesterday I had baked rice, and today suet pudding. My boy is an excellent cook, and generally makes a very good dinner.

Last evening I took my gun out for geese or teal, but could not get within shot of them. I shot a jack snipe, but could not find him on account of the darkness of the evening. Blake of ours is going with 50 men to Bunnee Bridge at 2 o'clock and I have asked him to take this with him so it will unavoidably be shorter than I intended. I am quite well, thank God, and have been with the exception of a day or two, ever since I left you. I sprained my ankle one day in Lucknow, and anxious to take my turn of picquet when it came round, I began to walk about before it was strong again. Consequently, it is now very weak and I frequently strain it. However, rest will set it right.

Your letter, dear aunty, gave me great delight; every word in it is good and kind like your own dear, dear self. Instead of length of time and long separation weakening, it only strengthens my love for you the more. Oh! darling aunty, you and sister, father and mother are in my thoughts waking and sleeping, and in my nightly prayers I thank God for having given me such good and kind parents, and so truly loving and affectionate an aunt and sister. I will, as you say, and indeed I do, and always have put my trust in Him who ruleth all things, and feel confident that He will keep me in safety to return again soon to those dear ones I so love.

Thank dear Macher for me for the kind and welcome letter enclosed in No.14, and tell both her and Chaper never to be anxious and worried if they do not hear from me; you all know that whenever I can write I always do, and so if you do not hear for even 3 or 4 mails consecutively, you may be certain that the post has been miscarried, or that some unusual circumstance like our being besieged in Lucknow has unavoidably prevented me from writing. I must now send this off or I shall be late for the mail. Blake will bring back the mail if there is one, and I will write again then. Give my best love to dearest Father and Mother and sister, and accept the same, dearest and kindest of auntys [sic]

from your loving nephew,
Hugh Pearce Pearson

"Jacko" desires to be remembered to "Juzzif's frebbend. He hopes in course of time to be introduced to him.

Letter No. 26

Camp nr. Allum-baugh, Lucknow
Sunday, December 20th '57

My own very dear Father and Mother,
    I only sent off No.25 to aunty and Emily on the 18th and consequently have as yet little or no fresh news to relate; however, since the day I sent off No.25 I have received your two delightful and interesting letters Nos.15 and 17 but the intermediate one No.16 has not yet turned up. I have also had a long letter from our old friend Drage, dated Tylden Detachment, Nr Queenstown, Frontier, Cape of Good Hope, in which he desires to be remembered kindly to you and writes something else in the same sentence which I cannot quite decipher, so I have enclosed the paragraph for you to see. I should have liked you to have seen the whole of his letter, for there are many parts in which he speaks very highly of dearest Chaper. He says he is in the midst of game, both birds and beasts, large and small.
    I cannot understand my name not appearing in the Gazette, for Kenny's death occurred on the 24th August and I get my promotion through him. It was indeed kind of dear good Taty to make me such a handsome present, but what you say is very true, i.e. that few nephews have so truly good and kind an aunt I will write something to her in this letter to thank her for such great kindness. As soon as I get it I shall sell the brace of Egg's pistols I bought the other day, and very likely the double-barrelled "Northallerton" also. I bought both these pistols from La Presle our doctor, and gave him 110 Rs. for the lot The revolver, you say, is either self-cocking or not, and this is exactly the sort I should have chosen; in fact, they are the only revolvers that keep in order. In my No.24 (I think it is) I say that this is the only kind I like. Hardy of ours who has just come out has one of them.
    I am now on picquet in the front of the camp, consequently have the whole day for writing. I have just finished a long letter to Drage and intend to keep up the correspondence.
    Our band master has just come up from Cawnpore, and the band has made great progress since his arrival. I see in the papers that the "Agincourt" has arrived in England. I should say you have ere this got my journal which was sent him by Mr. De Carteret. I see in the "Illustrated London News" a sketch of "Wheeler's Entrenchment" at Cawnpore; it is a very correct one indeed. I will give you a list

of the casualties amongst our officers since the date of the regiment's arrival in Bengal.

Name	Date of death	Wounds and action in which received
Lt. Maybury	June 15th	Died at Benares
Lt. Saunders	July 2nd	Killed in the massacre of Cawnpore
Capt. Currie	July 20th	From round shot wound recd. at the recapture of Cawnpore on the 16th inst.
Lt. and Adj. Browne		Sev. wounded 3 times at Unao, July 29th
Ens. Kenny	August 24th	Died of cholera at Cawnpore
Lt. O'Brien		Sev. Wounded in Lucknow garrison, July 16th
Capt. Willis		Slightly wounded at the relief of Lucknow on the 25th Septbr.
Capt. Pakenham	September 25th	Killed at the relief of Lucknow
Lt. Barry		Slightly at the relief of Lucknow 25th Septbr.
Lt. Oakley		Severely at the relief of Lucknow 25th Septbr.
Lt. Woolhouse		Severely (right arm amputated) at the relief of Lucknow 25th Septbr.
Lt. Poole	September 27th	Shot by a sentry 5th Fusiliers in Lucknow
Lt. Gibaut	October 6th	Killed in advanced garden of palace, Lucknow
Lt. Ayton	November 28th	From wound received at the taking of the Heron Khana, Lucknow on 16th Novbr.
Brigadier Russell		Severely, Lucknow November 17th. Was in Sir Colin Campbell's force
Capt. Anson		Slightly at Delhi (date unknown to me)

This is a correct list up to the 21st December. I do not know whether I mentioned in any of my epistles that Mecham (the son of old Col. Mecham who goes to St Luke's Church) is here doing duty with the 1st Madras Fusiliers. He was in the 7th Oude Infantry, and when that regiment was reported to have murdered their officers, he was given up by his friends as dead, but he managed to get into Lucknow and stayed there during the siege. He was blown up in a mine sprung by the enemy and badly bruised, but is now here all right and well. I made his acquaintance one day, and liked what little I saw of him very much.

You, dear Chaper, are not the only one who has remarked that our gallant regiment is destitute of Captains and Field Officers at the time when their presence is most required. As for the FO.'s, the two I have seen (Reed and McCarthy) are nothing but drivelling idiots (as the men call them) and I should be sorry if I could not command a regiment better than either of them. It is not however their fault, for they are both in their second childhood, and they certainly are to blame for not having retired years ago. As for the Captains, they are, with one exception, like policemen, never to be found when wanted, and one, viz. Captn. Snow, is, I have no hesitation in saying between ourselves, a down right c----- d. He has been twice sent up to Allahabad, and has twice contrived to go away sick, and now, when he was obliged to come up with the Chief's force, has taken some appointment or another down country. It is too bad and every one in the regiment is disgusted with him; here are all the juniors doing the work whilst the seniors are safe on leave. But I am happy to say there are exceptions. Captn. Willis has been everywhere with the regiment since the retaking of Cawnpore, poor Currie was killed at that action, Pakenham was killed the other day and Captn. Rolleston is now here with the regiment. Captn. Du Vernet who came out the other day with Chute on board the "Agamemnon", directly he arrived in Calcutta applied for a staff apointment there. I do hope he has not got it, for his place is with his regiment. Lightfoot came up with Sir Colin's force as a.d.c. to Brigadier Russell, and Anson came up too on the Chief's staff.

I read in one of the papers a glowing account of the 64th and 78th taking that gun on the Cawnpore road at the retaking of Cawnpore. Now it happens that the 78th had nothing whatever to do with the taking of that gun and it was captured by the 64th and 84th alone. But the Madras Fusiliers and 78th were two pet regiments of Havelock's, but in reality they did nothing more than the poor old 84th wh. is so shamefully deprived of its just amount of praise. The 78th had no more to do with capturing that gun than the Brigade of London shoe blacks, and not so much as a single grape shot went near them during our advance up to it. That they should have all the keudos does certainly stick in my gizzard most awfully.

I have found out an important fact since this campaign began, and that is, that British soldiers carry all before them as long as they are advancing, but once give them the word to retire and they are worse than a rabble. I have too frequently seen this myself, and I will just tell you an instance that I did not see myself, but which I know to be true.

Owing to the absence of the Chief's force from Cawnpore, the Gwalior Contingent came down and attacked it: it was then occupied by H.M.'s 88th, 42nd, 60th Rifles, 82nd Regt. and various detachments. Our force under General Windham (consisting of the above corps) went out to attack them, and when they got under fire, the 88th Connaught Rangers positively flung away their arms, and went as hard as they could go to the entrenchments, this was when they were ordered simply to retire. The colonel of the 82nd actually refused to lead his regiment against the rebels, and has been sent home under arrest. The 64th went at 'em with a will, and though awfully cut up, entirely routed them (the 64th lost 7 officers killed in this affair). What makes it so provoking is this. Some of the Gwalior Contingent were afterwards taken prisoners, and when sentenced to death they said that they had come to Cawnpore to die, but never expected to see the sahibs run away from them.

This is not the only case. Look at the 10th at Arrah, and at the 32nd at Chinahut near Lucknow, how they ran helter-skelter for miles and it was a case of "devil take the hindmost". On the 29th September when I went out with a party to take some guns, the men went on irresistibly in the face of guns showering grape with terrible effect, and this, not from one battery, but from battery after battery on the road as we advanced, but, when having fulfilled our purpose (viz. blowing up a 24-pr. gun) the order to retire was given, all discipline was cast aside and not only did the men run as hard as they could back to entrenchments, but they positively left many wounded (5) behind to be cut up, and it was with the utmost difficulty that they could be got to take away any of the wounded.

The Hero of the Redan (Genl. Windham) has got in a nice mess and has been sent by Sir Colin to Amballah out of the way. I imagine he will come down a peg or two in the estimation of the British public. The officers in Sir C.'s force have been behaving shamefully; at this present moment 2 are to be tried for murder, 3 or 4 for insubordination and many more for other crimes. Sir C. is being very strict and stands no nonsense. Several are to be tried for looting. The men in this brigade are not behaving as well as they might do, and floggings are very frequent. A man of the Artillery and 1 of the 5th Fusiliers who were flogged the other day have gone over to the enemy. That is what the men say; at any rate they are not to be found.

There is nothing going on here, and I believe Sir C. is not coming up here again for some months, so that will be a nice respite from war's alarms. Next time we go at Lucknow there will be very little fighting, for we shall pound them from all sides with 68-pr. and 13 in. mortars before we attempt to go in. The Chief has now got at, or rather 6 miles from, Cawnpore a force of at least 17,000 men, and there are 3000 here. He is now forming a large brigade to come up from Benares direct to Lucknow, without going to Cawnpore at all. It is to take Fyzabad, the ancient capital of Oude, on its way up. Col. Berkely 32nd is chief of Outram's staff here, but I do not know him personally. I intend making a few little ground plans of the position we occupied in Lucknow, and of that we now occupy. Of course it will not enlighten you much as to distances but I will do my best to make it as intelligible as possible.

I must write to Aunty in a separate letter or this will be too heavy. Good bye my own dear Chaper and Macher. Give my best love to Aunty and sister and accept the same

from your very affectionate and loving boy,
H. P. Pearson

Letter No. 29

Camp nr. Allum-baugh, Lucknow
New Year's Day, 1858

My own dearest Mother,
I sent off three letters to you, Nos. 26, 27, 28 all on Xmas Day, so, as you may suppose, my stock of news is very inconsiderable. However, what there is I will tell you at once and then put the letter by till another day. The best news is that I yesterday received your anxiously expected No. 18 in which you first make mention of my being a lieutenant and also one from Uncle Pearson about the same date as yours.

January 2nd. This morning I was refreshed by the sight of dear Chaper's handwriting, and the Drum Major put the lost No. 16 into my hand. What an odd thing both your 16 and mine went wrong!

On the 30th of December a draft of 185 men for the 84th arrived under command of Captn. Du Vernet and Lieut Chute: they are a remarkably fine set of men and many are decorated with Crimean medals and clasps, and a few have still to receive gratuities for distinguished conduct in the field. Chute told me he saw poor Woolhouse at Allahabad looking very ill, but he left this place little more than a skeleton so he couldn't be much worse. I have no doubt that when he once gets on board ship, he will from that moment get better.

I see it is in General Orders that Havelock's force are to get 6 months batta. I shall I suppose draw lieutenant's batta. On the 28th ult. I sent in a claim (to the E.I.C.) for compensation for my personal property which was left at Cawnpore, and destroyed by rebels belonging to the Gwalior Contingent, I being at the time on active service in the field, to the amount of 910 Cos. Rs. It was counter-signed by Willis, who stated that to the best of his belief the loss did not arise from any neglect on my part, and that at the time it was destroyed I was on active service. I bought one of poor Ayton's shell jackets for 10 Rs. It is short for me and a little too tight, but can easily be altered. Nothing very particular has occurred of late. Nine thousand Ghoorkas are expected to arrive soon. This will be an immense assistance for the sepoys both hate and fear them.

I wrote a letter to Uncle P. on Xmas Day and posted it the same day. It contained a plan of our position here and that of the enemy. I asked Uncle to send it to you when he had looked at it, so you have in all probability got it when you receive this letter. In this, I enclose a plan of the position occupied by the old garrison before we relieved it on the 25th Septr last. *(Fig)* If you are writing to Bourton you may as well send it, for although it is done from memory, and very badly too, yet it will perhaps give some idea on the subject.

By the last mail a letter addressed to Captn. Willis arrived from poor Kenny's father, thanking all the officers for their kindness to his dear boy. It went on to say that he had given his two sons to the 84th, and that he had not another to give them, but nevertheless would always watch with the deepest interest the welfare of the regiment. It was a beautiful letter and deep must have been the poor parents' grief. It (the letter) contained no murmuring, no angry expressions or passionate lamentations, but a quiet and calm submission to God's will, who gave him sons and whose right it was to take them away. I never read a letter so beautifully written as was the bereaved father's to those who had shown kindness to his boy.

I bought the pony which belonged to my old chum (Kenny) for 70 Rs. The animal was a great pet of his. His rifle (which I bought at his sale) was one which he found in Cawnpore on our entrance into that place on the 17th July, and was destroyed with my other things by the Gwaliors. I have not yet received the pistol, but have written to the Secretary of the P & 0 Company about it and expect an answer by next mail.

I have just heard that a convoy goes down to Cawnpore to-morrow, so I must finish this if I want to send it. I suppose you saw in the papers Lieut. Wm. McGeachy Keats from the 84th to be Captn. without purchase in the 2nd battn. 7th Fusiliers. This gives Hardy his Company. Humphries is still looking hard for an exchange, and so is Oakley. And now, my own dearest Macher, good bye, give my very best love to dear Chaper, Aunty and Emmie, and believe me to be,

Ever your most fond and affectionate boy,
Hughey

P.S. I sent nos. 26, 27, 28 on Xmas Day. I am going to write again soon to Uncle.

Letter No. 30

In the Allum-baugh, Lucknow
January 8th 1858

My dearest Emmie,

I am now on picquet for a week in the Allum-baugh, which is a house in the centre of a very large garden about ½ a mile from our camp, and I am sure I cannot employ my leisure hours in a more pleasant manner than in writing to you.

This very day, about 1 p.m., an artillery officer named Gordon was killed in the right front battery whilst directing the fire of his guns. A round shot struck the poor fellow on the head and dashed his brains out. He was buried in the evening by lamp light.

Saturday 9th. I was much amused by reading your little stories, especially the one about the Prussian soldier: You now must be able to speak French like a native. News arrived yesterday that Sir Colin had taken 15 guns near Futtegarh and that Colonel Seaton had taken some more, 8 or 10 more, at Furruckabad.

Sunday 10th. This is our last day at "Allum-baugh"; to-morrow we shall be relieved and return to camp. It was reported that we were to be attacked last night Consequently we were obliged to keep on the alert, but I suppose their courage failed them for they never came.

Thursday 14th. Since Sunday last I have been perpetually on the move, but as I am now quiet again for a space I will resume my pen. We were attacked last Sunday night about 9 o'clock, but we gave them two rounds of grape and they retired at once. We were relieved from Allum-baugh on the following morning and returned to camp on Tuesday 12th. inst. The enemy made a very bold and daring attack on the whole of our position, but were repulsed with great loss to themselves (viz. 400 killed and wounded) whilst our casualties amounted to 5 wounded. Rolleston, Barry and myself with 100 men were sent to reinforce, and subsequently to relieve, the party at Jellalabad. We arrived just as the enemy retired and had some fine shooting, though the round shot were flying about pretty thick. Barry, myself and 50 men were left as a picquet in the tope all that night and following day, and this morning we were relieved and are now in Jellalabad fortress. Jacko doesn't like round shot at all and barks at them like a dog.

Friday 15th. I went out shooting last night, and saw lots of duck, but my shot was not big enough for them. To-morrow we expect H.M.'s 13th Foot and 7th Hussars to arrive in camp. This will be a fine addition to our little force.

Now dear Emmie I must say good bye for I anticipate a "turn out" just now, and I shall be too late if I delay posting it. Give my best love to dearest Father and Mother and dearest Taty, and believe me to be

Dearest Emmie,
Your affectionate brother
H. P. Pearson

P. S. Du Vernet and Chute with 200 recruits arrived on 30th ult. I recd. a letter from the Secretary of the P. & O. Compy. saying he made over my revolver to Messrs. Grindlay & Co. I have written to them but have as yet had no answer. H.P.P.

Letter No 31:
[Missing–this letter went down in the *SS Ava* off Ceylon, but was ultimately recovered and arrived in a faded and hardly decipherable state.]

Letter No. 32

Camp Alum Bagh, nr. Lucknow
February 12th 1858

My dearest Father and Mother,

I sent off No.31 on the 24th January and since then I have received your delightful and welcome letters Nos. 20 and 21. There is so little to write about now, that you must not be surprised if my letters are not as long as they used to be, and if this is not as long as usual it is merely from the want of news.

The Chief is daily expected from Cawnpore with his siege train of 100 heavy guns, of which 9 are 68-prs., and by the end of next week most probably Lucknow will be in our possession. There will be some awfully severe fighting before the city is ours and more especially on their side, for the niggers have devoted all their time and talent to fortifying. that part of their position where the danger threatens most, and have, as far as we know, quite neglected the rest. Several large convoys have come up from Cawnpore within the last week, and one has just arrived consisting of 2000 carts of stores for the force coming up with Sir Colin, and also 800 of the Royal Sappers and Miners for the erection of batteries etc.

I have several times been out with my gun, and have never yet had a blank day, though the game is not by any means plentiful, nor is it easy to be got at, as it is all in the jheel and swampy ground which separates us from the enemy, and of course a certain amount of danger (though very small) must be incurred in pursuit of it. We always go out well armed and in parties of 3 and 4, and as yet only one shot has been fired at us. The season is now over, and I do not intend going out again. We are accoutred day and night in expectation of an attack, and to-day they were to have come out in overwhelming force, but I suppose they have changed their minds for there is no appearance of anything yet. I have just drawn a bill on Calcutta for 463 Rs. and am going to send home 400 deducting the odd 63 Rs. to pay my shoe bill. I shall have it placed to my credit at Cox's, as I did the 500 Rs. which I sent home a few weeks back.

We have had races here to amuse us, and several very good ones have been run. A steeple chase is coming off this afternoon, and several pony races. I of course shall go to see them.

We have now, I am happy to say, lots to eat and drink: and on the whole I am as jolly as can be expected under the circumstances. On the 15th inst. Brigadier Franklyn and Whittock with 40 men from Gyah join head-quarters. The Brigadier has now command of the left brigade, and Russell has the right (both 84th officers). I wrote a long letter to Uncle P. on the 1st. inst. which by the time you get this will have reached him. I have been sent down once to Bunnee Bridge on convoy duty, and dined with H.M.'s 34th the same night, returning to camp next day.

Monday 15th. I have just been relieved from a 3-day picquet and am therefore going to finish this letter immediately. H.M's 75th Regiment have been ordered down country and left here yesterday morning for Cawnpore. The road from here to Cawnpore is literally covered with troops. At Bunnee (10 miles off) there are the 79th and 42nd Highlanders, the 34th, 38th, Queen's Bays, 7th Hussars, a wing of the 9th Lancers, a troop of Royal Horse Artillery and 76 heavy guns. At Nawaubgunge there are some more troops, and so on all the way to Cawnpore. It is calculated we shall have 15,000 infantry and 4000 cavalry on this side alone. In about another week or ten days we shall commence operations.

Now my very dearest Father and Mother I must send off this letter for the dust is so terrific that it almost chokes me, and it is impossible to write whilst it continues. I shall write again to you just before we go into Lucknow, and as soon after as I can. Give my very best love to my dearest sister and aunty, and accept the same yourselves

from your most affectionate boy,
Hugh Pearce Pearson

P.S. I hope Joevelly is well and happy.

Letter No. 33

Camp nr. Alum Bagh, Lucknow
February 22nd 1858

My own dearest Father and Mother,

Although only a week has elapsed since my No.32 went on its way, yet many little things have occurred which I have no doubt will prove interesting to you, and if I can only recollect all that is in my head, I shall be enabled to send a much longer letter than the last.

As I sent my No.32 on the 15th I will begin by telling you what happened on that day and then follow my journal up to the present day.

On the 15th Febry. The enemy showed in numbers all round our position but more particularly on the left flank, whither Captn. Olpherts was sent with 2 guns of his battery and a troop of the Military Train. They came within 400 yards of the enemy, and the guns were then unlimbered and 2 rounds of grape from each gun were sent into them, killing (as was discovered by our spies next day) 8 and wounding 5, amongst which last was the "Moulvee" (slightly). A convoy came in from Bunnee Bridge.

On the 16th inst. Went out shooting with Penton to a large tank or jheel in rear of the left brigade. I got 1 duck (the first I ever shot) and Penton also got one. A large convoy arrived escorted by 2 companies of H.M.'s 34th which latter returned to Bunnee the same day. At 5 p.m. the enemy made a very bold and determined attack on our position which lasted till 10 p.m. The force all turned out on the alarm, and as the attack seemed to increase in strength towards night the picquets were all reinforced: our right wing was sent to the left front light gun battery, the left wing with 2 guns occupied the space between the heavy gun battery and the Alum Bagh. The enemy several times came within grape range and their loss was considerable. Before we were withdrawn, 3 rounds were fired at extreme range from the 2 24-prs. and 8 inch howitzer in the heavy gun battery, and the shells flying high in the air looked extremely beautiful.

On the 17th. I was on orderly duty and inlying picquet. The force was turned out at 11 a.m. and a second time at about 12 o'clock when the 84th was marched down to occupy the space between the Seikh lines and the half way picquet. The enemy retired without making any serious attack. Whilst we were standing there, some Seikhs got up on a bough of an old tree to look out, never noticing that the bough had been sawed three parts through. It broke, and the bough fell upon the neck and shoulders of Mecham, who is a son of Captn. Mecham in Jersey. He was a good deal hurt but fortunately no bones were broken. I went to see him yesterday and found him much better. The paymaster (Captn. Eddy) rejoined us from leave, bringing with him a corporal and 12 men of our regiment from Dum Dum. A large convoy arrived from Cawnpore.

On the 18th. One captain, 2 subalterns, and 100 men went to relieve the party at Alum Bagh. To-day the weather is most intensely hot and sultry.

On the 19th. I was on cattle guard, i.e. I had to go with 30 cavalry and 20 infantry to guard 100 camels and 27 elephants whilst they were cutting down forage and sugar cane for the gun bullocks; we went some 4 miles away from camp. On this day I received No.22 from you and also a letter from Mrs Kenny which I enclose for you to see. A convoy of 3000 camels laden with stores arrived at 3 p.m.

On the 20th. I went shooting with Chute and killed a very fine mallard at about 70 yards distance! Chute got 1 snipe and some red-shanks. A magazine belonging to the enemy blew up, having been ignited by one of our shells. I was invited to dine with Sir J. Outram at quarter past 6 p.m. and of course I went; he seemed to notice me a good deal and said I should be made quite a hero of at home. He asked me if my friends knew I had been shut up in the Residency and said he thought they would be very anxious about me. He said he remembered seeing me in Lucknow, but did not recognize me when he first saw me that evening in my new coat, and asked me where I got it. (I borrowed it from Barry for the occasion but did not tell him so.) Colonel Berkeley was also there, and took great notice of me.

On the 21st. I was on picquet in the heavy gun battery with Keats and Humphrey. The enemy made a very bold attack on all parts of our position with the usual success. At Jellalabad they had the impudence to bring scaling ladders within 150 yards of the walls and were severely punished for their temerity. They carried off most of their dead, but this morning we buried between 50 and 60 at Jellalabad alone. Our casualties amount to 2 men slightly wounded, 1 horse and 1 gun bullock killed, whilst they must have lost at least 200 and probably many more. During the attack a round shot came through the officers' hut at the picquet, and stopped on my bed: had I been lying down it would have bruised me but I do not think it would have seriously injured me.

On the 22nd (to-day). I was relieved off picquet by Hardy and Barry. This morning we breakfasted at mess for the first time and our first dinner will be this evening at 7 p.m. The 1st Bengal Fusiliers are hourly expected. I have now given you a detailed account of the occurrences of each day last week, and will now put my letter by till another day.

Tuesday 23rd. Yesterday evening the 1st Bengal Fusiliers came into camp escorting a large convoy of provisions. No news has been heard regarding the Commander in Chief, but it is supposed that he will soon come up. I have written to Hely about my pistol and told him either to bring it up himself or to send it by Williams, our new ensign. I have no doubt I shall be in possession of it before we enter Lucknow again.

Wednesday 24th. This morning I received a letter from Hely of ours dated Dum Dum 17th Febr. saying that he had got my revolver from Grindlay & Co. and had sent it up by a Captn. Hume 1st Bengal Fusiliers, so that I shall most probably get it in about 3 weeks. We have just been turned out in expectation of an attack, but as all seemed quiet we were dismissed. This morning Genl. Outram went out with 4 guns and all the cavalry to our left flank, it is supposed for the purpose of cutting off the retreat of some of the rebels who were defeated yesterday with the loss of 6 guns by Brigadier Grant, at a place 10 miles distant from here. The party has not yet returned. I have just finished writing an answer to the enclosed letter and have told poor Mrs K. all I know about it. You see I have put a stamp on this letter. Hely sent me up 5 Rs. worth so I intend to stamp all my letters to you as long as the stamps last.

Thursday 25th. The party of cavalry and artillery which went out yesterday under Genl. Outram did not see anything particular. They caught one sepoy and brought him back to camp.

(Thursday 25th confirmed). Yesterday evening one squadron of H.M. 7th Hussars, 1 troop of Royal Horse Artillery, and the whole of Hodson's horse arrived in camp from Cawnpore, and pitched their camp close to that of the Bengal Fusiliers.

Today, the usual monotony of the camp was agreeably interrupted by an incident which I will at once relate, and I must then think about bringing this letter to a close as the mail leaves Calcutta in five days from this, and unless I despatch this tonight I shall be unable to send you a letter by the present mail.

A force consisting of the right brigade (1st Madras Fusiliers, 84th and 5th Fusiliers) with all our cavalry (H.M.'s 7th Hussars, Hodson's horse, Wales' horse,

Military Train, Volunteer Cavalry, and 2 regiments of Punjaubee Cavalry) and 2 troops of Artillery (1 troop horsed, and the other, horse artillery) under Brigadier Russell set off at 10 a.m. this morning towards our right front. We had not gone far before we came in view of the enemy and opened a very hot fire of guns upon him. All our cavalry (about 850 in number) together with the horse artillery then set off at a canter and shortly came upon 2 guns of the enemy's, viz. a 24-pr. howitzer and a 9-pr. both our own) which for some reason or another did not fire at them. The enemy's infantry who were by the guns showed a very determined resistance, and as soon as they had fired off their muskets, closed with our cavalry and fought with their talwars. I need hardly say the guns were captured by our brave fellows, though not without some loss. Three of the Military Train were killed and 6 wounded. Amongst the officers wounded were Colonel Berkeley of the 32nd (slightly in arm), Lieut. Gough of Punjaub Irregulars (slightly) and Lieut. Moorsom, H.M.'s 52nd, our Asst. Qr. Mr. General. The guns taken were our own, horsed, with limbers and ammunition waggons complete, all of which I am happy to say were taken. An officer of the Military Train told me that 7 of the enemy climbed into the trees, and fairly bothered our cavalry–grape was fired into the trees, but without avail, and finally some infantry had to be called up who soon put an end to their fun, and brought them out of the trees with a..."squelch"...like so many rooks. We burned one of their villages, and arrived in camp at 2 p.m.

26th. In the evening of yesterday (25th, today is Friday 26th) we were turned out to resist an attack made by them to recapture the guns we took from them in the morning. They certainly never made a bolder or more spirited attack and they kept up a very heavy fire indeed till midnight. The 84th (notwithstanding they 'had been out all the morning) were dispatched to the left flank, and remained there till 12 o'clock at night. We had 5 men wounded but only one severely. Chute was hit in the thigh by a spent ball, but he has not returned himself "wounded" as it is too slight. Whilst we were standing there 2 or 3 round shot came "uncommon" close, and one pitched a few feet in rear of our company.

26th inst. (contd.) I am today on magazine guard and will therefore have lots of time to write. Two guns and some infantry have just come in from Bunnee and the artillery officer told me that the 42nd and 79th Highlanders with the 1st division of the siege train were within 3 miles of our rear picquet, and would be in camp in the course of the day. I shouldn't wonder if the Chief arrives before this day week.

I always take "Jacko" on picquet with me because he is such an amusement for me as I have no books etc. He barks like a little dog when he hears a shot coming and always takes very good care to get in a safe place. He is the tamest and most affectionate little monkey I ever saw, and is more than usually mischievous. He has just been amusing himself by upsetting my ink, and then by tearing a large hole in the tent. He is so tame that I frequently let him loose for an hour or two, and he invariably comes back by himself. After getting on all the tent tops in our lines he goes into the cook house and comes running to me with a potato in one hand and perhaps a spoon or a lump of butter in the other, and followed by half the native population in camp who have complaints to lay against the "sahib's bunda". I give him a piece of red baize about a foot square and is most amusing to see him wrap himself up in it at night, or in the day when the sun is too hot for him.

To understand the accompanying letter from poor Kenny's mother you must know that on first hearing of her son's death I wrote to Captn. Raikes, 1st M.F., who was a great friend of his and also of mine, telling him about it and saying how much I liked him: it appears that my note was forwarded by Captn. R. to

Kenny's uncle at Madras, who in his turn sent it to Mrs K. in Ireland. I wrote the other day to Mrs K. and told her all I knew, at the same time expressing my deep regret at losing so kind and valued a friend as her son. I concluded by copying out an order from the Regtal. order book which as I dare say you wd. like to see, I will copy again.

Camp Cawnpore, 24th Aug , 57

Regtal. Order by Captn. Willis Comg. 84th Regt

No. 6.   *It is with deep regret that the Commanding Officer announces to the Regiment the death of Ensign Kenny by cholera at noon this day. Ensign Kenny was a most promising young officer, and on more than one occasion of late was conspicuous for his gallantry and steadiness under fire.*

And now I really must send this off or it will be too late, and so in conclusion I must ask you to give best love to dearest Sister and Taty and accept the same yourselves, my darling Chaper and Macher,

from your very very affectionate boy,
Hugh P. Pearson

Letter No. 34

On picquet in the Fort of Jellalabad
March 4th 1858

My own dearest Emmie,

My last letter to you was No.30 and so I think it has come round again to your turn to get another. To-day is my nineteenth birthday, and if I could take a peep at you now I daresay I should find you in the mysteries of a plum pudding made in honour of the occasion, and I can imagine too that my health will be drunk by you all in some nice wine–possibly "Simkin". I have just been drinking your healths but only in ginger beer!! I can fancy too that "master's man" will get a share of the plum pudding, indeed I am sure of it.

This day last year I joined my regiment in Rangoon, and little did I then dream of what important events would happen before another 4th of March came round. My last birthday was spent at Rangoon, this one on a lonely picquet at Jellalabad, and where will my next be spent? I hope with you all in that peaceful isle of Jersey.

Since I sent off Number 33, only 5 days ago, great and important events have happened. Sir Colin Campbell has at last advanced on Lucknow with a large army and a force of artillery that has never yet been used in Indian warfare. He marched on Tuesday 2nd inst with the first division of his army and yesterday morning he captured the Dil Koosha. He is reported to have said to Outram, when asked by him to allow this division to lead into Lucknow, "No! These noble soldiers have suffered enough, let them rest a while." I think we shall have very little more fighting to do, perhaps no more. This morning the 2nd Dragoons, 2 Battalions Rifle Brigade and a troop of horse artillery passed through this fort on their way to join the Chief. Long before you read this letter Lucknow will have fallen, and it is then impossible for the rebels to make another stand. The fighting will then be over and in 3 months more I should not be surprised to find the 84th on its way to Calcutta.

I will now answer your letter enclosed in Chaper's No.22 and then will tell you about "Jacko". I hope the mumps have disappeared, and that you are all of you in the best of health and spirits. I should much have liked to help you to consume the loving cup and the Chaumontel Pears. You asked me in one of your letters to tell you the pieces of music I like. "Ben Bolt" is a very pretty air indeed, and one piece of music I heard our band play a day or two ago struck me as being peculiarly sweet; it is called the "Angel's Whisper". You cannot be wrong if you get any of Russell's music: his "Far far upon the sea" is a pretty thing.

I hear (as I write) the thunder of the Chief's guns in the distance; he is probably taking the Martiniere College. In a week from this Lucknow will be in our possession, and a terrible retribution will have been wreaked on those dastardly murderers of women and children. I will now put by this letter till news comes from the Chief.

Saturday 13th. Our regiment is now at the Martiniere College, and we are expecting to get the order immediately to go to the front and join our brigade which is now the foremost of all. We have just been transferred to General Franks' division and so have the 90th L.I. and Seikhs. The 90th are now in front and I rather imagine Brigadier Russell will not let his own regiment be far in rear. We have already taken their 1st and 2nd line of defences, and are now breaching the 3rd and last. This afternoon their 3rd line of defences is to be stormed and then comes the key of the city, viz. the Kaisar Bagh or New Palace, the taking of which will be something fearful.

Yesterday "Jung Bahadoor" arrived with 10,000 Ghoorkhas and he has gone to take up our old position at the Alum Bagh. Of all the regiments that were there only ourselves, the 90th and Seikhs have come to the front. The 78th have gone to garrison the Alum Bagh; the 5th Fusiliers have gone to garrison the fort of Jellalabad. The enemy's losses have been very heavy the last day or two; when we took their 2nd line of defence 600 bodies were found and in several other places the same has happened. The well known Captn. Hodson of Hodson's Horse was killed yesterday, so was Lt. Moorsom of H.M.'s 52nd and many officers of other corps.

Camp, Martiniere College, Lucknow
March 18th

Lucknow has fallen! The 84th have had very little fighting and only 3 men have been wounded. The Great Kaisar Bagh was taken with very little opposition, and now there is not a sepoy in the whole city. The army is now breaking up and I expect the 84th will soon be on its way to Calcutta. The Madras Fusiliers are going back to Madras in a few days, the artillery recruits have been ordered up to Meerut, and the 75th have already gone up country. I have looted a nice scarf (Cashmere) which I am keeping for you. I have got a small cannon which was put in position against us and intend to take it home as a curiosity. Brigadier Russell is going home on sick certificate, and all his things are to be sold this afternoon. You will be very glad to hear that I have got another little monkey to play with Jacko; it is such a little beauty.

Some of our officers have got very valuable loot. Willis has got 2 or 3 very large diamonds and lots of pearls etc. I am now going to send this letter off, but will write again in a day or two. Give my very best love to dearest Chaper, Macher and Taty and accept the same my darling Emmie
from your most affectionate brother
Hugh Pearce Pearson

The last received from you is No.23. I hope none of my letters have gone down in the "Ava" .

Letter No. 35

Camp, La Martinere College,
Lucknow
March 21st 1858

My own very dear Father and Mother,

I posted No.34 for Emily on the 18th inst and although nothing of importance has taken place since then, yet I will begin this letter to-day and will tell you a little about the late fight at Lucknow. The niggers made a very determined stand for the first 3 or 4 days until we got into the Begum's Palace, after which a panic seemed to have seized them, and little resistance was offered after that. At the Begum's Palace they showed good fight, and when at last we got possession of it 560 of their bodies laid inside it—our loss on that day was 112 killed and wounded.

The Kaisar Bagh, which we all dreaded, turned out to be a very mild affair; indeed it never was meant to be taken when it was, and our people got in it through a mistake. The niggers never expected us in that day, so it was a very good piece of luck altogether. In the houses all over the town, but more especially in the Kaiser Bagh, were several hundred tons of gun-powder, not in magazines but lying loose all about: this caused more damage to our men than any of their firing, for half the men were smoking, and of course great explosions resulted. In one street the niggers put 3 or 4 hackories laden with powder, and covered them over with silks and shawls etc. When the men saw it they thought it was loot, and rushed to it, when a nigger left for the purpose fired the the train and 31 men were blown up, amongst whom were 2 officers.

There were mines all over the Palace and fanatics left with them to set fire to them when opportunity offered. These brutes would wait days till they had a chance and would fire the mine when no one suspected danger. Had we not taken the Kaisar Bagh so suddenly our loss would have been much heavier, for we found the whole road mined and they were only prevented from firing them by the rapidity of our movements. I cannot tell you how many guns we have taken but it is something like 74, their largest was the 8 inch howitzer which they captured from the 32nd at Chinahut and afterwards used with such effect at the Residency. There was also a 13 inch mortar, a 10 inch ditto and several smaller ones.

I have just read a general order to my picquet warning the men against straggling about the town, in consequence of an officer and a soldier having been found murdered near one of our outposts. The brutes wait till they catch one or two men alone and then rush out and kill them.

Many of our officers and men have found a good deal of loot. I have got a nice Cashmere scarf, a pretty little cannon (which was fired against us), a handsome mouth piece for a hookah made of glass mounted with gold, and a curious glass bottle with 4 different compartments. Nothing I have is valuable except as a remembrance of Lucknow.

I have got another little monkey to play with Jacko. It is the most eccentric little old-fashioned thing you ever saw and is only a month old.

By some mismanagement 90,000 of the rebels have escaped: 30,000 have gone to Bareilly, 30,000 to Fyzabad and the rest somewhere else, so I dare say we shall have a little more to do yet. I hear that all the regiments here are being distributed over the country for the hot season; I hope we shall go down country.

Give my best love to dearest Aunty and Emmie, and accept the same,

My own dearest Chaper and Macher,
From your truly affectionate son,
Hugh P. Pearson

I hope the brown pet is webbel.

Letter No. 36

Camp Jungjipore, en route to Benares via
Sultanpore and Azimghur
April 2nd 1858

My own very dearest Father and Mother,
I am now, as the heading of this letter shows you, on the line of march from Lucknow to Benares, and am 42 miles from Lucknow. The 84th now compose part of a flying column under Sir E. Lugard, the other part of the force being H.M.'s 10th and 34th Regts., the Military Train and 2 Regts. of native cavalry, a half battery of Royal Horse Artillery, a battery of Madras Artillery, and a battery of heavy guns. The object of our journey is to relieve a wing of H.M.'s 37th who are besieged by the rebels in Azimghur. This done, the 34th are to stay there with the 37th, the 10th are to go to Dinapore, and ourselves to Benares. Azimghur is 140 miles from Lucknow and Benares is 60 from Azimghur. In 8 days more we shall arrive at Azimghur and when all is settled there we shall be off to Benares, and then down country preparatory to going home.
My revolver arrived about 10 days ago, and I am delighted with it; it is one of the only sort I like, and it is admired by all.
I received your No.24 on the 24th of last month and was just going to answer it when the order came for us to move. I managed to get poor Gibaut's sword but the scabbard was burnt when he fell into the fire. I have the sword all right and will bring it home with me. I imagine we are sure to go home this year and the report is we are to do so at once. I hope we may. We are marching through a most lovely country and one full of game. I saw a man of the Military Train who is on picquet with me in this tope kill a hare with his sword about 10 minutes ago, and yesterday 2 hares were killed by our own regiment.
This is a very short letter but if I don't send it by the post which leaves for Lucknow at ½ past 4, I may not get another chance. I am writing under great difficulties as you may see by the blots etc, but I could not get good materials, so I was obliged to put up with what I could get. Good bye dear ones, give my best love to dear Aunty and Emmie and to all at Bourton and Ardsley when you write, and believe me to be dearest father and mother,
Ever your most affectionate son,
Hugh Pearson

P.S. I shall not write again till I get to Benares. H. P. P.

Letter No. 37

(See page 101 for sketch of Alum Bagh)

Camp Juanpore,
nr. Benares
April 10th 1858

My very dearest Aunty,

In my last letter to dear Father I concluded by saying that I did not intend to write again till I arrived at Benares, but as I find we may not arrive there for a week or 10 days, I think I had better seize this opportunity or I may not get another for some time. If you look on the map of India you will find this place situated about 39 miles N.W. of Benares, and 32 miles S.W. of Azimghur. We came here in a straight line from Lucknow, through Sultanpoor, at which last place we encamped on the 5th inst. "Jungjipore" (the place I last wrote from) is 2 days march the other side of Sultanpoor. We march for Azimghur tomorrow, and after two days march shall in all probability come across the 40,000 rebels under "Koer Singh", and after disposing of them return to Benares.

This place is exceedingly pretty, and there are still some bungalows standing in which Europeans have been murdered. It is the most civilized place we have been in for a long time. Will you ask Chaper if I ever had any relation an assistant surgeon out here, because in the churchyard there is a tombstone with J. P. Pearson son of Asst. Surgeon Pearson, died 1838, on it. You will have seen by the papers that our Serjt. Major and Qr. Mr. Serjt. have both been promoted from the ranks, also that Hardy has got his company. Bodkin of the Military Train was telling us just now that he had seen a letter written by a person in Azimghur which said that there were 300 of H.M.'s 37th, 300 of H.M.'s 13th, and 60 of the 2nd Dragoon Guards now in Azimghur, and that "Koer Singh" was there with 40,000 rebels including 5 regiments of Sepoys. It said that our fellows could go out and smash all the sepoys easily but it would be madness to go out against so many as 40,000. Crohan of ours who has been sick ever since the commencement of the campaign is going this afternoon to Benares and from thence to Calcutta. Four of our officers are left sick at the Dil Koosha, viz. Rolleston, O'Brien, Chute, and Humphrey. Of those who are here with the Regt. 5 are sick: Du Vernet, Whittock, Willis, Pratt and Crohan, so you see the work is pretty severe.

We are up every morning at 3 a.m. and yesterday we got up at ½ past 1 and marched 22 miles. I was twice on Rear Guard and was each time in the sun all day, however thank God it has done me no harm.

It is generally reported that we are to go home this year, and I see no reason why it should not be true. I cannot expect any letters from you till I get to Benares, the last I got from you was No.24 received on 24th March. Many thanks dearest Taty for the revolver wh. I got safely before we left Lucknow. It is a remarkably nice one, and the only kind I like. I fired 2 shots out of it on the march and it carried beautifully.

Now dearest Taty, good bye for the present. Pray give my very best love to dearest Chaper, Macher and little Emmie, also the dear ones at Ardsley when you write, and accept the same dearest Aunty,

From your most affectionate nephew,

Hugh Pearce Pearson

P.S. (12th April) You will be glad to hear that Captn. Lightfoot who commands the Regt. has given me charge of a company, although there are several officers now present with the regiment who are without companies. Tell Chaper this. H. P. P.

Pearson's sketch of Alum Bagh.

Letter No. 37 (continued)

18 miles from Juanpore
April 12th 1858

I was unable to send this letter when at Juanpore but to-day Whittock of ours is going to Benares to join his father's column in Madras, and I shall ask him to take it as far as Benares.

Yesterday we received intelligence that a lot of rebels were within 3 miles of us, and at 3.30 p.m. the whole of the cavalry and 3 horse artillery guns set off at a gallop across country, and soon came across the brutes in a narrow road. The Military Train and Seikh cavalry charged into them, captured 2 native guns (one 9 pr. and one 4 pr.) and killed between 60 and 70. No one was hurt on our side except Lieut. Havelock, the old General's nephew, who was shot through the head and is now lying in a very precarious state. His life is quite despaired of.

We are now on the road to Fyzabad instead of the one to Azimghur, and came here with the intention of preventing the enemy's escape in a northerly direction; whether we shall go on this road any further, or strike across country on to the Azimghur road remains a matter of doubt, however, tomorrow will shew.

In Father's last letter to me No.24 he mentions poor Gibaut's sword: tell him I have got the sword but the scabbard was burnt in the fire into which poor Gibaut fell. I will take great care of the sword and will bring it home with me.

I am happy to say we are to have another 6 months' batta given to us, Rs. 730 or £73. I shall send most of it home to Cox's, where I have already sent £96.6. 0.

You must indeed have been delighted to receive my Nos.23 and 24, as much so as I was to get your Nos. 13 and 14 after being so long in Lucknow without seeing your ever welcome handwriting. I sent off my last letter (No.36) at some outlandish place on the march, and I very much doubt whether it will ever reach you, so I may as well tell you again that I got my revolver all safe before leaving Lucknow and am more pleased with it than I could tell you. I wear it every day and feel more comfortable with it on than I did before I had it.

Dear Father asks me to send the names of all the actions I have been in, and their dates, so I will now put them down.

		Date	
	Futtehpore	12th July 1857	
	Aoung	15th do.	
	Pandoo Nuddee		
	*Cawnpore	16th do	
Oude	Unao	29th do.	
"	Busseerethgunge (1st time)		
"	*Busseerethgunge (2nd time)	5th August	
"	Busseerethgunge (3rd time)	12th do.	
	Bitthoor	16th do.	On Cawnpore side of the river
Oude	Mungrawar	21st September	
"	* Alum Bagh	23rd do.	With Genl. Outram
"	*Relief of Lucknow	25th do.	
"	Final capture of Lucknow	from 10th to 14th March 1858.	

These are the regular fights, and I will now put down the skirmishes and minor affairs which cannot be called actions, in which I have been.

Skirmish with the enemy on crossing the river into	
Oude the 2nd time	19th Septbr. 57
*Sortie on the enemy's position in Lucknow	29th do.
Taking of the "Heron Khana", Lucknow	16th Novbr.57
Taking guns at Alum Bagh	25th Febry. 58

Those marked with an asterisk * are the most severe ones of all, but we had lots to do in all of them. The next hardest fought to the ones marked * was Bitthoor.

Tell dear Chaper that as he has so kindly offered to get me a "trustworthy blade" when I return home I shall not buy a regimental sword at Calcutta but shall borrow one till I come home. I lost my own wretched skewer going into Lucknow on the 25th Septbr, it was sent flying out of my hand just as we were charging the bridges and I could not stop to pick it up. I got poor Pakenham's when he fell, it is a cavalry sword and before Pakenham got it, it belonged to Currie and after him to Kenny.

Tell Chaper I committed a great piece of extravagance when we were at Alum Bagh in buying a double barrelled rifle and gun (on the same stock), maker Forsyth. I gave Hardy of ours 300 Rs. for it. It belonged once to a celebrated sportsman in the 75th named "Smith" and he sold it to Hardy for 300 Rs. It is a beautiful rifle and I have amused myself greatly with it.

Now dearest Taty, good bye once more. I expect we shall be in Benares in another fortnight when I will write again. If however, an opportunity offers before I will avail myself of it Good bye, best love to all and believe me to be, Dearest Taty,

your most affectionate nephew
Hugh P. Pearson

Letter No. 38

Camp Senpore
April 22nd 1858

My very dearest sister,

I am now at a place called Senpore at the confluence of the Ganges and Gogra and not more than 16 miles from my birthplace "Dinapore". We have been pursuing the beaten remnants of Koer Singh's army and have literally driven them into the river. Koer Singh himself has for the present escaped, but most of his army have been killed by us or have been drowned in the river and the two guns he had have been taken by us. My last letter was written at "Tiggre" on the 12th inst. and was taken by Whittock of my regiment to Benares where I suppose he posted it; since then I have had no opportunity of writing till now. I will briefly tell you what has happened since then.

We first met the enemy at "Azimghur" but only our artillery and cavalry were engaged. We then halted for one day there and left on the 16th inst. in pursuit of Koer Singh: our force now consists of a half troop of the C. troop of Royal Horse Artillery, a light field battery of Madras Artillery, a troop of the Military Train, and 250 "native" cavalry, a wing H.M.'s 37th, H.M.'s 84th, 3 companies Madras Rifles, and a company of Punjaubee Sappers, the whole under Brigadier Douglass, one of the greatest idiots to command a flying column that you could possibly pick out. Ever since the 16th inst. we have been pursuing the rebels by forced marches and have come more than 130 miles from Azimghur in 6 days. My regiment has got no shoes, or stockings to put on and we are brought to a standstill on that account. Unless we can speedily get boots and shoes the men will be unable to march. We have been coming at the rate of more than 20 miles a day, and what with the heat, want of sleep, and want of shoes the men are so done up that many are unable to stand.

I am extremely sorry to say that we have lost our paymaster Captn. Eddy, who died a few days ago from the effects of the sun. He was greatly esteemed by every one, and his loss will be greatly felt by the regiment.

We have had 3 or 4 little skirmishes with the enemy, and have had 9 or 10 men of the 84th wounded, but none killed. Two companies of ours were sent out as skirmishers one day and came across an ammunition waggon filled with rupees. Du Vernet who was commanding the 2 companies got about 5000 rupees, Griffin who was promoted the other day got 2000 and the doctor who was with them got some 1500. The men each got as much as they could carry.

The 84th have taken a gun and the regimental and Queen's colors of the 28th N. Infantry since we left Azimghur. We have several times been close to Koer Singh, but things have been so shamefully managed that he has always escaped. I suppose you know we have got 6 months more batta, 730 Rupees for a subaltern.

Both my "Jackos" are in excellent health and spirits and the little one is very tame. He is never tied up but always runs about loose. I hope dearest Joevelly is well. I often look at his locks of hair and think of him. I suspect this letter will go by a steamer which is now in the river. The mail closes in half an hour, so I must now conclude. Give my very best love to dearest Chaper and Macher and dearest Aunty too. Accept the same yourself,

my beloved little Emmie,
from your most affectionate brother,
Hugh P. Pearson

P.S. I will write again at soon as I can. The last I had from home is No.24.
I have just reopened this to tell you I have this moment received your long-expected and welcome letters Nos. 25 and 26 but have not time to answer them now. Tell Chaper I will make enquiries about poor Gibaut's money and let him know.

You ask me where I spent my 19th birthday, on picquet at Jellalabad. I will write a long long letter to "all hands" when I get to a place where I can sit down to write in comfort. Tell my darling Mother, Father and Aunty that I am in excellent health and I may say in safety. I anticipate a move in 3 or 4 days to Dinapore or Ghazipore.

I have just been able to get 2 bottles of beer, 2 of sherry, 2 of port, and 1 of brandy from the Commissariat and I can assure you it is a great treat. I shall send home another £50 when I get my batta. What I want is a medal: no money can compensate for the privation of that. Good bye for the present. H. P. P.

Unnumbered Letter

Camp Singhah, right bank of Ganges
April 30th 1858

My dearest Uncle,
Doubtless you will think I have been very neglectful in not writing to you for such a long time but I have been on the move ever since the reduction of Lucknow, and the last letter I wrote, except those to my Father, was the one I wrote to you bearing the date 28th February. I am now about 10 miles from Arrah, to which

place we expect to go in a day or so and from there to "Jugdispore" where Koer Singh has entrenched himself very strongly.

You have I feel sure heard of the proceedings of my regiment up to the taking of Lucknow from my Father so I will at once begin the history of its wanderings after that time. News arrived at Lucknow that the 37th were shut up in Azimghur and would not be able to hold out much longer; a column was then formed to proceed by forced marches to their relief and my regiment formed a part of that column. The regiments ordered to form the column were H.M.'s 10th, one wing 34th and 84th, half of the F troop Royal Horse Artillery, a Madras Light Field Battery and 4 heavy guns: in cavalry we had the 2nd Battn. Military Train, a very strong regiment of native cavalry and about 20 mounted men of the 10th Foot; a company of Punjaubee Sappers completed our little army.

The whole under command of Sir Edward Lugard left Lucknow on the 29th of March and arrived at Azimghur on the 15th of the present month. On that day our cavalry and artillery had a slight skirmish with the enemy, but the infantry never came into action. It was ascertained by Sir E. Lugard that the enemy on hearing of our approach had deserted the town and were making for a small town called "Doliar" which is situated at the confluence of the rivers Ganges and Gogra, at which place they intended to cross into the Shahbad district and immediately another column was sent by our chief to pursue the rebels and drive them into the river. This column consisted of H.M. 84th, the wing of H.M.'s 37th which we relieved at Azimghur, a company of Madras Rifles also relieved by us, the company of Punjaubee Sappers and a few Seikhs; in artillery we had 4 guns Madras Artillery and the ½ troop R.H. Artillery; in cavalry one squadron Military Train and half the native cavalry. Sir E. Lugard sent his Brigadier (Douglas) in command and remained at Azimghur himself with the 10th, 34th, one squadron Military Train, some native cavalry, the remaining 2 guns of the Madras Battery, and the 4 heavy guns.

Now our hardships commenced in earnest, for we were expected to catch these ruffians who had already got a day's start of us and you, I daresay, know how they can go when they like. We followed them up close for two days sometimes being within 2 kos (4 miles) of them, and at last one fine day we came up with them in a village and after a sharp skirmish sent them flying; they got off with their 2 guns and we instead of following up sharp halted for 4 hours before we again advanced!! Our wounded were then sent back to Azimghur. After 4 hours halt we again pursued them and so hotly that many of their numbers were unable to keep pace with them and these falling out became an easy prey to our advanced guard. Their cattle were exhausted and the road was strewed with bullocks, horses, camels and elephants dead and dying from sheer fatigue. Some of the rebels who were unable to keep up tried to hide in villages and topes, but the villagers, dreading our anger, gave them all up. So wearied were they that nearly 100 men were killed singly or by twos and threes. Four who tried to swim the river were drowned.

At length one fine morning at 6 o'clock we came up with their rear guard who were cooking in a tope and they being unable to run were cut up where they were; some climbed into trees and our men amused themselves by what they called "rook-shooting" and the sepoys came down with a "squelch" from trees 20 and 30 feet high: others hid themselves under bundles of straw or faggots and were bayonetted by the men; 18 were found under one bundle. One of their guns was taken, and we found the horses so exhausted that they were obliged to be left and our own horses put in the gun.

Our horse artillery and cavalry then galloped to the front and on arriving at a small village on the river bank discovered them swimming the stream and opened with grape. More than a hundred sepoys were found in the village without arms or accoutrements which they had thrown away in the hope of passing for villagers; they were all killed. The remaining gun was found abandoned in a village and was brought in by our rear guard. Many hackories and waggons were seen by our cavalry but they could not stop to take possession of them and they fell into the hands of two companies of the 84th who were skirmishing: they were looted by them and every man got as much as he could stagger under. The 3 officers who were there got 2000 Rs. each and the captain (Du Vernet) 5000 Rs. One man captured from a sepoy the regimental and Queen's colours of the 28th B.N.I These two companies charged and captured one 9 pr. gun (one of our own) and got great credit for what they did.

The force halted in a tope by the river-side for 3 days, after 5 days of the hardest work that we have ever had in marching, having marched 123 miles in 5 successive days!! The 84th had no boots or shoes fit to march in, and when a return of boots was called for, my company stood as follows: without boots or stockings 7 men; with very bad boots 34 men; with tolerably good boots 4 men. So you see in my company alone there were 7 men absolutely bare-foot, and I have seen some men do their 24 miles without a shoe to their foot. So bad were we that Brigadier Douglas reported the regiment as "unfit to move". We have now had some boots and clothing sent up from Dinapore. I will now proceed with my narrative.

We halted, as I said, in a tope for 3 days and on the evening of the 24th inst. news came to us that H.M.'s 35th had gone out to cut up the niggers who had escaped from us across the river and that instead of thrashing them they (the 35th) had been thrashed themselves and had lost 2 guns which they had taken out with them. This turned out to be nothing more than the plain truth, and off we went again to take back the guns that a British regiment had lost to an equal number of niggers! Our men are horribly disgusted and I only hope we may not meet the 35th or in all probability there will be a row. We crossed the river Ganges on the 25th inst. for the purpose of going to retake the guns lost by the 35th and had fallen in yesterday to march for Arrah when the order came for us to halt and pitch tents in the same place as before; we did so and have had no order since.

I have now told you all the movements of the column to which the 84th (or "Lucknow-wallahs" as we are called) belong, and I will now tell you of the movements of two other columns in our immediate vicinity, viz. Sir E. Lugard's (which we left at Azimghur) and Lord Mark Kerr's. Sir E. Lugard's force, it appears, were ordered soon after we left to go also in pursuit of Koer Singh and went accordingly a few days after we did: they went to Ghazipore, then to Buxar, and are now coming down to join us; they are within 2 days march of this place. Sir E. Lugard left the 34th to garrison Juanpore and Azimghur and only has the 10th and a few guns with him. The other column under Lord Mark Kerr consisted of a wing of H.M.'s 13th L.I, a company Madras Rifles, 100 of the 4th Madras Cavalry and 2 guns. He was also after Koer Singh and was in communication with our force from Azimghur to the river. He never came across the niggers at all, but joined our force yesterday. To-day the 13th recrossed the river, and are now going to Goruckpore, where it is said their other wing has met with a reverse, having been repulsed from a fort with the loss of 20 per cent of their men:

This is the history of my travels since the 29th ult and after "Jugdispore". I trust we may be sent to Dinapore or some other station to have a little peace: it seems very hard that the old 84th which has been in the field since last July and done such excellent service, should be made to work still now whilst other corps just out from home are enjoying themselves in comfortable quarters. We are, and always have been, the "fatigue regiment" of Bengal, and it is because we are commanded by a captain; were a colonel at our head, justice would be done to us, but they listen to the remonstrances of a captain without heeding them in the least. This is why the regiment has never been mentioned in despatches as it ought to have been. Unthanked and unapplauded, the good old corps has always done its duty well, and I know right well it always will. Nothing is more discouraging to both officers and men than to think they have been passed over. However, the day will yet come when the gallant old corps shall get its due meed of praise, and till then it will rest satisfied with the consciousness that it deserves the highest praise. I could say much more but I find I am almost without knowing it at the end of my paper. I will write again shortly. Till then goodbye. Give my very best love to dearest aunt and cousins, all of whom, I hope, as also yourself, are well, and dearest and best of uncles accept my most affectionate love,

Hugh Pearce Pearson

Letter No. 39

Camp Arrah, nr Dinapore
May 2nd 1858

My dearest Father and Mother,

The 84th is now at Arrah, 29 miles from my birthplace, and we expect to stop here for 3 or 4 days when Sir E. Lugard's column will be here, and then we shall all move towards "Jugdispore" for the purpose of dislodging the rebel force which has taken up its position there.

I yesterday met a young fellow in the 35th who was a great ally of mine at Chatham, and he gave me the following account of that unfortunate affair which took place near Jugdispore on the 23rd of last month. Two companies of H.M.'s 35th and about 50 sailors with 2 12 pr. mountain train howitzers went to Jugdispore on the 23rd ult. for the purpose of thrashing the rebels who had succeeded in escaping from us on the other side of the river. The British force under Captain Le Grand (35th) only numbered some 300 men. The rebels were 4 or 5000 strong. A belt of very thick jungle encircles Koer Singh's house near Jugdispore, and the house itself was approachable only by one narrow road which is flanked by a high bank on each side. Our men were going along the road when the sepoys poured in a volley from these banks and killed a great number of the 35th. The rest, taken by surprise, turned and ran to the guns in great confusion and loaded them with shell; as one was being loaded the fuse of the shell slipped and the shell became immoveably jammed in the muzzle of the gun, thereby disabling it for the time. The men then got panic stricken, and cried "the cavalry are on us—the cavalry are on us" and then ran for it as hard as they could lay leg to the ground. The officers tried their best to stop them, but were unable. When the cavalry were supposed to be coming, Captn. Le Grand who was in command completely lost his presence of mind, and gave the order to retire. The men then thought all was over with them and ran for their lives. The enemy's cavalry pursued them to within 1½ miles of Arrah, and out of 140 of the 35th and 5 officers who went out that morning, only 38 men and 2 officers (of which latter my friend is one) returned alive to Arrah. One hundred and two men and 3 officers of the 35th were cut up and not one wounded man ever reached Arrah. All the gun ammunition and 125 Enfield Rifles with the men's pouches full of ammunition fell into their hands, and the 2 howitzers also. My friend told me that there was no use in attempting to disguise it, it was a most disgraceful affair. Of course I asked no questions as I knew he would not like it being his own regiment that behaved badly, but all he told me I have told you. The officer who commanded, Captn. Le Grand, was killed. When the 84th marched into the tope where Parsons and I were standing, he said "Your men are the right sort I can see, and I'll be bound they will not lose their guns."

Hardy of ours was just now at the magistrate's house when one our spies came in. He said Koer Singh is dead, and that to prevent the sepoys from hearing of it, his brother buried him in one of the rooms of the Zenana at Jugdispore instead of burning him as his caste are. He said they have 3 guns, 2 they took from the 35th and one little one they had before. They muster 7000.

I wrote a very long letter to Uncle P. on the 30th of last month, but I greatly fear it will not be in time for the mail leaving Calcutta on the 4th inst. The letter chiefly contained the history of the movements of the 84th since the reduction of Lucknow. In my last letter to you I misstated the rate of our marching from Azimghur to the river's bank; instead of doing 130 miles in 6 days as I said in No.38, we did 120 miles in 5 days–being an average of 24 miles per diem!! I forgot in my letter to Uncle to tell him of the safe arrival of my revolver, but very likely you would mention it in your letters to him. If you write soon, tell him how delighted I am with it. I also forgot to congratulate Hugo on his promotion to midshipman, which I was very glad indeed to hear of.

I called a barber this morning to cut my hair, and I told him to cut it short. The wretch cut it all off before I knew what he was doing, and by way of adding insult to injury had the impudence to ask 1R. for doing it!! I was very pleased to see O'Brien of my regiment has got his brevet-majority. He is an excellent fellow, and deserved it right well. Willis has gone sick with sore eyes to Dinapore en route for Darjeeling or Calcutta. He is a regular "schemer" and has been trying the "sore eyes" dodge a long time. I do not recollect Morris of the 75th being at Alum Bagh when I was there, and I made enquiries for both Major Faber and Captn. Blackall but did not succeed in finding them out. The 35th officers behaved very kindly to us, and sent us a lot of beer, wine and brandy when they heard of our arrival on this side of the river.

My little monkey is exceedingly tame, and is now lying on my knee asleep. I never tie him up, so he is unusually tame, and comes when I call him. The big monkey is always tied up but he is very tame too: if the big one was not here the little fellow would run away. The little one is very small indeed, not more than 8 inches tall and is a great pet. I heard a great noise in the tree over the tent just now, and in going out discovered the youngster perched on a bough tête à tête with two owls whom he had not seen till he got close to them: he dare not move and was uttering the most piteous cries, so I got my pellet bow and drove the owls away, very nearly killing one. He then came down and jumped into my arms with great chatterings and other demonstrations of joy, which were loudly responded to by her eldest sister Miss Jacko, who during the above scene had been very much alarmed about the safety of her adopted child. The "butcha" is very mischievous and draws the corks of all the bottles in the tent. I enclose a letter from Col. Impett which you may like to see. I have no more news now, so I will say adieu till another day.

3rd May. No news. Little Jacko hurt his arm last night and is very cross in consequence. I hope Dashy is all well. I am going now to settle with my company for April, so good-bye.

6th inst. Sir E. Lugard arrived here yesterday with H.M.'s 10th, half of the F. troop R.H.A. and 2 8-inch howitzers. We shall I think go to Jugdispore tomorrow, and we are to take 4 days supply of water with us as the sepoys have poisoned all the wells. I have got lots of beer and wine so I shall do pretty well.

I enclose an extract from a private letter from Sir J. Outram to Lightfoot in which he speaks highly of the "glorious old 84th" as he calls us. I feel sure you would like to read it.

My friend Parsons of the 35th is coming to dine with me to-night, indeed we are always dining with each other, I dined with him last night.

Bye the bye, dear Father, next time you see Mellish de la Taste will you tell him that I made the acquaintance of an old friend of his, Captn. Hicks of the B.N.I. (18th I think but am not sure) who desired to be remembered to him when I next wrote. I dined with him on the 26th of February at camp Alum Bagh. Nearly all our officers' wives are now at Dinapore, and supplies are daily coming from them to their husbands.

Yesterday the corporal of my company brought my grog (ration rum) in a large gallon measure with the grog of the whole of my men: whilst he was pouring mine into a bottle the big "Jacko" got hold of the can in which the remainder was and upset every drop of it. The idiot of a corporal had put the can close to the monkey instead of leaving it outside the gate. I had to pay for the grog 4 Rs. There were 64 drams. Jacko knew he had done wrong and tried to hide himself from me.

I must now conclude as I imagine we are off to-morrow early and the last post will leave this for Dinapore to-night. Give my best love to dearest aunty and Emily and to all at Bourton in your next, and accept the same my own very dearest Father and Mother,

from your most affectionate son,
Hugh Pearce Pearson

N.B. If you can confirm the news about the names for the monument in Trafalgar Square I shall be delighted. Is there any talk of a medal?

[Enclosure]   *Regimental Order*

By Captain Lightfoot

Camp Tiggre, April 12th 1858

No.6. the Commanding Officer has much pleasure in publishing to the men of the Regiment the following extract from a private letter from Major General Sir James Outram, G.C.B.

Lucknow 28th March 58

"A private letter is hardly a proper medium for giving expression to the strong feelings I bear to the glorious old 84th, but the feelings I do bear it are very strong and every officer, non commissioned officer, and private of the corps is, and ever shall be, regarded by me as my comrade and my friend.

I suspect the order for breaking up my Division tomorrow or next day, when I shall take the opportunity of officially recording my sense of the conduct of the troops composing it. May success and further glory attend you and your gallant corps."

Very sincerely yours,
(signed)   James Outram

To Captain Lightfoot,
Commanding H.M.'s 84th Regt.

Letter No. 40

Camp "Arrah"
May 14th 1868

My very dearest Mother,

For the first time during the campaign I am away from my regiment when it is in the fields, and yet I can hardly call it being away from the regiment, because I am on detachment with 2 companies, but what I mean to say is that whenever any part of the regiment has been engaged I have always till now been with it: and very sorry I am too at my being away from it now, however, I could not help it, they would send me. We all left the place (under Sir. E. Lugard) for Jugdispore on the 8th inst. and marched to a place called "Beehera" within 5 miles of Jugdispore that day. Two companies of the 84th, 1 company Madras Rifles, 2 guns, and some cavalry were then ordered to proceed early next day to Arrah, and my company was one that had to go. We came according to order, and arrived here at 11 a.m. We have been encamped here ever since.

The following day the force under Sir E. Lugard took Jugdispore, with trifling loss on both sides. On our side 4 men were wounded, 2 bheesties killed. The enemy only lost 20 killed! The company of our regiment being detached saw a gun frowning at them through a neat embrasure; they charged up to it in their usual style and to their disgust found it was. . . a wooden one!! I believe they are greatly quizzed about it, but everyone knows they would have charged it whether iron or wood. The rebels managed to get off with the 2 guns they took from the 35th, but we got some of their ammunition, and they took 2 camel loads of ours also. They have had one or two actions with the enemy but never could get at them owing to the intense thickness of the jungle. I will now relate to you a little incident that occurred which will shew you how thick the jungle is round Jugdispore, and then I will put this by till another day.

16th May. I was interrupted when writing the above by an order to go and see the men's beddings brought from the fort, so I could not tell you the tale then but this is it: a corporal and 4 men were told to patrol about 150 yards in advance of their picquet, but so thick was the jungle that the enemy managed to cut them off from their picquet, and they had no resource but to strike into the jungle and trust to God's mercy to save them. They wandered here and there, continually falling in with bodies of the rebels and at last one of our spies saw them, and brought them safely to Arrah (17½ miles). They lost one man in the jungle, but he managed to get back to the picquet. I sent the spy back to Jugdispore with a letter to Lightfoot telling him of the safe arrival of the men, and he was rewarded with 100 Rupees by the General.

The destination of our regiment is fixed for "Juanpore", so I think you had better direct your future letters to "Benares". Juanpore is a very pretty place, and is only 30 miles from Benares. It is not the place I should have chosen above all other, but still it is better than many places I could name. I have had several chits from our fellows at Jugdispore. There is not much news. We have not done much harm to the niggers, and they captured 24 camels from us one day.

19th May. There is still no news. Our people are remaining inactive in the jungle for although the niggers are within one or two miles of them, yet we can do them no harm. Lugard has written to the Chief for instructions and will not do anything until he hears from him.

I am going to send this letter off now, or you will not get one this mail, and I am sure you would rather have a short letter than none at all. Give my very best and dearest love to darling Father, Aunty and Emily, and accept the same yourself, my own dearly beloved mother,

from your most affectionate son,
Hugh Pearce Pearson

P.S. Your last letters are Numbers 25 & 26 received at Senpore (junction of Ganges and Gogra) on the 22nd April. My poor little monkey's hind legs are paralysed and he is utterly helpless. I hope all are well and happy. Tell Chaper I made enquiries about poor Gibaut's money but can ascertain nothing till I see Rolleston who was President of the Committee on his effects. Ask Chaper to remember me kindly to Saville when he next sees him. I will do my best to find about poor Gibaut's money.

Letter No. 41

Camp "Narainpore" nr. Jugdispore
May 31st 1858

My own very dear Chaper,
This morning I had the inexpressible delight of receiving your kind and welcome No. 28, the latest date being 30th March, and although most of my writing materials are at Arrah, yet with what I have I can manage to tell you a good deal. I will commence by giving you a list of my services in the field.
Marched from Allahabad on the 30th June 1857 with 2 companies of the 84th which formed part of a column under Major Renaud (1st Mad. Fusiliers). Our little force was joined by Genl. Havelock at 12 p.m. on the night of the 11th of July, and on the 12th, after a march of 17 miles, we met and defeated the rebels at "Futtehpore"; on the 15th we twice defeated them, once at "Aoung" and in the afternoon at a bridge over the "Pandoo Nuddee". Next day we fought them in a plain before "Cawnpore", and after 6 hours very hard fighting routed them with great slaughter. In this action I received a slight graze on the right temple from a musket ball, but was not returned as wounded. Crossed over into Oude, and was present in all the engagements with the enemy, viz. at "Oonao" and "Busseerut Gunge" on the 29th of July, at "Busseerut Gunge" on the 5th August and at "Boorbeake Chowkee" on the 12th August. Was at "Bitthoor" on the 16th August and carried the regimental color in that action. Recrossed the river into Oude on the 19th September and was engaged with the enemy who endeavoured to prevent our crossing (skirmish). Served in the actions of "Mungrawar" on the 21st, "Alum Bagh" on the 23rd, and at the relief of Lucknow on the 28th September. Took a part in the defence of that city from the 25th September to the 25th November and commanded a company in the sorties of the 29th of September and 16th November (on which latter day the Heron Khana, King's Stables etc. were stormed and taken). Served with the army of occupation in Oude under Sir J. Outram, and whilst there was constantly engaged in repelling attacks of the enemy. Was present in the skirmish with the enemy on the 25th of February 1858, and also at the final taking and fall of Lucknow by Sir Colin Campbell from 10th to 21st March. Served with the Azimghur Field Force under Sir E. Lugard, and was in all the minor affairs which took place during the pursuit of the rebel chief, Koer Singh, by that column.

I have written my services in such a way that you can cut them out of the letter without having anything else on the other side which perhaps you would not like every one to see.

This is the full and detailed account of everything that I was ever engaged in, but the one I sent to the Army List [Hart's] (we were all ordered to send our own services in) is as follows:

> *Lieutenant Pearson served with Genl. Havelock's moveable column in the advance from Allahabad in the actions of Futtehpore, Aoung, Pandoo Nuddee and recapture of Cawnpore, at Oonao and Busseerut Gunge on the 29th July, at Busseerut Gunge on the 5th August, and at Bitthoor (carried regtal. color). Was present in all the actions from 19th to 25th September including the relief and siege of Lucknow from 25th September to 25th November. Commanded a company in the sorties of the 29th September, and 16th November. Commanded a company in the sorties of the 29th September and 16th November. Was present with the army of occupation in Oude under Sir J. Outram, and at the final capture of Lucknow. Served with the Azimghur Field Force under Sir E. Lugard and in all the minor engagements with that column.*

You see I have in the above endeavoured to put as much substance into as small a space as I could, and in several instances instead of naming the action I have merely said "served in all the actions from–to –" and as I was not returned as wounded I thought I had perhaps better say nothing about it. How truly delighted I shall be that I have been through all this if "my services" do you any good, and I would gladly receive a severe wound if by so doing I could get you some nice lucrative appointment which would enable you to live luxuriously in the future! You know I would, dearest Father, don't you? I would indeed undergo anything for you.

I received your No.27 on the 21st inst at Arrah and was about to sit down and answer it when the order came for us to move. In that letter you ask me to tell you all about how I am living, and what servants, horses etc. I have. I will give you a history of them all. I have just now only one servant, my old boy "Jack", having sent away "Mallipah" for drunkenness some months ago. Jack and I agree very well together; one good thing about him is he can do without pay for 5 or 6 months at a time and never bother me about it. I have 3 coolies to carry my charpoy and portmanteau, an old fellow and his 2 sons: he is a very good and faithful old man, and I have had him ever since I first crossed into Oude with Havelock; by getting his two sons I ensure always having some one to carry my traps, for they would not run away and leave their father behind.

In horseflesh my only one is a strong, ugly, and extremely vicious black galloway which once belonged to poor Kenny, and consequently has been through the whole campaign. He is quiet to ride, but when tied up is a devil incarnate, and no one but the syce dare go near him. I was in an evil moment persuaded to sell my little mare, and I have much regretted it since: a man ought always to have two nags on a campaign in case one "knocks up" or to mount a friend. You ask what baggage I lost, and whether my gun and rifle are safe? Yes, I am delighted to say they are safe. The dear old "spout" you gave me is, I am rejoiced to say, still "in the family". It would indeed have been an irreparable loss had it gone, for Manton's finest gun would be of no value to me compared with that, because it was your gift dear, dear Father.

I have not been very well for the last 4 days and have had a nasty boil on my jaw which has irritated me much; however, I am happy to say that thanks to our good doctor's pills I am again myself and ready for the niggers again too.

My iron bedstead and chest of drawers were both left at "Dum Dum" as well as my gun and rifle. We have but sorry accounts of the state of our things at Dum Dum, and I am sadly afraid all my nice kit exists "but in name". Crohan went the other day to get his boxes out, and wrote to say that all his clothes were a mass of dust, mildew and white ants, so I am afraid it is a bad look-out. When the order came for all our heavy baggage to be sent over from Rangoon everything was taken down to the beach and left without cover for a week exposed to sun, rain and wind. When they arrived at Dum Dum they were put in Hely's care, but it seems he left them too long in one place, and the white ants got at them. They are now at the agents and nothing has been heard about them lately. However, neither white ants nor anything else could hurt the iron work of the cot or the gun, at least I hope not.

Doctor Innes of our regiment received a letter this morning from Doctor McMaster 78th Highlanders at Lucknow, and in it he says: "I met a cousin of Pearson of your regiment; he is attached to the 42nd and belongs to some native infantry corps". As he does not mention his name, of course I do not know who it is.

A man of our regiment has written several very clear articles in the Bengal Hurkaru about sending us down country, in the last paper he put one in headed "First in the field, and last out of it". It is an extremely clear and well written effusion, and recapitulates the services of the regiment together with a list of officers and men who have been killed since the commencement of the outbreak. Lightfoot has been exerting himself to his utmost for the good of the regiment, and wrote to the Chief (Sir Colin) to say that the 32nd have been made a Lt Infty. regiment of, and have been allowed to carry "Lucknow" on its colors, and asking why should not we have the same done to us? He has written to all the heads of the army requesting we might be sent down country, but has, as yet, had no answer. Willis, Crohan and Blake have gone home, and now we have not an officer per company!! Rolleston, O'Brien, Chute, Humphrey and Williams have been ordered down from Benares to join; the 4 first were left sick, the latter has brought up a detachment of 40 men from Calcutta, and has not yet joined Hd.Qrs.

There has been a pretty considerable "row" here about that money that Du Vernet looted, and an order came out from Lugard saying "he had not behaved as a gentleman" or words to that effect. It is not safe to put everything on paper but I can tell you a good deal about that individual when we meet.

There is a young fellow in the Madras Artillery here of the name of Chamier, whom I have taken a great fancy to; we were on detachment together at Arrah and as he both plays the guitar and sings nicely we used to pass our evenings together singing duets. If I knew the words of a song he used to accompany me with his guitar, and we were very happy indeed.

We are now I suppose the only column in the field, all the rest are in quarters; however I hope in a day or two we shall go to Arrah. We were told our summer residence was to be "Juanpore" but nothing is certain. It is just possible we may be quartered at Dinapore; when I know for certain I will not fail to tell you. Well, good bye for today, as I am tired of writing.

June 1st. I am now on picquet with nothing but dear old Jacko to disturb me. You must not mind the writing for I have most horrid pens. There is no news in camp of a move in any direction, though I feel sure we shall move soon. In your No.28 you say that most likely a letter or two of mine has gone down with the Ava. I don't think any did, but if you have not yet got No.31 I suppose it must be the letter you mean. According to the little piece of paper you gummed on to the top of your letter I shall have a medal and two clasps, for you must recollect it is for the' "relievers of Lucknow and Cawnpore". I suppose they mean the taking of Cawnpore on the 16th July. I am glad the Felstead boys behaved so well at the burning of the mill. I knew Mr Ridley well but I doubt if he would know me now.

I am happy to be able to tell you that the 2 12-pr. mountain train howitzers taken from the 35th on the 23rd April were recaptured by the despised old 84th and are now safely "parked" amongst the spare waggons of the R.H.A. They are pretty little pop guns, but useless beyond 650 or 700 yds. I am living on the best of "drink", though not by any means on the best of "wittles". I got 2 doz. of best Allsopp's (English bottled) from Dinapore, also 4 doz. of soda water, 1 doz. of sherry, and ½ doz. Exshaws for the cold nights. I got a few tins of sardines, and 2 or 3 pots of inferior Strawberry jam. The beer is uncommon nice.

I wrote a letter to my old chum Morgan of the 19th but have not yet heard from him. What ship is cousin Hugo in now? Is he still in the "Brunswick"? I hope Jane and Mary are well, and also dear uncle, aunt, and all at Bourton. Give them my best best love when you write. I wish, dearest Father, you could fly over here and spend 24 hours with me. What a lot I could tell you to be sure. Willis has gone home, it is supposed, to take "substantive rank" which will give another step. If dear mother could only see the pitiable ragged state I am in what would she say? One white sock and one red sock; a shirt minus a sleeve; a flannel waistcoat without a back; and a pair of odd shoes is part of my valuable property. Is dear mother glad the shooting season is over? How funny of her to be anxious; however it is over, there is no mistake about that.

I am now in a "single fly" tent with the sun about 113° in the shade, so hot that I keep a wet towel on my head, and a hat over that again. My revolver hangs by my side, and my trusty blade peeps grimly out of its black leather sheath as if wishing for something to do. The flies are fearfully troublesome and old Jacko looks as if he wishes he had not eaten that sweet mango which has "smeared" his jaws all over with sweet juice and made the flies settle on him as thick as currants in a barrel. Everything is still and everything is asleep except the sentry who looks as if he was half inclined to go to sleep too.

I have now told you all the news, and must say adieu. Give my very best love to dearest mother, aunty and Emmie and accept the same my own very dear father,

from your truly affectionate boy,
Hugh P. Pearson

P.S. Write and tell me if you have got what Uncle was trying to get for you. Jacko desires to be remembered to Juzzif and his flebbend. I hope you are all well. I am quite right again now and as jolly as I can be when away from you. H.P.P.

Letter No. 42

Camp at Buxar
June 13th 1858

My very dear Father,

My last letter was posted on the 1st inst. and ever since that day I have been on the move. Only yesterday we came back from a wild goose chase, and tomorrow we expect to be off again, goodness knows where. It is cruel to work this poor regiment like they have been, and are being worked, and I very much doubt whether the men will stand it any longer. Twice it has been given out to the men on parade that "this is the last day's fighting you shall have" and twice the promise has been broken. As for myself I am nearly finished, and am so weak from fatigue and constant exertion that when I get up in the morning my legs can hardly support the weight of my body. All I want is 3 or 4 days rest to make me all right again.

We are now under a brigadier who is I should say "the most mutton-headed idiot in India", who works the men off their legs, and when he comes up to an enemy he halts to let them get away again, and then next day rushes after them as before, but only to encamp within a mile of them. He is very fond of putting out a great many picquets, and out of our regiment alone I have known 6 companies on picquet at a time! It seems we are never to go into quarters, for I believe we are off again tomorrow.

We have been fighting in the Jugdispore jungle, and have succeeded in driving the brutes out of it with a loss of about 150 of their number. Williams has joined us and so has O'Brien, Humphrey and Chute, who were left sick at Lucknow. Magrath and Oakley are both under arrest, and it is supposed will be tried. They had a squabble about something, and Oakley threw a basin of water over Magrath, calling him a blackguard. M. immediately took a stick and broke it across his back, and then walked into him with his fists, and ended by kicking him out of the tent, whilst brave Mr. O kept calling out "Help me, help me, he is hitting me". Oakley actually took no notice of it, and the adjutant who heard it all put them both in arrest. Lightfoot says he will never associate with a man who has been kicked and thrashed without reporting it, or even attempting to defend himself. The men were spectators of the scene and testified their satisfaction by clapping of hands and shouts. The whole affair has been reported, and every one says they will be tried.

I am very sorry my letters to you and uncle have been lost, but it cannot be helped. I can hardly think the bill of exchange was lost for I only posted it on the 15th Febr., whilst No.31 was sent off on the 24th Jany. Perhaps though it was the first bill (for 500 Rs.) posted on the 22nd Jany. and not the one for 463 Rs. However I will write to the paymaster and get the 2nd of exchange.

I received your No.29 yesterday in which you ask a very important question, viz. Am I as fond of my profession as I expected to be? To that I can answer "I am", and if possible, fonder than I expected. I am greatly grieved that dear mother has been poorly and sincerely hope she is now recovered. There is very bad news from Gwalior, but you will see the account in the papers long before you get this letter.

The post closes at noon today, so I must post this now or it will not reach you when it ought. This is a short letter but I will make up for it in a day or two by writing a good long one. I will then tell you all I have not told in this. Give my best love to dearest mother, aunty, and Emily who are all I hope well. I see in the papers Edward Boultbee has got his commission in the 15th. Morgan is in Barrackpore with his regiment and I had a letter from him a few days ago.

Now, dearest Chaper, good bye for the present, and believe me to be your most affectionate boy,

                    Hugh P. Pearson

Letter No. 43

Karuntadhee, opposite Buxar
June 20th 1858

My dearest Father and Mother,

I received your No.30 yesterday but could scarcely read it I was so unwell, having an attack of fever. Today I am quite well again, but still rather weak. I yesterday got a letter from Mrs Kenny which I will send to you as soon as I have answered. I was delighted to see in the "Home News" of the 10th May that the 84th is to return to England this season. I only hope and trust it may be true. I am on detachment duty with 2 companies of the 84th for the protection of the Government Stud at this place, and we are likely to remain here for a fortnight, when we shall be relieved by H.M.'s 77th and go up to Benares by steamer to join the regiment which marched from Buxar this morning for that place.

We have been very comfortable during the 4 or 5 days we have spent on this side of the river, and as our neighbours are so very kind I have no doubt that the next fortnight will be a very happy one. Captain and Mrs Siddall who live close here have been exceedingly kind and attentive to us, and out of the 5 nights we have been here we have dined 3 at their house. Now that it is determined that we are to stay here the Siddalls have sent us tables, chairs, a carpet, and lots of books and papers to make us comfortable, and I think that living as we are in a nice waterproof stable we shall be much jollier than the rest of the regiment, more especially when the rains come on.

Whilst at Buxar, I saw some English ladies, the first I have seen since 18th June 1857, a year all but 3 or 4 days! I positively stared at them, and I am sure they must have thought me very rude, but had they known the cause I know they would have forgiven me. I hear old Reed has sent in his papers, and Radcliffe is moving heaven and earth to get back into the 84th. Whether this is true or not I can't say.

Du Vernet of ours is, I should say, "up a gum tree". I should be sorry to give 6d. for his commission. He is now under arrest (with a sentry over him) for being drunk when Field Officer of the day, and when I tell you that 2 months ago he was put under arrest for being drunk when in command of the Rear Guard I think you will say with me that he has a bad chance. He is a man who is drunk day and night for 3 weeks at a time, and on the march from Azimghur he was drunk every day for a week, and 3 of those days he was on responsible duty. One day he was in command of the Rear Guard and I was on too, he got drunk 3 different times that day, and had to be taken off his horse and put in a doolie by myself and a private of H.M.'s 10th Regiment!! The next day he was in command of the Rear Guard again, and got drunk again, when he was reported, put in arrest, and got off with a slight reprimand on his solemn promise of better conduct for the future. He is married to a very beautiful and talented young lady, and has only been married a year and a half. The gentleman who was kicked out of the tent the other day has got off with a slight reprimand!!!

Now to answer your letter. I was very sorry to hear you had not received No. 34 written to Emily from the Martiniere College, but doubtless it reached you soon after you posted No.30. I will take your advice about keeping my mind and body as much engaged as possible, and even now I always go out either riding or walking mornings and evenings. The difficulty is to find something to engage one during the heat of the day, for it is positively too hot to do anything; however the rains are coming on and it will then be cooler. I have heard nothing as yet about letters from here to England being prepaid, but will make enquiries. Hely ot ours at the depot will always send me up stamps. I am very very sorry to hear dear Macher has been poorly and sincerely hope she is now quite well.

I am in hopes that we shall be coming home this year. The regiment has been reported unfit for further service to Genl. Lugard and by him to the C in C, so I hope that may be of use in getting us home quick.

I am now going to post this letter, but you may expect letters much oftener now as I shall have lots of time to write. Give my best love to Aunty and Emmy and accept the same, my very dear Father and Mother,

from you most affectionate son,
Hugh P. Pearson

P.S. I think you had better direct Benares for the future. Little Jacko is defunct; Big Jacko sends love to Joseph and his friend. My next will be to Emmie. H. P. P.

Letter No. 44

Karuntadhee, opposite Buxar
June 27th 1858

My very dearest Emmie,

In my last letter I promised to write to you next, and am now about to fulfill my word. I am going to answer all your numerous questions first, and then put a lot of my own. Your first questions are about "Jacko", his habits, and manners etc. He is of temperate and regular habits, and has only once been convicted of "drunkenness". He takes his meals when he can get them, und when he cannot, as a matter of necessity, he goes without. His food consists of grain, bread, a little bit of meat now and then, fruit of every kind, vegetables (especially potatoes) and many other curious things. For medicine he (like Juzzif) eats grass. His color is "dusty colored" with head and legs of a reddish brown. He does drink out of a cup, but is not particular. I have seen him drink coffee out of a soda water bottle, holding it in his hands like a man. He is about 14 inches tall when standing on his hind legs. He does know his name, and if asleep when I call him, always wakes. So much for "Jacko". Now for your questions respecting me. I am not living in tents now, but in stables: 14 days ago we were in tents. We have not fought any battles lately. It is not very hot at present, but very cloudy and windy, and lastly, there are few, if any, flies or mosquitos. Jacko has short hair.

Now I have answered all your questions about Jacko and myself, and am now going to ask you some. Shall I bring Jacko home with me? If I do, will Juzzif promise to behave kindly to him, and let him look for flebbeas in his hair? Do you know "The last rose of summer"? Do you know "Shades of Evening close around us" or "Excelsior"? Does Chaper take nice walks like he used to do? Have you bathed this year, and if so, did you like it better than you used? Has young Mr Woolhouse returned to Jersey yet? How are you progressing in French and music? Have you commenced to collect lichens and sea weed? Do you go to the pier on steamer days as formerly? How did your Mid-summer tree look when finished? What did you give Miss Dodd for a birthday gift? Tell me all about the pic-nic and what you did, and where you went to. How did the "charades" come off? Did you act, if so, how did you like it? Is there anything in the papers about a "medal" or about our names being on the "Havelock Monument"?

There is a fine lot of questions for you to answer, besides which I want you to tell me all about your school, and about dear Juzzif and his "bow-legg'd frebbend". Do you know how I amuse myself during the day? I will tell you. I get up at 5 a.m., ride or walk till 7½, and write letters till Breakfast (8½), after breakfast, write letters till 12 noon, then read or play with Jacko till "tiffin" which is about 1½ p.m., read till 4, play cricket, ride, walk, practise with my rifle or revolver, or make calls till 6½, and then dine, and go to bed about 8½ or 9 p.m.

I like being on detachment very much, and have been especially fortunate in being sent to such a nice place as this. I am close to the river, and see all the steamers which go up and down. We generally have one coming by every 3rd day. The Military Train are encamped under the walls of the Fort of Buxar which directly faces us on the opposite bank, and when they discharged their carbines yesterday the bullets came across the river, which is here about 850 yards broad, and one or two came into the very compound and knocked up the dust under our noses. It would be very unfortunate to be shot when one is never thinking about it, especially after having gone through so many dangers as I have, don't you think so? At any rate, we thought so and lost no time in sending a flag of truce to our cavalry friends which had the effect of making them depress their pieces a little more.

I am sure you would be delighted if you could see all the Government horses here that we are sent to guard. Such fine beautiful stately creatures with flowing manes and tails; then you would be astonished to see what care is taken of them. I declare they are treated more like infants than great big strong brutes as they are. Each one has a groom to itself, and every morning and evening they are taken out for a walk, and then brought back and put to bed on a fine straw bed. In another stable are all the little foals and they are turned out twice a day into a large field with high banks where they play and frolic together for an hour or two, and are then put into their stalls again.

Did you see Mr De la Taste's schooner launched? I suppose you have not much time now that you go to school. I wonder when this letter will reach you! I will make a guess, and you must tell me how many days I am wrong. I say about the 16th of August, which is the anniversary of the battle of Bitthoor. Do you know, Emmie, my poor little "Bunda" is dead (bunda is Hindoostanee for monkey), not Jacko, but his companion and playfellow. He got paralysis in the limbs, and died at Arrah not many days ago.

I shall be very glad to get the book marker you are making for me and shall prize it much for your sake; it was very kind of you darling one to think of making it for me, and shews that poor old brodie is often the subject of your thoughts. I am indeed happy to have such a good, kind, and affectionate little sister as my Emmie. I hope our best and dearest of auntys is well, pray give my dearest love to her and say I am going to write to her next, so when you see No.45, recollect it is for Miss A. and not Miss P. I am going to tell her about some shawls that I got possession of in Lucknow but which I am sorry to say I have not now. However, "more of that anon".

As I have, and in all probability shall have, little else to do than write for 3 months to come, I intend to write to Aunt Micklethwaite, and for fear of mistakes shall send the letter first to Aunt A. who will forward it for me to its destination; however, that will do in a week's time.

I gave Juzzif's message to Jacko, who took it very unfeelingly, at least so I thought. Perhaps on more mature consderation he thought better of it. I asked him if he had any message to send to Juzzif, but as yet he is silent on the subject. Now dear Emmie, I must bid you good bye for the present, but you may expect

many more letters for the future than you have had hitherto. Give my best love to dearest Chaper, Macher and aunty, and accept the same
> my much beloved Emmie,
> from your very affectionate brodie,
> Hugh Pearce Pearson

P.S. Jacko has just awakened and begs that I will say that, doubtless a wag of the tail when sent by a dog of Juzzif's standing in society is a mark of the greatest esteem, but that he (Jacko) not being in the habit of wagging his tail, begs to send a shake of the hand (not paw, mind) and a broad grin to Mr Juzzif, and hopes in the course of a few months to make his personal acquaintance.

Letter No. 44

> Karuntadhee, June 27th 1858
> Left bank of the Ganges

My dearest Father,

I have written to Emmie according to promise but there are one or two little things I want to tell you which would not interest Miss P., so I decided upon enclosing one sheet to you. I should have written yesterday or the day before but my time on those days was fully occupied, yesterday in answering the enclosed letter from Mrs K. and the day before in paying and settling with my company for April and May. I yesterday wrote a long letter to my uncle P. and in it sent several messages to you under the impression that I should not have time to write to you by this mail; as it is, this letter must go to Buxar today or it will be too late.

Du Vernel is still under arrest, and the charges have gone to the Commander in Chief, so I think it is all "up" with him. His unfortunate wife came from Dinapore to Buxar yesterday and when she arrived did not know about the affair. It was of course a sad blow for her. I hear she has written to the C in C to try and beg him off. Mrs Keats and Mrs Browne also came by the same steamer to meet their husbands.

The regiment is still in quarters (stables) on the opposite side of the river, and I am still on detachment with 2 companies for the protection of the stud on this side. I believe we are now settled for the rains, but rumours came this morning that Douglas has received orders to organize a column to clear this district. Whether the 84th will form a part I don't know, but one thing I do know, and that is that your humble servant does not mean to go if there is a way of helping it. You had better direct "Buxar" for the future for I have made up my mind to stop here.

About the money I sent home. I wrote two days ago to Parry & Co.; when an answer comes I will let you know. I find what you say in your letter about letters being prepaid is to take effect from the 1st September next. However, I have laid in a good stock of stamps, and it makes very little difference in the end. I sent No.43 to the post just a week ago, so probably you will get it at the same time as this. In all probability I shall send £50 more home at the end of this month, which will make £146.6. in Cox's hands sent home by Parry.

Gwalior is taken but no particulars have arrived, except that the Ranee of Jhansi was shot The nujeebs (native police) of Gyah have mutinied, murdered their chief native officer, and taken treasure to the amount of 18 lakhs. The 10th are to go to Ghazipore, and the 77th to Dinapore. The 3 companies of the 54th that were here went to Benares four days ago, but I hear they are to form part of this force which is to clear this district. In that case they will come back here. I never had time to find Pawlett in Lucknow, as we left a day or two after I got your letter telling me about him.

I took my rifle down to the river yesterday evening and made some <u>first rate</u> shots, smashing 3 bottles in the first 3 shots and a 4th bottle during the evening, all at 80 yards. I have made some very good practise with my revolver, which I keep in splendid order as I know neglect in that respect might cost me my life. I sent 500 Rs. to Parry a day or two ago to enable me to pay my tailor and shoemaker and Wilson.

I am obliged to get some boots from Calcutta as country ones are worse than useless and I am now in a pair of country "ammunitions". I have ordered 3 pr. to be made and sent up without delay.

I am very happy here and have everything I want except boots and clothes which I have written for. I think I told you before that I have made valuable friends here, and the comforts that come to us in the shape of tables, chairs, books, papers, carpets and fruit prove that the fair sex at least are mindful of the hardships we have undergone during the late campaign. I hope dearest mother will not give way to desponding thoughts about me, for I have all I could wish except the presence of those I love best. A few short months and we shall be on our way home, and then how joyful we shall be. I am now once more in perfect health and have made myself very cosy for the rains. Has No.31 turned up yet? Has uncle heard from Cox about the money I sent home?

Well good bye dearest Chaper, and God bless you all. Best love to darling mother and Taty (Emmie I have written to) and accept the same my own dearest Father,

from your affectionate son in haste,
Hugh P. Pearson

Letter No. 45

Karuntadhee, near Buxar
July 1st 1858

My very dearest Father,

I intended this letter to be to Aunty only, but many things have occurred since No.45 was posted which I should like to tell you. Perhaps this part of the letter to you will be very short, but we shall see as we proceed; if any fresh news comes, of course it will be longer but what I have at present to say will not occupy more than two sides.

Du Vernet is, as my No.44 tells you, in a very nasty mess and as the charges have gone to the C in C he cannot get off; there is a chance (though a very slight one) of his being allowed to sell; if so, Blake is the first for purchase. But yesterday Pratt got a letter from his father saying that his name (Pratt's) had just been returned for purchase, so that he will get the step in case of D.V's being allowed to sell. (2nd piece of news) Willis wrote to Chute the other day saying he would take substantive rank for £700. Both Chute and Pratt have written to offer him £500, so in all probability he will go. (3rd piece of news)

Pratt's father, who is (or will be in a few gazettes more) a Major General and has great interest with the authorities, says in his letter to his son that he is sure the 84th will come home the end of this year or early next, is not that capital? (4th piece of news) Keats is going home immediately. (5th piece of news) Reed and McCarthy are both about to retire. (6th piece of news) If the regiment goes home Snow cannot go with it, for two great reasons, first, because he is deeply in debt in this country, and second, because he is worse in debt in England, so bad indeed that he was obliged to leave, hid in a cart of straw!

One company of our regiment has gone on detachment to a village called "Doomraon" 10 miles from Buxar, and another to a place called "Beloutie" some 20 miles farther: the object of this is to keep the road from Buxar to Arrah free from budmashes and sepoys.

You say you hope I will re-write my journal. I am sadly afraid that will be impossible, but I will write a long and detailed account of all that I can remember from the time of my leaving Barrackpore to the present time. I could not write a journal, because there are many dates I cannot recollect.

2nd inst I went across the river yesterday afternoon to see some of our fellows with the regiment, and saw two letters from Brigadier Russell of our regiment (who you are aware has gone to England on sick leave), one to Lightfoot and one to Innes. He says Reed and McCarthy have both sent in their papers. Reed's have passed the War Office, but McCarthy's have not yet, on account of some hitch about his having drawn Full Major's pay and not ever having done duty as one. This is the alleged reason, but I believe (so Russell says) that Radcliffe is trying to get back into the regiment, and of course is anxious for delay to give him time. If Radcliffe succeeds in getting back into the 84th it will ruin Seymour, who, if he got his Majority soon would probably get his brevet lieut. colonelcy, having been very highly mentioned in despatches. Russell says he is going to stop in London till it is settled and will do all he can to prevent the scheme from succeeding. He says "I dined last night with Sir G. Wetherall who told me that the 84th would come home this year. If the men volunteered well we might get home in autumn". This is good news is it not? There can be no mistake for I read the letter myself.

I yesterday wrote a letter to Mr Wratislaw. How surprised he will be to see it! You may tell Mr Gibaut that I have his son's sword but no scabbard, it having been burnt when the poor fellow fell into the fire. About my "piece of ordnance" you may make up your mind to see it, for despite Sir Colin's order, I kept the cannon, and even fired a young salute out of it for the fall of Lucknow. Lightfoot has one just like it, and as he didn't give his up, I didn't mine.

Pray remember me most kindly to old Briggs. I hope he is well, and ready to play me a game next March, about which time I calculate being at home. I am very glad indeed that my ill-treated old "Ava" No.31 has turned up. I think we ought to congratulate ourselves upon our letters all going so safely, not one is now missing of mine to you, and I have received all yours up to, and inclusive of, No.31.

I am very glad Spilsbury is made so comfortable and tell him from me when you see him, that when I return to Jersey I shall walk over to Noirmont to see him. I saw the appointment of Edward Boultbee to the 15th, and noticed it to you in a former letter. You were not very far wrong in mentioning Ghazipore or Dinapore as our summer quarters, we are, you see, between the two. I must read the pamphlet you mention "by one who has served under Sir C. Napier". Doubtless his censure of Lord Canning is deserved, for at the commencement of the mutiny he certainly lacked that energy and decision which is so essential to a man holding so high a position; but still he had, I think, a difficult part to play. I have changed my mind about the disposal of my six months donation batta and instead of only 500 Rs. It is my intention to send the whole of it, viz. 730 Rs. 8 ans. to Cox's.

I hope, dear Chaper, that if you change your mind about what I said in No. 31, you will not hesitate to make use of any or all the money I have at Cox's, for I would rather see every farthing I have go towards Emmie's education than that you would deprive yourselves of a single comfort to make you happy. How I should like to see dear Juzzif's likeness! It must be finished now I should think. Pray remember me kindly to Saville when you see him. I can well imagine you miss him, for he is the oldest and best of our Jersey friends, however, I dare say before many months more are over you will have me to walk with and talk to. What has become of that old man and his wife, I forget his name, but he was my grandfather's clerk? Of course you do not now receive the "Friend of India". I wrote to stop it long ago.

I have practised frequently with my pistol, and like it better every time I fire with it. I smashed a bottle placed on a skull 25 paces off, and hit the bone with another shot last night, but this was not my pistol, or I should have shot a bottle twice out of every three times at that distance. We play cricket or quoits every evening, so there is no lack of exercise for us. I dined last night with Mr. and Mrs. Hamilton and Captain and Mrs. Keats who are staying there. This is the third time I have dined out during the last 5 days, so we are well treated you see.

I have made enquiries about poor Gibaut's money as far as I can at present, but no one knows what bank it is in. I will see Rolleston who was President of the Committee, and if he does not know, I will write to Binny & Co. and the Oriental Bank at Madras. Well! I must now conclude as my sheet is exhausted. When I began I thought this would be a very short letter, but I am agreeably surprised to find it is not. The fact is, that my happiest moments are when I am writing to you or reading your letters. I shall send you a lot of very long ones now I have so much time.

Give my best love to dearest Mother, Aunty and Emmie, and accept the same, my beloved Chaper,

from your most affectionate boy,
Hughey

Letter No. 46

Karuntadhee, Buxar
July 6th 1858

My very dear Father,

I have just heard that a mail for Bombay closes here this evening, and though No.45 (to Aunty) was only sent on the 4th inst. yet I cannot but think that you will be glad to see my handwriting of two days later date, if only to say I am well and happy. I am in great doubts whether this will reach you as it has to go through the Gwalior district, but it will not matter very much if it does not for my last contains all the news.

During the last 2 days Du Vernet has written a letter requesting to be allowed to sell, and the Major (Lightfoot) has recommended him to be permitted to do so. If he does, it will give Pratt the step.

More letters have been received from different people, agents etc at home, and all agree in saying the regiment is to come home immediately.

I believe Williams is to get the Adjutancy; he is a relation of our Colonel's (Franklyn) and it has been promised to him for some time. I am glad he has got it for now these "rankers" just raised have no chance. I much prefer a gentleman to a man who has risen.

Snow has been ordered up, but I don't think he will come. We have seen the "Thackers Overland" of the 2nd June but there is no news to interest us. The rains have set in more than a week, though we have had no rain for two days. I am delighted to be able to tell you that our compensation for kit lost at Cawnpore has been granted, viz. £91.0.0. I have sent all my batta £73 1. 6. to Parry and requested him to transfer it to my credit at Cox's. I sent it yesterday.

Well, dear Chaper, good bye for the present and believe me to be

Your most affectionate boy,

Hugh P. Pearson

P.S. Give my love to all. Your last letter received by me is Number 31. Jacko is in good health. I hope Juzzif is too.

Letter No. 47

Karuntadhee, near Buxar
Monday 12th July 1858

My dearest Father and Mother,

The mail for England closes at Calcutta on the 17th and unless this letter goes by the post which leaves this at 10 a.m. today it will be too late, so you must not expect a long letter. I have no news, and am only writing because I know you would be uneasy if you did not hear from me by every mail.

The only news I have (It will interest Miss P. immensely) is that I have procured another monkey, a very little one. It is extremely mischievous, and possesses more than the ordinary amount of sense which monkeys are endowed with. My last letter (I grieve to say a very short one) was posted only last Tuesday (the 6th) so you must make allowances for this being so short, for six days is not much time to gather news in–I sent No.46 via Bombay and Marseilles.

I have sent home £73.0.0. more to add to my little fortune at Cox's, and have just paid £20.0.0. to different tradesmen in Calcutta for boots, uniform and clothes. I have now got more than £30.0.0. in Parry's hands at Calcutta, with which I intend to pay for anything I may get from Calcutta in the next 3 or 4 months. I have ordered up some boots and trousers which I shall pay for out of the £30.0.0.

Captain Doyly has returned to this place, and last night we all dined at his house: he is a very nice gentlemanly man, and is without exception one of the most beautiful amateur artists I ever saw. His sketches are superb. He has one of Elizabeth Castle, Jersey in a storm, and it is truly a masterpiece of art.

Rolleston has come from Benares, bringing with him Ensign Jones and 50 men. I am about to be relieved and sent to the Grenadiers as his sub. and Penton will come and take over mine. I have now had command of this company since April 12th and have been drawing £5 a month for it in addition to my pay. I thus draw £30.0.0. a month. I have been very fortunate in having had it so long for there are two or three of my seniors who have been acting as subs. whilst I had the command of a company: however, this was in a great measure their own faults. I shall when relieved return to Hd. Qrs. on the other side of the river.

Do you remember this day last year? Doubtless you do. It was the day on which we fought my maiden fight "Futtehpore". The year just over has been a hard working one for me, has it not?

There has been a bit of a skrimmage with the niggers on the other side of the river, in which about 100 were cut up. They have caught one of the rebel leaders on this side: I don't know his name. We amuse ourselves here by playing cricket and have had two capital matches. On Saturday we trapped a fox by smoking him out of his hole, and placing a net over one of his numerous exits. We afterwards ran him with greyhounds and after a short run caught him, and as he was none the worse we put him by for another run.

I am going to take a dose of oil today to put my interior to rights. For the last two days I have had a pain in my stomach, brought on I think from the want of vegetables. Now dear Chaper, I have nothing more to say and the time is drawing near to post this, so good bye for the present. Your last letter rec'd is No.31.

I am all right with the exception of the little pain before mentioned, and hope all of you are well. Nothing more has been heard about Du Vernet. Give my best love to dear Aunty and Sister and accept the same,

My dearest Father and Mother,

From your most affectionate boy,

Hugh P. Pearson

Letter No. 48

Buxar

July 21st 1858

My very dearest Father and Mother,

My last No. 47 was put in the Post on the 12th inst. since which date much has occurred to tell you. On the 14th Du Vernet's papers went in to sell, and Pratt gets the step. D.V. is going from here by the next steamer. On the 14th I handed over my company to Penton, on account of Rolleston having arrived from Benares and taken the Grenadiers from Penton who was left without one and who of course, being a senior, took mine. Williams will get the Adjutancy as soon as Browne is gazetted in the C in C's orders. The fellows all asked me to apply for it and had I done so I should have certainly got it, but I have found out that the Adjutancy of a regiment in India is no sinecure, and the pay, good as it is, does not compensate one for the immense amount of work required to be done. Perhaps when the regiment comes home I may apply for it, as Williams neither likes it nor wants it, and is quite ready to give it up.

Your No.32 came to hand yesterday and I will now answer the questions in it. Regarding the attacks on Alum Bagh which you say I have not mentioned in my services, I have looked at my diary and no attack is mentioned as having taken place on the 12th of February, but there is mention made of those on the 16th and 21st I was present in both. In the former, I was with our left wing in the heavy gun battery, and in the latter, I was in the same battery on picquet with Keats and Humphrey. In the last services I sent home (in letter 41) I do not mention these attacks individually but as "was present with the army of occupation in Oude under Sir J. Outram". As you say, I do think them too insignificant to name.

I should greatly like to see dear Juzzif's picture but I suppose I shall in a few months more. I should like to shew you my gun and rifle very much. It is really "a beauty". I told you in my last letter that our claim for compensation has been allowed; we shall soon draw it now. I almost think I shall send it all home for you to buy me a new kit with. Let me know if you think I had better. You may depend on it that I will not part with my "war sword". It is much too heavy for me, but is good metal, and would puzzle a nigger to cut it through like he would one of the common "regulations".

You say I must have been with Outram in the repulse of the enemy after crossing the Goomptee on the 6th March. No, I was not. Our regiment was then at Alum Bagh with its own brigade. Outram was sent to command an entirely new division and when we did go to the Martiniere we were in Genl. Franks' division, Russell's brigade, and Outram was the other side of the river. If I remember right, we did not leave Alum Bagh till the 10th March.

I sincerely hope you and Macher will accept dear Uncle's invitation to Bourton; it will do you a very great deal of good, and I am sure if you could get a gun in your hand again, you would feel much better.

I have been for the last 6 days on a "dour" at Balliah 30 miles off. We went down in a steamer but as soon as we disembarked our troubles began. Of course the niggers bolted directly we arrived, and 50 of our men on elephants and all the cavalry were sent in pursuit. They remained out 3 days, and at last the Madras cavalry came up with 200 of them marching in order. The niggers formed square and the Madrasees wouldn't charge but fairly turned and ran for it. The infantry killed about 20 sepoys and budmashes, and one woman who threw herself into a sepoy's arms just as one of our men fired; the ball went through both of them. We marched back and arrived here yesterday. The men are terribly disgusted at having to go out on wild goose chases like this when there is no chance of catching the niggers.

We have got up a nice mess here, and are jolly enough if they would only let us alone. I greatly regretted leaving Kuruntadhee for all were so kind to me there. I am sorry to say they are going to take 190 Rs. from me, being the difference between an ensign and lieutenant's six months batta. The reason is that I was not a lieut. in the Indian gazette when the first six months batta was given. It is an awful shame, but Lightfoot is going to try and get it back for us. We are going to amuse ourselves with pigeon matches, and we are going to challenge Penton who is on the other side the river. Hardy and I are going to shoot against Penton and Pratt.

Well, dear Chaper, I have filled up my paper so must say adieu. Give best love to all and kind remembrances to Saville and our friend Briggs. My next letter will be written and sent in two or three days more. Now good bye for the present and believe me to be,

Your most affectionate boy,
Hugh P. Pearson

Letter No. 49

Buxar
July 26th 1858

My dearest sister,

It is now your turn to have a letter, and though I have not very much news just now to tell you, yet I dare say by the time I post it I shall have lots to write about; at any rate I will answer the many nice questions you put, and ask you others in return.

Du Vernet of our regiment is going away and is selling off all his things. I bought several things of his, amongst which were a tunic for which I gave 80 Rs., a shell jacket 15 Rs., a sash 10 Rs., and several other little things. The tunic and shell jacket fit me to a nicety and the tunic has never been worn. Tell Father I have written to Parry & Co (my agents at Calcutta) about the bill which was lost in the "Ava", but have, as yet, had no answer.

The Military Train challenged us to play them at cricket and the match came off a day or two ago. Our side went in first, and got 181 runs, and when they went in they only got 32 runs altogether! I am sending home to you by this mail a pamphlet called My Journal, or what I did and saw between the 9th June and 25th November '57, by a Volunteer. It was written by an officer of the Volunteer Cavalry and is one of the most correct accounts I have seen of Havelock's march from Allahabad to Lucknow. As I was present in every one of the affairs he mentions, you will be the more interested in it. In some places he has made trifling mistakes, but I have altered them for you. The author is, I think a Mr Anderson, and certainly he has confined himself to facts in a very praiseworthy manner. As he was in the Volunteer Cavalry, he naturally mentions them most and certainly a braver or more useful little band of men never existed. I have made my own remarks in the margin of the book, so that you may better understand it.

My little monkey has been in hospital for the last 2 or 3 days, but is now, I am happy to say, perfectly recovered. The health of the elder monkey continues good. You ask if it is as large as a cat: the big one is, but the small one is only as big as a kitten. I must now leave off writing for to-day, as there will be a mess meeting in less than half an hour, at which we must all attend.

27th July. I have just now posted "My Journal", by a Volunteer, and have sent it via Southampton with a 4 anna stamp on it. I hope it will arrive all safe, and that you will all approve of it. I am on orderly duty to-day, and have no time to spare, so ta-ta for the present.

30th July. To-day is the last day I have to write in if I want to send it by the mail leaving Calcutta on the 6th prox. Penton is going home sick and leaves this for Calcutta the next steamer. I saw an extract from General Orders dated 23rd July in which appeared, Lieut. R. T. Pratt to be captain by purchase vice Du Vernet who retires. Ensign G. Lambert to be lieutenant by purchase vice Pratt. This of course gives me a step. I yesterday crossed over to Karuntadhee and "took over" again the company which I handed over to Penton on the 14th inst. I shall in all probability keep it for some time now.

I have for some time been anxiously expecting a letter from you, and cannot at all account for my not having done so. The last is No.37 received on the 20th July, and it is now more than time that No.38 should show his welcome face here. We are looking out for a river steamer from Benares which has got all the luggage of the 84th on board. Perhaps I shall now see the 4 boxes which I parted with on the 14th March 57, but I quite expect to see nothing but mildewy rags.

I have been amusing myself with firing at adjutants with my little Lucknow cannon, and made some good shots. I have been offered anything I like to name for it, but I am bringing it home for all of you to see, and it would never do to part with it, oh no! I have just got a new chain for the small monkey, which enables him to climb up a high pole, and if he likes, sit on the top. It has a ring which encircles the pole, and is so loose that Jacko can pull it up after him.

I had a great and protracted battle with a strange "Jacko" the other night, in which, though severely wounded, I came off the victor. It was a well contested battle, and twice I had to retreat and keep up a heavy fire of stones on the enemy, who, having no guns, was unable to reply. At length, by dint of repeated attacks and continued firing I so far got the best of it as to be able to close with the enemy and pour in successive showers of grape and canister (small stones) whence the courage of the enemy failed him and on his declaring himself conquered, I advanced with guns loaded (viz. a stone in each hand), in case of treachery and took him prisoner. I received no less than 5 wounds but the enemy suffered most severely. I must tell you I should not have made war on Mr Jacko, had he not in a most cowardly manner sprung from an ambush, and inflicted a severe wound on me. I gave an account of the action to my Jackos, who expressed their deepest indignation and requested to be led against the strange "Jacko". I complied with their wishes, but alas! when we came in sight of the enemy, one of my allies deserted to the foe, whilst the other was so intensely frightened that he retired behind me, nor could I get him to face the enemy. Being thus situated I thought it would be rash to proceed, so with a few parting shots I retreated, and left "Jacko" and his treacherous ally masters of the field. I held a court martial on the deserter, and sentenced him to be blown away from a gun, which was effected by firing the Lucknow cannon loaded with the ends of cheroots at him: after standing 4 rounds begged to be released, so I forgave him. I hope dear Juzzif is well, and also his "frebbend". I wonder if he will remember me when I come home! I hope he will.

Tell dear Chaper I shall not be able to send any more money home till September, on account of the numerous bills for carriage of luggage etc which are now due. I have sent home now altogether £169, besides which I have £30 in Parry's hands. Ask Chaper if this tallies with his account of what I have sent. Now dearest Emmy as I have come to the end of my paper I must bid you adieu for the present. Give my best love to dearest Chaper, Macher and Taty and accept the same, my dearest sister,

from your affectionate and loving brother
Hugh Pearce Pearson

P.S. Has Chaper seen anything more of Spilsbury? Tell Father to remember me kindly to Saville and all our friends. H. P. P.

Letter No. 50

Karuntadhee, Buxar
August 6th 1858

My very dear Father and Mother,

The day before yesterday I had the inexpressible delight of receiving your welcome No.33 and I intend today to answer your questions in it reserving any news I have for to-morrow. You mention having received my No.38. Have you yet got No.37? The reason I ask is because I entrusted it to Whittock of ours to post and it was ten to one against his doing so. He is so careless and forgetful. However, from your not mentioning its absence I conclude it arrived safe. You ask, who will get the adjutancy? I anticipated the question and answered it in a former letter. I felt sure you would say I was right to get the wine and brandy, and to the latter liquor I owe my escape from the exposure to rain and damp to which I was constantly subjected. On the subject of "medals", I was overjoyed to see in Thacker's of July 2nd (just in) that Gen. Peel in answer to Mr Kinnaird said that a design for a medal for the heroes of Lucknow had been approved of by Her Majesty, and that the subject was under the consideration of the Board of Control. As they have given or rather, granted a medal for Lucknow in particular, I should say they would give one for "the Campaign" as well: in which case I should have two.

Du Vernet was obliged to give up all the rupees he looted, and was severely censured in Gen. Orders by Sir E. Lugard for not having done so when the order came out that all was to be given up. I think the wording of the order was that "it was an act highly unbecoming an officer and a gentleman". Du V. has now left the 84th and is on his way to Calcutta. He is no loss. It was Oakley and Humphrey who intended to exchange and not Crohan, but I suspect both have changed their minds now Oakley is 3rd for his company, and Humphrey is next before me. I imagine neither will exchange, but Oakley may.

You mention the fact that Browne and Clery of the 32nd have only been a short time longer in the service than myself, and have been promoted. I am afraid you have little chance of getting mine yet. I am now ninth lieutenant (supposing Chute has got his company) and as to services, surely Magrath (who was shut up from the first in Lucknow) and Barry (who has been with me all along and has 7 or 8 years service) have prior claims! I am sadly afraid, dearest Chaper, it will be a vain attempt, and most certainly I do not expect success. I think myself more fortunate than 5 out of 6 subs, at being ninth lieutenant (without purchase) and having two medals (?) in the short space of 2½ years. I suppose you have seen my "services" in Hart's for April. Willis put them in, and has taken care to give himself the "lion's share", however, you will, I hope, soon see the alteration in mine which I sent to you in No.41. I mentioned in a previous letter that the compensation for baggage lost has been granted. We shall soon now be authorized to draw it. Donelan has written to ask permission to issue it. Donelan is, I think, the man recommended for Paymaster.

The story about Whittock and two companies of the 84th expecting to be attacked at Arrah must have been a pure invention of the papers. In the first place Whittock never was at Arrah or nearer to it than Gyah (some 80 miles off) and no companies of the 84th ever had the least apprehension of being molested there. You say several officers have made their fortunes by loot got at Lucknow. An officer named "Lance" of some B.N.I. Regt. found one diamond cross valued in Calcutta at £7500 and in addition to this he has loot which if he sells it will give him about £1000 a year. He has retired, and gone home to sell it. I have now answered your letter and will put this by till to-morrow, when I will tell you about myself etc.

7th inst. On the 3rd inst. Penton left Buxar in the steamer "Charles Allen" for Calcutta, to appear before a medical board which will, I suppose, send him home. Now if ever I happen to come across any good shooting there will only be Hardy to come with me, for no one else cares about it; however I don't think that is likely. Two or three days ago the men killed a cobra in this compound. It was quite young, measuring only three feet in length. I have got new houses for my beloved "Jackos" to live in. The little one is already in possession of his, and I expect the big one's today. The house is a box on the top of a bamboo with a little platform in front for them to sit on. I caught a rat yesterday and put it in the little monkey's house; when "Jacko" saw rain coming he went upstairs to take shelter. But Mr Rat disputed his right to the box and bit him when he tried to come in, however, strange to say, they made friends, and both occupied the box till the rain was over, when they quarrelled and had a "battle royal" which ended in the summary expulsion of the intruder, Mr Rat.

I yesterday dismissed my three coolies, syce, and grass cut according their request. They want to return to their homes in Oude at a village called "Mungrawarrah" (a place we were in for some weeks). I have given them all a good "backsheesh" beside their wages and character. The old coolie and syce have been just a year with me. The former was shut up with "Jack" my servant in "Alum Bagh" for two months, and the latter came in with me into

Lucknow carrying some few things of mine. Many a chuppatti has my syce given me when I was almost famished, and had I been a rich man I would have given him 100 instead of 20 Rupees.

On the 2nd inst. I wrote to Uncle Pearson, telling him that I had sent home "My Journal" to you. I had very little news at the time I wrote and the letter was not so long as I usually write. I received a letter from my agents at Calcutta, informing me (in answer to a letter of mine) that they had not yet received an acknowledgement of the money sent home to Messrs. Cox & Co. from that house, but expected to do so every mail. We play cricket every evening, weather permitting, and I take plenty of exercise. I have written to Cuthbertson and Harper at Calcutta for some English books, and to Wilson for ½ a dozen flannel shirts. If you, dear mother, could only see the ragged state your boy is in, how horrified you'd be! I had six old flannel shirts, and at last they got so bad that I was obliged to cut three up to mend the other three!! No two shirts were the same colour, so you may imagine what a mixture of patterns the patched ones presented. In a day or two the new shirts will arrive, and I shall once more appear in "gorgeous array". I received a pair of regimental trousers and a pair of braces "per banghy" from Harman last week, and have got a supply of "kha'ki rung" (or mud coloured) coats and trousers from Benares. I still want pocket-handkerchiefs, flannel waistcoats, and socks, but I will get those afterwards. I have sent the carriage of my little cannon to be mended: when it comes back I shall pack it up ready to bring home. The white ants are in great quantities here, and very destructive: we have to inspect our things every other day to see they are not eaten.

Well, my dearest father and mother, I have reached the limits of my paper, and as I have nothing more of importance to say, I suppose I must bring this letter to a stop. I will not post it till to-morrow in case this evening's mail should bring me No. 34, though that is not likely. Give my best love to my dearest and best of aunts and also dear little Miss P. and believe me, to be now as ever,

your most affectionate & loving son
Hugh. P. Pearson

Letter No. 51

Karuntadhee, Buxar
August 11th 1858

My dearest Father and Mother

Number 50 was posted at Buxar only 3 days ago. I am now going to tell you about little skirmish that took place near Buxar yesterday and then I shall put this letter by till another day. First, however, I must not forget to tell you that I directed my last (No.50) to care of Col. P., Bourton, anticipating from your letter that you would be there when this reaches England.

I told you some time ago that two companies of the 84th were stationed at Doomraon, 10 miles from Buxar. The rebels, it appears, were rather too close to our men to be pleasant, so 2 more companies of ours on elephants, all the Military Train, and some 100 Seikh Cavalry were sent after them.. The information the rebels had must have been very bad, as our people were on them before they knew anything about it. The elephants were lazy, and our men did not come up in time, but the M.T. and Seikhs charged and killed between 70 and 80 out of 300 that were there. The loss on our side amounted to 1 Seikh killed, 1 wounded, 1 horse killed, 2 wounded. They are now regularly dispersed in this part of the district.

We are going to have a cricket match this afternoon and I have been busy marking and levelling the ground all this morning. I will now put this away till some further day, so adieu for the present.

Thursday 12th (grouse shooting begins). I wish I were on some nice moor just now with my gun, how delighted I should feel! Yesterday evening a portion of the Fyzabad rebels were within 25 miles of this on their way to the Jugidspore jungles. It is said there are 600 sepoys and 1200 budmashes, that they had lots of money and ammunition but no guns, and that they were making for a ford somewhere near "Balliah". Yesterday afternoon the troop and a half of the Military Train and 2 companies of ours left Buxar for Doomraon on a dour; probably this force was sent to oppose the enemy crossing the river. When more news arrives I will tell you it, in the meantime I will scribble a few everyday occurrences for your edification.

Last night I had an addition to my stock in the shape of two kids. I visited them this morning, and cruel to relate, speculated as to how long it would be before they would be fit for the table. Yesterday our cricket match came off, and we had a very nice game; my side were vanquished by about 30 runs; I only got 8. Just now my little cannon came back from being mended. It is now in thorough repair and I am getting it cleaned, after which I shall take it to pieces, and pack it up. I received a letter yesterday stating that my 3 pr. boots had been sent off from Calcutta, so that I shall probably get them about the 18th inst. To-day is the anniversary of the 3rd fight at Busseerutgunge. As I gave in one of my letters (No.45 to Aunty I think it was) a calendar of our battles and skirmishes for the month of July, I will now give the same for August.

Aug. 5th. Advance on, and 2nd taking of Busseerutgunge. This was one of our hardest fights. It was, if I remember right, in this action that I was sent to support Gibaut with 24 men when he was defending a disabled gun carriage. On the 12th Aug (to-day) we advanced on Busseerutgunge for the 3rd time and fought at a small village called "Boorbeake Chowkee" about 3 miles from Busseerutgunge. On the 16th August we fought the action at Bitthoor on the Cawnpore side of the river. On the 24th poor Kenny died of cholera, and on the 25th of this month I shall have been one year a lieutenant. These are all the remarkable events that happened in August, at any rate they are all that I have chronicled.

I am taking advantage of the temporary quiet we are enjoying to get all my clothes, boxes, etc mended and repaired, so that if required to move I may be in good order and ready to do so. My good old "rifle" cloak has served me well and is rather the worse for wear in the lining. I am getting a "dhirzee" to mend it, and I shall then iron it and brush it, so that it will be as good as new. I am also getting a pair of regimental trousers "turned": this saves 16 rupees.

If any vulgar little London urchin were to put the favorite question to me of "how are you off for soap?" I am afraid I should inadvertently reply "uncommon bad", and moreover when I got home I should be induced to look in the glass to see if the brat had any reason to ask the question, for, without joking, you cannot get soap here for love or money. I sent to Dinapore for some on the 16th of last month, but none has come, nor do I think it will now.

Old "Jacko" is monstrously fat, and saucy in proportion; he is too lazy to climb up his pole, and when he does get up it is only to sleep till his next meal arrives. He was very indignant just now with some crows who ate a lot of his rice, and evinced more energy in scolding than I could have believed him capable of. The young one is also getting fat and naughty. I have just had a new chain made for him, very light indeed, so that the wretch does not know he has one on.

Well, good bye for today; tomorrow I shall most likely be able to give you intelligence of either the niggers or the "dour" party that left yesterday afternoon.

Friday 13th. No news today. Dine with the Siddalls.

Saturday 14th. The party that went to Doomraon came across the enemy at noon. Two guns (12 pr. howitzers sent from the fort on the morning after the party left) were sent to the front and fired several rounds but were soon recalled, as it was thought that the enemy were outflanking the main body. The cavalry were, however, sent on and made a brilliant charge, in which 40 or 50 sepoys and countless badmashes were slain. Our casualties amount to 2 M. T. men wounded, 1 Seikh wounded, 3 horses wounded. Captn. Nason of the M.T. was nearly shot; the bullet cut his shoulder knot in two. I have had the inscription on my cannon translated, and enclose a piece of paper with the result.

How is dear Joevelly? I hope he is well, and does not forget his master. Well dearest Father and Mother, I have told you all the news, and as I intend to send this by tomorrow's post, I may as well finish it now. Give my very best love to dearest Emmie, Aunty and all at Bourton when you next write and accept the same yourselves,

from your most affectionate son,
Hughy Pearson

P.S. I am sorry to say my poor goat died yesterday. The kids are being nursed by another of my goats.

Letter No. 52

Karuntadhee, Buxar
August 20th 1858

My dearest Father and Mother,

I sent my last letter by the post which left Buxar on the 16th, but although it is only four days ago, yet many things have occurred which will be news to you. Yesterday 4 companies of ours, 1 troop of the Military Train, and 1 of the Seikh Cavalry left in two steamers for Balliah, whence they march to a village called Russerah to relieve a company of Seikhs who have been besieged there for the last 3 days. As I do not intend to post this for a week I shall be able to tell you in it the result of the "dour", and in the meantime I will write on other subjects.

We have received the "Overland News" of the 9th and 17th ult. how rapidly papers are sent so long a distance! On the evening of the 17th of August we were reading the paper of the 17th of July! I expect this afternoon to receive your No.34; at any rate I shall get it before I send this off. The gazette of July 9th took us all aback considerably, and one part of it (Lambert to be Adjt.) was received as anything but agreeable news. The fellows had all been congratulating themselves upon having a gentleman for an adjutant, and Williams had actually been doing the duties of one for a fortnight, when the gazette overthrew all his hopes, and conferred a much prized appointment on a puny and undeserving snob. No one yet knows why, or for what he got the Victoria Cross. Certainly it was not for "distinguished conduct", and I think even he himself would be puzzled to know why he got it.

I was delighted beyond measure to see that our medals are to be sent out to us. I shall have two clasps according to the wording of the answer to the Duke of Newcastle's question in the paper of the 9th July. One clasp for the defence, and one for the taking of Lucknow. How jolly it will be!

Sickness is very prevalent amongst the Europeans in India just now; Hely writes that 8 and 10 die daily at Dum Dum, and in our regiment 12 men died within

8 days of dysentery and cholera. All the officers, with one or two exceptions, are more or less ill. Donelan, our Qr. and Actg. Pay Mr. has been seriously, nay even dangerously ill. He had Neuralgia in the head, and inflammation of the brain. Even such a great and mighty warrior as your hopeful son does not escape entirely, having had the dangerous disease called (don't be alarmed, mother) "a bad cold in the head", from which he has happily recovered. Chute is very ill, so is Pratt, and you would not find two officers in the regiment that are "really well".

Brigadier Douglas has sent to all the regiments to hold themselves in readiness to go into the Jugdispore jungles in a week's time. Lightfoot has written to say that the 84th can't go as the whole regiment is sick, and we have more than 90 men in hospital. Fancy a jungle in the rains! I pity anybody who goes there before November, for the doctors all agree in saying that the miasma which arises from the decayed vegetation is fatal, yet this thick-headed dolt persists in going; if he does, I hope he will be the first victim.

Three officers and 60 men will arrive here on the day after tomorrow in the steamer "Koel" for the 84th. The officers are, I hear, Forster, Wolseley and Horan. Lady Canning is also on her way up and intends visiting the Karuntadhee Stud, so we shall have a grand day of it. I got from Calcutta a day or two ago 3 flannel shirts, and 3 good prs. of English boots, so now I am not ashamed to call upon the ladies. I am much pleased with the things I got and the charges are very moderate. The men are waiting to be paid so good bye for today.

5 p.m. I have again sat down to tell you of a book I have just been reading. It is called "Campaign in Afghanistan under General Pollock" by Lieut. Greenwood, H.M. 31st Regt. In it he speaks most highly of the officers of the 49th Regiment, so no doubt you, dear father, know him. The book is well written and most interesting: you ought to buy it, for I am sure you would all like it: it was published in 1844 and the publishers are Colburn & Co, Gt. Marlborough St, London. I dare say the man is dead who published it, but you ought to be able to get it in Jersey. If you can't, let me know and I will get it out here. I will write out for you the passage in which he speaks so highly of your old corps, but must first tell you that it was a bad fever which brought him in contact with the regiment, and it was a Dr Robinson of the 49th who attended him in it. He says, "When I began to get about a little, I experienced the utmost kindness from the officers; they all seemed like a set of brothers; a more pleasant or united corps it never has been my lot to fall in with. They have lately distinguished themselves very much in China, and with such a commanding officer, and such a feeling as there was throughout the regiment, it never could be otherwise.

23rd Aug. (Monday) Poor Chute of ours is dead. He died at Doomraon on the 20th inst. of erysipelas in the head: he had been sick for several days before he died, and it was thought nothing of till the 19th when he became dangerously ill. His gazette to captain probably never reached him, as communication with Doomraon is not regularly kept up, and it is only once in a way that letters etc. go to and come from it.

Yesterday I had the satisfaction of receiving your No.34 dated 30th June, and before I give any more news I will answer it. I fully expected that my short service would preclude any chance of promotion for the present, but the answer given by the Duke of Cambridge to the Mily. Secy. is a much more favourable one than I could have expected, and I have no doubt that in a couple of years' time I shall meet with success. I think we ought at least to wait till that time without again mentioning the subject, for if it is brought forward too often the C. in C. will get annoyed, and think it a great piece of assurance in one so young in the service to ask for such a gift as a company. I don't think I ever came under Sir

J. Outram's notice sufficiently for him to know me, however he perhaps may. Whatever he may say, I think it would be best to keep it quiet for the present, and in two years more I imagine I shall have no mean chance of promotion.

Lady Canning passed by yesterday in her barge on her way to Allahabad. Her first intention was to visit the stud here, but it came on to rain and the idea was given up. I see the flag at the post is hoisted, so the Koel with 60 men and 3 officers for us must be in sight, as she is the next steamer expected. I am now, by poor Chute's death, made 8th lieutenant. Much as I like promotion I would rather be without it than get it by death steps. To think of a poor fellow who yesterday was talking with you to be dead next day is very awful.

As soon as the India medal comes out you should have it painted on my portrait. How many clasps shall I have? One or two—if a clasp is given for the final taking of Lucknow I shall have two, but in any other case but one only.

It is very kind of Dr. Bird to think of me and I can assure you I often do of him, as well as all our old Chelmsford friends. I intend putting by £20 for the express purpose of paying for a trip I intend to make to Essex if I am alive and well next year. I will go and see the old Felstead school where I passed so many happy days, also Ingatestone, to Chelmsford and Colchester.

It was very kind of Uncle Key to do so much for me: I hope, dear Father, you will write to him and tell him how sensible I am of his kindness, and how exceedingly obliged I am to him for it. As to dear Uncle P, it is nothing new, for ever since I can remember, he has always been the kindest friend I had (of course excepting all of you at Jersey) and is in point of goodness the counterpart of your own dear self. I am indeed fortunate in having such good and true friends, and I hope I shall shew by my actions and conduct that I am grateful for it.

The news you mention about Major Lightfoot being attacked at Arrah is, as I before told you, all bosh. I see nothing more in the papers about our regiment returning to England, but I heard that the order for it to do so was now in Calcutta, and that as soon as the G.G. and C. in C. get troops to replace us we shall go. At any rate we must, I should say, leave India in the commencement of next year. There is a good deal of sickness about; the 84th alone have above 100 men in hospital. No news has been heard of the force gone on the dour, but I hear the niggers split up into parties, and separated on the approach of our people. Very probably this was the case, but this is only a bazaar rumour.

The Siddalls (our kind friends) have been in great trouble this last day or two on account of one of Mrs Siddall's sister's children having been seriously ill. I believe the poor little thing was almost gone when Burton our doctor took it in hand and literally snatched it out of the jaws of death. It is yet far from out of danger but it has been rapidly improving, and will I hope get over it. Burton, who has only been married a year or two, has just heard of the birth of his first child, and is as proud of it as every one in his position always is.

I intend sending this by the mail leaving Bombay on the 7th prox. and must send it from here at latest to-morrow, however, I will leave it open till then and I may hear some more news in the meantime. I have said my say for today and will put it by for tomorrow.

24th (Tuesday) I must send this off in an hour or two to be in time for the mail, and am sadly afraid I shall not have time to write much now, however, I will try. Last evening I dined with the Siddalls and had some delicious iced beer. The little baby is a little better, and is in a fair way of recovery. The steamer Koel arrived here yesterday afternoon with our recruits on board. I do not know what officers have come with them but have sent over to see. The weather is wet and cold and it has been raining incessantly since 3 a.m. The "Jackos" have shut themselves up in their houses and do not even show a finger lest they should get wet. How is dear Emmy now the tooth is out? Have you, dear mother, and aunty commenced sea bathing yet? I long to get a glimpse of the sea once more, and when I do, I hope it will be on my way home.

Penton left Calcutta in the P. & O. Steamer "Nubia" on the 20th inst. Is Woolhouse yet in Jersey? Tell me if he calls on you and what he says.

Now I must send this off as there is no more news and I am afraid of being late for the post. You have I suppose received my No.41 long ago. I mention it because in it is the list of my services which has been sent to Hart's Army List. Give my very best love to dearest Aunty and Emmy (to whom I shall in all probability next write) and accept the same my very dearest and kindest father and mother,
from your most affectionate son,
Hughie Pearson

Letter No. 53

Karuntadhee, Buxar
August 29th 1858

My dearest Emmy,

I sent No.52 via Bombay and posted it at Buxar on the 24th inst this letter will go by the mail that leaves Calcutta on the 7th of September, and I intend to post it about the 31st inst or 1st prox.

The "dour" party have returned wretchedly tired and disgusted, having done nothing, and slept every night for a week in a pouring rain without shelter. Poor Donelan of ours is dangerously ill; in fact he cannot recover except by a miracle. The "neuralgia" in his head has turned to inflammation of the brain, and I am afraid it is all up with him. Our Serjt Major was buried yesterday: he died of consumption. This is the 2nd Serjt Maj. we have lost since the mutiny began. Poor Hamilton died 2 days ago, and his poor little wife is frantic at her loss. I have often told you in my letters how kind they were to us since we came to Karuntadhee. I am happy to say I am quite well; this I attribute in a great measure to the great amount of exercise I take daily. I crossed the river to Buxar two days ago, and saw our new ensigns, Horan, Forster and Wolseley. I have not had sufficient opportunity of judging, but I dare say they will turn out well.

Yesterday I received 3 flannel shirts from Harman, and like them very much: they are, however, very dear. I wrote to Uncle Pearson and sent the letter off on the 25th inst. I doubt whether it will be in time for the Bombay mail, but it may.

The weather has been very disagreeable, and for the last 5 days it has rained incessantly, however, it is seasonable, so we cannot complain. I have amused myself during the rain by making percussion shells for my rifle. They are very tedious to make, but when made are formidable weapons. I shot an adjutant with one and the effect of the explosion was terrific. I should like to catch sight of an enemy's ammunition waggon when I had my rifle with me loaded with one of these little shells.

The "Jackos" are looking uncommonly well, and the big one is so fat that he can scarcely climb his pole: when he jumps he comes down with a grunt like a prize pig. I have promised him a medal and clasps for his services during the war, and he seemed much pleased at the idea. The young one will get no medal as he has not been under fire but I may perhaps give him six months' batta. I tied old Jacko to a pariah dog this morning and he jumped on his back and had a nice ride about the compound, much to the pariah's disgust.

Our drafts arrived on the afternoon of the 24th (I sent No.52 in the morning) and the recruits are as fine a set of men as one could wish for. Captain Snow of ours came up with them but has gone on to Allahabad with other troops. He is expected down in a day or two. I will now put this by for a day or two when perhaps I shall have more news.

Tuesday 31st. I hear poor Donelan of ours is dead: it must be him, for a native came across yesterday and said an officer was dead and was going to be buried in the afternoon. This makes the 23rd casualty in the 84th since it came to Bengal in March 57!! I see in "Thacker's Overland News" that the 49th are under orders for India, and some time ago I saw Gilson's promotion to a lieut. in H.M.'s 22nd.

On Sunday last (29th) guns were heard in the direction of Doomraon and soon after O'Brien of ours who commands there sent in to say the rebels were all about him and that he had fired several rounds from the 12 pr. howitzers at them. A reinforcement was sent out but no fresh news has come in. The rebels are very impudent now and often come within 8 miles of Karuntadhee.

I was greatly pleased with the piece of poetry you composed on "the Rose". I should have liked to have been at the "Midsummer Tree" and to have seen you all enjoying yourselves. You should have put the little ring I sent you on the tree. It would have sold for a good deal from the fact of its having come out of Lucknow. Don't you think so? Well, good bye for today as I really have nothing more to tell you. What a pity I have so little news!

5 p.m. I am going to devote this evening to writing instead of taking my usual ride, for I have this moment received your No.35, latest date 18th July, and cannot rest till I have, at any rate, partially answered it I knew you would all be delighted to hear about my getting a medal and clasp. I hope eventually they may give a clasp for the final capture of Lucknow. Your next letter will doubtless acknowledge the receipt of my No.41. I am rather anxious to hear you have received it safely, as it contains my revised "War Services", which have gone to Hart's Army List. When Chaper next sees Saville or De la Taste, tell him to remember me kindly to them. Dr Jackson, who exchanged with Dr Popplewell, arrived at Buxar yesterday. It was, as I supposed, poor Donelan who died yesterday.

Late last evening a party of 120 men of ours and 50 M.T., the whole under Barry, went out to Doomraon to the assistance of O'Brien, who expected momentarily to be attacked. I fancied I heard guns just now in that direction, but when I hear further I will let you know. The light is failing, so fare thee well till tomorrow!

September 1st (partridge shooting begins) I'm not likely to forget that I think. I dare say dear Chaper is enjoying himself now with his gun at Bourton. I hope he is, for I know how fond he is of shooting. Dear Chaper mentions in his letter about Jacko upsetting the tin of grog; strange to say, I have just got the bill for it, which amounts to Rs. 5.4.0 or in English money half a guinea!

I will answer your questions about little Jacko now. He will not, I think, grow any bigger. He has no tricks except tumbling head over heels, and that he often does. He will eat out of a spoon or cup or any vessel; he is not particular in that respect. I am very glad you have learnt "Far far upon the sea"–it is a very pretty tune and a great favorite of mine.

As to little "Jacko" whose hind legs were paralysed, I told you of his decease some time ago. There are no mosquitos here, indeed I have scarcely felt any at all since we left Barrackpore. Report says that a very large British force is going to collect in this district in the cold weather, and no rest is to be given to the rebels, but they are to be hunted down and killed wherever they may go. The papers, and all our people in Calcutta, say that we are to be relieved in a few weeks by H.M.'s 77th and the 10th by the 19th. I trust this is true. As the weather is so bad I shall allow this letter one more day to get to Calcutta in, and send it by this morning's post instead of tomorrow's. Even if I kept it I doubt whether I should have any more news. Give my very best love to darling Chaper, Macher and Taty, and believe me to remain now, as ever,

Your most affectionate brother,

Hughie

P.S. Jacko's compliments to Joevelly. I hope the "man" is well and fat as ever. H. P. P.

Letter No. 54

Doomraon, near Buxar
September 12th 1858

My very dearest Father and Mother,

My last No.53 was posted at Buxar on the 1st instant, and since then you see I have changed my quarters to Doomraon. The reason was that Captain Snow has joined the regiment and taken over his company from me, and I have now come here to take over No. 10 Compy. from Williams who is junior to me. I am afraid this will not be in time for the mail leaving Bombay on the 23rd so I shall send it by the Calcutta mail which also leaves on the 23rd. I am happy to say that there is a chance of our not making a second campaign in Jugdispore, for report says that all the rebels have dispersed to their homes in expectation of an amnesty being granted to them.

13th inst. We were turned out yesterday morning in expectation of an attack but only a few sowars came. We returned to Doomraon at 12 noon. I have been twice to the Rajah's deer park and gardens. He has a large tank full of tame fish which come and eat out of your hands. There are some very large fish in the tank: some weigh 15 or 16 pounds. He has a menagerie too, and two of the largest and finest rhinoceroses I have ever seen. Doomraon is a most beautiful place and is a nicer place than Karuntadhee, at least it is for a change. In the park (which is only about ¼ of a mile from here) are all sorts of deer and other game. I saw some splendid black bucks, antelope, spotted deer, and nylghu. There are also hares and partridge and pea fowl innumerable. I should like a day's shooting there very much indeed, but the old Rajah has never offered it, and I don't like to ask for it.

We have a good big force here now under O'Brien of ours: there are 490 of the 84th, 150 Seikh infantry, 1 squadron of the Military Train, 300 Seikh cavalry, and 50 of the naval brigade with 2 12 pr. howitzers.

With regard to the regiment, I think there is but little news to tell you. Pratt is sure to get his exchange into the 69th; Rolleston talks about taking substantive rank; Griffin will probably get the pay-mastership, and I suppose someone will be promoted from the ranks to the vacant quartermastership. Wolseley will exchange into the 90th as soon as he gets his lieutenancy, and Browne is making arrangements to exchange. Penton is in the Indian Gazette vice Chute, and those I think are all the moves at present. I have no doubt the regiment will go down country very shortly, say in the beginning of November, and we shall, I dare say, embark about February. I think we may calculate on spending Midsummer Day at home. In a few days our papers relative to compensation for loss of kit will come from Calcutta and we shall then be entitled to draw the £91 claimed. I intend to send at least £50 home to buy me a new kit. The men have erected a very nice tomb over poor Chute's remains and are preparing an inscription for it. We have lost 4 men (including Chute) from disease since we have been here.

16th inst. H.M.'s 19th Regiment are daily expected at Dinapore and the women of our regiment write from Dum Dum to say we are to go down immediately. I expect we shall be on our way to Calcutta before this reaches you. To-day is a very miserable and rainy specimen of the rainy season in India; ever since 8 p.m. last night it has been literally pouring. I hear there is always one good day's rain to finish up the wet weather with, and I dare say this is it, for we have had very fine weather now for more than a week.

Whilst Gregory (our assistant surgeon) was riding through the bazaar here a day or two since, a native picked up a stone and threw it at him. He was immediately knocked down and brought in and O'Brien ordered him to be well flogged. This was done under the superintendance of the soldiers and sailors, and, as you may imagine, very effectually. Gregory would have been quite justified in shooting the fellow on the spot, but had no pistol. For the future I shall always carry my revolver whenever I go out, so that if a nigger takes it into his head to hurt me I may not be without the means of defending myself.

I saw a splendid nylghu in the deer park yesterday and also a fine buck sambre or elk. I never saw a more beautiful animal than this nylghu, it is a deal larger than a bullock, and must be about 18 hands high, of a beautiful mouse color, and small elegant horns.

Your last letter received by me was No.35 but I am expecting one every day. This letter must leave Buxar tomorrow morning, and I am now going to send it in per coolie. I am sorry this is such a short epistle, but I must make amends in the next. Remember me kindly to Saville and all our other friends when you meet. Give my best love to dearest aunt and Emmy, and believe me to be, my very dearest Chaper and Macher,

                          Your most affectionate son
                          Hughie

P.S. I send you a very nice piece of poetry I copied from a book of songs: it would do nicely for Aunt Pearson. I see the "Brunswick" has gone to Cherbourg with the Queen.

Letter No. 55

                                              Doomraon, near Buxar
                                              September 23rd 1858

My dearest Father and Mother,

My last letter was sent off on the 17th inst. and I think was remarkable for nothing but its extreme brevity. Doomraon is not a place where much goes on, so I cannot promise much news, and the greater part of this letter will, I imagine, be about myself and monkeys.

First, however, I will tell you what little news there is. The sepoys in Jugdispore jungle have, with the exception of 4 or 500, all returned to their homes in expectation of an amnesty being granted to them: such a move is, I believe, in contemplation and the papers say it is to come out on the 23rd (today). I shall not be sorry if an amnesty is proclaimed, for I have had a fair share of all that has passed, and should certainly be sent to Jugdispore if the sepoys still remained there. Freeman, 3rd Seikh Cavy. has just gone out on a dour with 40 men, he having heard that 50 of the enemy's sowars were looting a village

4 miles off. I sincerely hope he may catch them and give them what they deserve. Col. Walter of our 35th attacked a village full of rebels near Arrah, and killed 60 or 70 of them; this was 10 days ago. One hundred men of the 80th with 2 officers (Captn. Arniel, Lieut. O'Connor) are staying with our fellows at Buxar: They came up the river in a sea steamer, and were going to Allahabad, but the steamer drew too much water, and they are obliged to wait for another to take them on.

I received your long expected No.36 on the 18th inst. and was glad to hear you had got my No.41 and approved of the way I had written my "War Services" This is the anniversary of the action at Alum Bagh, and I put this night down as the anniversary of the most wretched night without exception that I ever experienced during the campaign. I recollect it rained the whole night and we had not even a tree to shelter us. None of our boys were up with grub or clothes and we slept accoutred, in momentary anticipation of an attack. The day after tomorrow, you will, I know, remember. We are going to have a grand jollification in commemoration of that dreadful day and so are the men. A memorandum has just been round to say that it is proposed to erect a handsome tablet or monument in York Minster to the memory of all the officers, N.C. officers and men of the 84th who have fallen or died during the late campaign, and soliciting subscriptions for it. I am glad of this, for I think every respect ought to be paid to the memory of those brave men who laid down their lives in such a noble cause, for I cannot help thinking that but for God's great mercy I too might have been among them.

Pratt's papers to exchange into the 69th went in 3 days ago, so I suppose he will soon be off. I am having a cup, or drinking goblet, made out of the silver I got in the Kaiser Bagh. It is pure silver, gilt inside, and is worth between 47 and 50 rupees. The silver was taken off the wheels and body of a state carriage belonging to the King of Lucknow, and was found by Burton (now in the 6th Dragoons) from whom I got it.

I will do what I can to get home overland when the regt. is under orders, or rather when it goes down country, and will not forget to tell you when the route comes. The compensation for our kit at Cawnpore has been granted, and we are now waiting the arrival of some papers from Calcutta, without which we cannot draw the sum. I wrote down to Messrs. Parry & Co. telling him that I had 4 boxes there and asking him to look after them. He wrote to say that he had taken over the officers' things in a hasty manner and that many of the boxes were broken or damaged; that he had made strict search and could only find one box with my name on, but that there were a great many without names on, anyone of which might be mine. I can only hope that my name may be rubbed off; if not, I suppose they are gone. However, he said he was about to make another search soon, and would let me know the result. I think I told you I heard from Parry & Co. about the money I sent home, and that he had not heard from Cox but wd. let me know when he did. I have not heard from him since, but mean to write again about it. How is young Woolhouse getting on? Have you spoken to him yet? Our fellows have it that he was obliged to undergo another operation and was very ill in consequence. Is this the case? It is now getting dark, and I am going out for a ride, so good bye for today.

Septbr. 28th. On the 25th inst. we had a fine jollification here and though we could not get champagne, yet we managed to enjoy ourselves on what we had. I fired a salute of 21 guns out of my little cannon in honor of our going into Lucknow on that eventful day, and came to the conclusion that it is better to be near a miniature gun firing blank from you than to be near a 24 pr. firing grape at you. I used my silver cup that evening for the first time, and drank a jolly good bumper out of it to those at Home. I christened the cup "crumbs" in remembrance of Inglefield of the Military Train who goes by that nickname. Crumbs is now undergoing the process of gilding inside: when this is done I intend having "Doomraon, 25th September 1858" inscribed on the bottom of it, and it will then be finished. I hope when I bring it home it will (as the shopkeepers say) "meet with your approbation".

I killed a very venomous snake called a "Kerait" with my pellet bow as he was gliding about on the top branches of a mango tree. I believe it is one of the most poisonous reptiles in existence. I have got a tame squirrel as a pet. I found it one day in a small tope behind my tent. It is getting very tame and runs loose all about the tent. I am sorry to say that there is every chance of our paying Jugdispore another visit in a day or two: indeed, carriage has been indented for and orders have been received for the regiment to hold itself in readiness. Lightfoot seems to think we shall not go to Jugdispore itself, but to Sahessram or some other place on the Grand Trunk Road, in order to cut the rebels off should they attempt crossing over to the Rhotas Hills. However, there is very little doubt as to our moving somewhere and that very soon too. Probably after a little more hammering about we may march down the G.T.R. to Raneegunge, and over there we shall be tolerably safe.

And now I must bid you good bye, having arrived at the end of my paper, and this being the latest day to catch the mail of the 7th prox. from Calcutta. Give my very best love to darling Emmie and Aunty, and to Uncle and Aunt P. when you write and accept the same,
my very dear Father and Mother,
from your most affectionate son,
Hugh Pearce Pearson

P.S. When I know where we are going I will write and tell you. Our subscription to the tablet to the dead officers is Rs.50.

Letter No. 56

Doomraon, nr. Buxar
October 8th 1858

My dearest Father,

My last letter was sent off on the 28th ult., and in it I told you of our intended move. We were to have taken the field on the 1st of this month, but the ground was in such bad order from the heavy and continued rain, that it was thought advisable to postpone operations till the country was thoroughly dry, more especially as no tents are to be taken. We have had no rain now since the 3rd inst, and the weather has been intolerably hot, so we shall in all probability make a move about the 12th or 15th. There are several different forces organised, and the 84th will be split up into several parties, of which the largest is under Lightfoot and is to march straight to Jugdispore where Douglas will assume command of it. The Hd. Qrs. and most of the regiment will be in this column (my company amongst the number); 100 men of the 84th under Oakley are to be left here to form part of the garrison of Doomraon to be commanded by O'Brien. A third party of our men (1 company) is to go to a small village called "Roopsungor" 20 miles from here; the officers to go there are Snow and Horan; the post itself to be commanded by Major Carr, Madras Rifles. One company of ours is to remain with all the sick, stores, etc. at Buxar, and is to be commanded by Rolleston with Wolseley for his subaltern. The rest of the regiment goes with Major Lightfoot.

I see Penton's name in the gazette as captain vice Anson transferred to 10th Hussars: this gives Barry his step vice Chute deceased. Russell has gone, and if his step is filled up (of who there are great doubts) Oakley will be promoted to his company. Willis is doing his best to get Woolhouse and Blake provided for, and also Crohan, but the latter has no chance, I should say. Blake and Woolhouse have a very good chance of promotion, especially the latter. If these steps go I shall come home pretty high in the list.

Do you see the comet in Jersey? There has been a beautiful one here for the last week or 10 days, and it has done a great deal of good to us, as the niggers think it is a sure sign that their time is up. We have had several dours out against the rebels, and last Sunday we went to a place called "Morar", shelled it, and burnt it. The day before yesterday a gunboat with some of our men on board went 17 miles up the "Kurrumnasa" (a small river flowing into the Ganges 8 miles above Buxar) and the cavalry went up the banks. A letter has just been recd. saying 2 officers (one Mily. Train and 1 Mad. Cav.) were wounded, but no particulars are given. From this I should imagine there was a stiff fight.

I find, much to my disgust, that Havelock's force is to be considered as engaged in the relief, and not defence of Lucknow, so that we shall only get the same clasp as Colin Campbell's force. This is rather too bad after being shut up for 2 months.

I went out yesterday afternoon with my gun into some fields just behind my tent to see if I could not find a hare or partridge. We saw some partridge, but they went into the Rajah's park where we did not like to follow them. Later on in the day Freeman who was with me shot one. This is a beautiful country for snipe, but strange to say there is not one here. Buxar is just the same. Today I received a new forage cap from Harman's. I have now all the uniform, full and undress, except a shako. The little monkey played truant for 4 days, and I at last discovered him in a tent occupied by our men.

(5 p.m.) I am sorry to tell you that 2 of our best cavalry officers were killed yesterday in a fight with the niggers; one was Captn. Nason of the M.T. and the other Captn. Douglas 4th Mad. Cav. Nason had a very narrow escape the last time he was out; a bullet cut his shoulder strap in two, and I recollect his telling me he was not born to be shot. He was a very plucky fellow, and had the dash so requisite for a cavalry officer. It appears they were both charging a long way ahead of their men, and both fell shot through the stomach. Nason was killed on the spot, and Douglas lived till 5 this morning. No other casualty on our side, 47 pucka sepoys killed, and 8 or 9 budmashes. I knew them both very well, and am sincerely sorry for them. All the arrangements for Jugdispore altered, and no column to go from Buxar. I hope now we shall not go.

9th inst. 7 a.m. No more news from Buxar so I shall now answer your No.37 recd. on the 2nd inst. With regard to your first question as to whether I have heard of the acknowledgement of the money sent home by me. I have heard nothing more, but am sending to Parry to-day, requesting him (if he has not heard from Cox) to forward the 2nd of exchange, or in some way take immediate steps to ascertain whether the money has arrived or not. I hope in my next to be able to tell you that all is right. Perhaps it would be as well for you or uncle to write to Cox and ascertain how much has been sent to him through Parry on my acct. My first bill sent to Parry was one for Rs. 500 from Alum Bagh on the 22nd Jany., my second was one for Rs. 463 sent also from Alum Bagh on the 15th Feby.: my third was one for Rs. 730 8. 0 sent from Karuntadhu on the 5th July. This makes altogether a total of Cos. Rs. 1693 8. 0, or in English money about £169. 7.0.

I am delighted to say that Havelock's force is to get another six months' batta for the entry into Lucknow. I shall send this home as soon as I can draw it.

Your second question is of more importance, and I have well considered it. I shall write by this mail to Willis, who commanded the regt. in Lucknow, and under whose eye I was during the whole time, and after this affair is over I intend to get some testimonial from Lightfoot. I think however it would be of little use to write to either Outram or Lugard, and Berkeley I was never under. Outram never noticed me except when at his table and probably does not know there is such a person, and I do not think I ever distinguished myself sufficiently for one so high as he is to remark. I am now getting well up the lists of lieutenants, and by the time the regiment goes home I shall be 2nd on the list, or at any rate not lower than 4th. My services alone would in two years more be a great claim for promotion, and till I am thoroughly versed in both the theoretical and practical part of an officer's duty I wd. sooner remain a subaltern. When the regiment gets once more into proper quarters I shall attend drill till I am perfect in it, and intend to apply myself diligently to learning everything a good officer should know both on parade and in the interior economy of a company. The fates have smiled on me as yet, and if I do not get my company in 3 years from this day I shall still consider myself fortunate.

The 3rd subject you call my attention to, viz. the examination for a company, I will pay every attention to, and as soon as we go down country I will apply for a board to pass me. The examination is easy enough, but still one must study for it a little. I will not forget what you mention about coming home overland, and probably my having been through all this mutiny will not be overlooked when I request permission to go by that route. I have gummed a small piece of newspaper on this letter to show you what Mr Layard's opinion of the old 84th is. I also send some native pictures done on talc: they are badly done, but Emmie will like them I dare say. Please give them to her and tell her I have got 10 more to send to her.

The latest safe date from here via Bombay is the 10th (tomorrow) so I shall keep it open till then, and send it in by "Jack", who is going to bring some shot and powder for me in case we got to Jugdispore. We have just heard that one of the Rajah's tigers has broken out of his cage and gone into the deer park, so I suppose it will be scarcely safe to walk or ride there now. The night before last the Rajah gave us a grand nautch, and sent elephants and carriages for us. We also went to it, I riding on a huge elephant. It was very slow work, but it was a novelty to me, and I was wishing dear Emmie could have been there to see it. After the dancing was over, a large silver tureen with rose water in it was brought in, and the Rajah squirted a lot of it over each of our heads and faces with a handsome silver syringe, after which he put a drop of otto of roses on each of our handkerchiefs, and we then took our departure, and came home in state on the elephant. About 4 p.m. in the afternoon he sent us a grand dinner: this consisted of about 250 different dishes each borne by a man dressed in "gorgeous array". I thought everything on the table nasty, and so it was to European ideas, but our servants had a grand feed on it after we had done. I made my four coolies each bring a plate of sweetmeats to "Jacko", and made them salaam to him and call him "bahadoor" and "koodawan" (your majesty). He cared more about the sweetmeats than the obeisance made to him, and I am ashamed to say behaved in a very greedy manner, but his greediness brought its own punishment, for whilst trying to kill a hornet which came to partake of his sweets he got a severe bite in the foot, and the pain made him grin and chatter in a ghastly way.

In looking over a Madras Army List the other day, whose name should I stumble across but that of an old chum and schoolfellow of mine who you may remember at Felstead? I mean Francis Walker Merritt, now an ensign in the 24th M. N. I. I am going to write to him soon.

Have you got me a sword yet? Could I have "First relief of Lucknow 25th Septr. 57" put on the blade? I must have my medal and clasps put on my likeness when I come home. What do you say to it? In a day or two more we shall be entitled to draw our compensation for kit destroyed at Cawnpore, Rs. 910. I shall send most of this (if not all) home. If I send all home, and also the 6 months' batta we are to have, I shall have sent over £300 to Cox's. But I will wait till it is safely lodged there before I "count my chickens" as the expression is.

Tell Emmie I have invented a monkey language and converse with Jacko daily. The weather during the day is fearfully hot, but the nights are as cool as one would wish, so much so that I always sleep covered with a thick blanket.

Now my dearest Chaper I must conclude, as I have positively told you all the news. Give my best love to darling Macher, Taty and Emmie, and accept the same, best of fathers

from your most affectionate boy,
Hughie

Letter No. 57

Peeroo, Jugdispore jungle
October 27th 1858

My dearest Father and Mother,

We have been knocking about over the country ever since I wrote my last letter, but now I think we shall stay here for a week or so before we again move, and I hope to be able to send you a long letter. The force I am with is under Captn. Snow of the 84th and is now at a place called Peeroo at the extreme south of the Jugdispore jungle. There are no rebels near us, and we have at present nothing to do but shoot. I go out shooting every day, and always bring home some game. The game here consists of pig, deer, wild fowl, partridge, quail, plover, snipe, and now and then a stray nylghu. I have had six shots at deer but have not yet been so fortunate as to get one. I was out yesterday afternoon with an officer named Freeman, and he knocked over a fine young boar. We had some very nice pork chops for breakfast this morning out of him. I am now as happy as I can be in India, because I am in such a beautiful shooting country, and my ambition is now to shoot a deer.

I have been much troubled with the toothache lately, and have passed some sleepless nights, but now the tooth is as well as ever. I have also got an abscess on my heel from the chafing of my boot but it is to be cut open to-day, and will soon be all right.

My force has not had much fighting this time and I have only once been under fire, viz. at a village called Chougein. We had one or two men wounded and one killed: the sepoys lost about 60. The Hd. Qrs. have had harder work, and in one fight we (the 84th) lost 3 men killed, 1 officer (Jones) and five men wounded. Jones was severely wounded by a ball through the fleshy part of the thigh: the last accounts of him say he was getting on as well as could be expected, but the ball had not been taken out. The rebels have lost most fearfully lately; at one village young Havelock killed one thousand and fifty with his cavalry, and since then they have been caught twice. They have now gone south to the Rhotas Hills followed closely by Brigadier Douglas and Col. Walter.

I see by the papers that Woolhouse has been promoted into the 16th: this makes me now 6th lieutenant, not so bad is it? We have also got some new ensigns from other regiments. A few rebels attacked Buxar the other day and I hear they came so close that the fort guns opened on them. The rebels are now scattering themselves by twos and threes in the surrounding towns and villages, and we are getting them in and hanging them daily. Now good bye for today: I will finish this another time.

Hurpoor (Degree of long. 84°) October 31st. You see we are still on the move. We are in pursuit of a body of rebels under Meghu Rhao which went to the west of the Kurrumnasa river and thence down southward to the Rhotas Hills. I was sent with my company to the force under Major Carr, and Snow's force to which I belonged was sent from Peeroo to Jetoura Bungalow in the centre of the jungle. It seems an extraordinary thing that I am never allowed to rest quietly after all I have gone through. It is the same with Barry. We two have seen more work than any of the other officers and hoped we should have been left with our companies at Doomraon or Buxar, but they left young Wolseley instead, a fellow who has never seen a shot fired and who was burning to distinguish himself.

I am now myself again. The toothache has entirely disappeared and my heel is quite well. We (or rather our cavalry) cut up about 50 of the rebels in a village yesterday, among whom was a jemadar of some consequence in the rebel army. We had only one Seikh slightly wounded. We are now encamped in a tope full of monkeys, and this morning I let Jacko loose and sent him up the trees to catch me a small one. He caught one and made friends with it by catching fleas on it, but it would not come down with him. We are in a beautiful country, but I have seen no game except a few quail. We have had some delicious veal for the last day or so. We caught some nice plump little calves, and kept them to eat. I never enjoyed veal so much before. We had a goose too, but he was not kept long enough, consequently was very tough.

Young Havelock is close on the trail of Ummar Sing, and the last we heard of him was that he left a small village 6 miles from this just 2 hours after the rebel chief had passed through. I think Ummar Sing will be caught ere long, for Havelock is a splendid hardworking fellow, and will give him no rest. When I was under Snow's command we were once or twice in a very critical position, and then it was apparent how foolish it is to send a man in command of a force who had never before seen a shot fired. Snow was, however a man of sense, and did not hesitate to ask the opinion of one so young as I am, knowing that having seen so much service I must know better than himself on some points. There were but six officers with the force, and I was the only one, except Jackson our Asst. Surg., who had ever been under fire. Snow is a really good officer and only wanted a little experience in this guerilla warfare to make him a first rate commander. We were all uncommonly happy under him, as he did all in his power to please us and make us comfortable, and I was very sorry indeed to leave his force.

One evening when we were in sight of the enemy Snow sent his cavalry out to the front to draw the niggers out of the jungle. I suggested to him that if I were to take some men and lie in ambush I might spoil a few of the rebels and he assented. I took a sub-division of my company and laid down behind a bank. Our cavalry drew them out, and they were already within 300 yards of us still advancing, unconscious of our presence, when unfortunately, Snow, thinking we might get in a mess, sounded the "Retire", and then they immediately "smelt the rat" and pulled up uncertain what to do. I saw at once that I should not get a nearer shot, so taking a rifle from one of the men I took a steady aim at a man who appeared to be their leader, mounted on a splendid black horse, and fired. The ball fell a few yards short, but ricochetted and broke the horse's fore leg: the men then fired a volley and emptied their saddles. Had they been more careful of their aim they would have done much more execution. The enemy then retired, and revenged themselves by annoying us all night with firing at our sentries, two of whom they killed. I shall now conclude for the present, but shall not close the letter till I post it, which at present I cannot do as we have no communication with Buxar.

Rajpoor. Nov. 2nd. Some sowars are going immediately to Buxar, so it is a fine opportunity to post this and as I am not likely to get another for some time I ought to take advantage of it. Give my best love to dearest Aunt and sister and believe me to remain,

Ever your most affectionate son,
Hugh Pearce Pearson

P.S. I shall not forget the 7th. and 20th. of November [father's and sister's birthdays].

Letter No. 58

"Hatha" at the foot of the Rhotas hills
November 11th 1858

My dearest Emily,

I posted my last letter on the 3rd inst. and on the same evening had the inexpressible delight of receiving No.39 from Father who was then at Doncaster, and also another No.39 from yourself, mother, and auntie. Your No.38 is as yet not forthcoming, but will, I dare say, turn up when I least expect it. When I received your No.39 it was just a month since I had heard from you before, so you may imagine how delighted I was.

We are now at a nice town just under the Rhotas Hills, and expect the order to go into them soon. The niggers are about 4 miles from us in the hills, and a few days ago they came down and attacked us with all their force: their cavalry behaved very well, and came within 300 yards of the village we were defending, but the Enfield Rifles made them pay dearly for their rashness, and emptied 7 or 8 of their saddles in less time than it takes me to narrate it They were well met on all sides, and must have lost heavily, whilst the damage we sustained was 1 Seikh Cavalry man very slightly wounded. This is a splendid country for shooting and I have already bagged 4 couple of teal, and 1½ couple of duck. I am now going out again to see what I can get, so good bye for today.

Bhuraree (28 miles from Benares) Novbr.15th. We are now 8 miles to the west of "Hatha" and 28 miles E.S.E. of Benares, close under the hills, and in the most magnificent country for shooting of all sorts that ever I was in. I went out at daylight this morning with my rifle and had not gone 500 yards from camp when I saw a herd of about 70 deer and antelope feeding. I walked up to within 80 yards of them with my rifle slung on my back, and in 20 yards more I should have been behind a bank from where I could easily have shot one, when Gibson of the 87th who was out with me fired at another herd, and those in front of me immediately jumped up and saw me. Before I could unsling and cock my rifle, they were 150 yards off, and though I sent both balls very near, yet I did not hit them. However, I am going out again in half an hour to have another try.

Yesterday afternoon whilst wandering through the hills with my gun I saw at a distance what I took to be a man sitting under a tree and therefore I paid no more attention to it. On my approach it jumped up, and I saw before me one of the most magnificent monkeys I ever set eyes on, it was bigger than a greyhound, of a white colour, and with a tail at least 2 and a half yards long by which it hung from trees. Subsequently I saw upwards of 50 of these beautiful animals. Round the edges of a small pool of water in a valley we saw the footprints of tiger, <u>deer</u>, and <u>pig</u>, and every small pool we saw had its edges regularly trampled down by the two latter animals. There are also, besides the game I have mentioned, nylghu, <u>bear,</u> sambre, peafowl, <u>partridge</u>, hares, cheetah and <u>quail</u> to be found on the hills: those animals whose names I have underlined thus, <u>deer</u>, literally swarm in the valley and I hope yet to bag some of them. Now good bye for the present. I am off again, and I hope when I continue this letter to be able to tell you I have bagged my first deer.

"Hatha", 17th Novbr. I went out yesterday afternoon after all sorts of game but only got a brace of partridge and a few quail. I got a running shot at a deer, and went very close to it.

We have now moved back to our old ground, so good bye to sport for the present. Col. Seymour of ours has joined, and has now gone to the hills in command of a column. This of course takes the command of the regiment from Lightfoot.

The Amnesty goes into the enemy's camp to-day, and I sincerely hope they will accept it, come down, give themselves up and go quietly to their homes, then perhaps we shall be sent down country and have a little rest. We march again to-morrow, if anything else occurs I will resume my pen when we arrive at the new halting ground.

(Novbr. 21st. Ramghur Ghant) Yesterday, my darling Emmie, was the anniversary of your birthday, and I drank your health and many many happy returns of the day to you in a glass of sherry. Last night the rebels made an attack on one of our posts about 4.5 miles from here, but were driven back into the hills. their loss is not yet known, but they must have suffered considerably for our guns fired no less than 43 rounds of canister and shell into them in the course of the night. About 1 o'clock last night a large tiger came to within a few yards of one of my sentries, and began licking his lips in anticipation of a nice tit-bit for his supper when the man fired and hit it, but not mortally: it roared a good deal as it went off, and a few drops of blood were seen this morning sprinkled about. I saw a bear come down to drink about 2 a.m. today, but did not like to fire, as I should have alarmed the camp. I saw a chit just now addressed to Major Carr from a Mr Denison, a Magistrate, saying that he surprised the enemy yesterday, and killed 50 of them. And now, dearest Emmie, I must bid you good bye for the present, as I have no more news, and this letter has already been too long detained. Jacko is well, and sends his love to Juzzif. Give my very best love to dearest Chaper, Macher and Aunty, and accept the same, dearest sister, from your loving and affectionate brother,

Hughie

Give the enclosed letter from Messrs. Parry & co. to father.

Letter No. 59

Hatta, Rhotas Hills
December 10th 1858

My dearest Father and Mother,

My last letter was dispatched on the 21st ult. and since then I have received your Nos. 40 and 41 dated from Wales. The best news I have for you is that the 84th have now every chance of being in Calcutta before the end of next month, and every one says that we are to be relieved by the 29th, which is by this time at Sahessram. Fifty of our men and one officer have already gone to Calcutta as an escort to the King of Delhi, and I hear that all the regimental baggage which was left at Buxar has also been sent down country. This looks uncommonly like a move for us, and I really believe we shall go this time, notwithstanding our former disappointments.

Our force is now the only one in the field in the Shahabad district, all the rest having returned into quarters at Doomraon and Buxar. The rebels are all giving themselves up, and going to their homes, and there are not 10 armed men together in the district. Three cart loads of arms, and upwards of 100 horses have been taken from them during the past fortnight, and at Ghazipore a great number have delivered up their arms and persons, relying on the well known lenity of the civil power to save them from punishment.

I was very glad to see you had taken advantage of some of the many invitations sent to you. A little excitement and change of air would I am sure be good for you, and it pleased me to see how kindly you have been treated at every place in which you stayed. I am heartily glad to hear you talk of settling in England when uncle has bought an estate, for Jersey, though a nice healthy little island, is not at all the place for a permanent residence. I hope none of the wettings you got on coach tops did you any harm; how unfortunate you seemed to be, as you never spoke of being on a coach top without there being heavy rain. I should greatly have liked to have been with you on your visit to Hampton Court Palace and grounds, but we may yet go there together.

I went out shooting yesterday by myself and shot 2 hares, 1 partridge, and 3 and a half couple of quail. I got one of the hares in a very lucky way. I first saw it when about 60 yards from it, and immediately fired. I saw the shot strike all round it, and knew it must have been hit, but it went away apparently unhurt and I saw it when about 350 yards off, going through the bushes at a great pace. I then went on shooting for an hour or so longer, and when I came back I made the coolies beat the bushes in hope of seeing my "friend": when I got about 400 yards from the place where I had fired at it, there lay "Pussy" as dead as any nail in any door. It was a great "crow" my getting it.

(11th Decbr.) I went out again yesterday afternoon with my gun, and bagged a brace of partridges, and 4½ couple of quail; I shot 1½ or 2 couple more quail than I bagged but did not get them owing to the thickness of the "dhol khets" in which they were. There is a Captain Simeon of the Bengal Artillery in this camp, a great sportsman, and a man who has shot a great deal in Cashmere and Thibet. He has taught me many useful things about shooting that I never heard of before, and has given me a good deal of information about guns, ammunition, rifles, etc. I go out with him nearly every day, and always learn something fresh. He is a beautiful shot, and rarely misses.

We have had two (what they call in this country) "hauks", i.e. what I imagine they call at home "battues". The game we expected was pig, tiger and deer:

we beat two or three miles and saw nothing, and then tried the plains: there were two splendid boars driven out of a "ket" and they were coming straight for me when a beast of a pariah dog drove them back into the "dhol khet" and we were obliged to leave them as it was getting dark. I have often, when out shooting, seen large droves of pigs, but never got a decent shot at them.

We are daily expecting the order to move towards Buxar or Sahessram, and from there down country. The 29th are said to have arrived at Sahessram, so we shall in all probability hear something in the course of the day.

(12th Decbr.) This morning the 2 guns under Simeon, one company of Madras Rifles, and a troop of Madras Cavalry were withdrawn from this place, and ordered to go, the former to Arrah, the latter to Buxar, and the Rifles to Amabad [? Ainabad] on the Grand Trunk Road 12 miles from this. At the same time Carr received a hint that the whole force would be withdrawn very shortly, so that in 2 or 3 days we may expect to move. A letter from Buxar says that the Military Train have all been ordered to assemble at Arrah, preparatory to marching down country and then home. I received a letter from Hely yesterday. He says that the news he gets from England is that we are to be at home in the spring, that lots of troops are arriving at Calcutta daily, and that the 50 men under Wolseley who escorted the King of Delhi down country are at Chinsurah with our depot, waiting for the regiment to come down.

(14th Decbr) I have just seen the gazette of the 26th Octbr. in which Penton, Pratt, and Barry get their companies vice Chute, Anson, and Russell respectively, and Jones, Wolseley, Horam, Driberg, and Forster their lieutenancies, all without purchase. There yet remains Du Vernet's purchase step to be filled, and either Crohan or Hely will get it, unless it is filled by some-one from another regiment. One of our own men received a letter this morning saying that our Head Qrs. have been ordered to Dinapore. This looks like breaking us up into other regiments. The order for us to go to Jehanabad on the G. T. Road has been sent, but has miscarried somewhere. I fully expect that ere many days are over we shall be on our way down.

I yesterday went out deer stalking but could not get within range as the ground was as level as a billiard table and no cover could be got: I saw one black buck with horns nearly a yard long, and would have given 50 Rupees for a shot at him, but he was very wary, and kept 400 yards from me all the time. I then tried for duck, and was more lucky with them, getting a brace with each barrel. I afterwards shot a couple of snipe, and a like number of quail, when I was obliged to cease shooting owing to my shot having run out. I have however sent to Benares for a fresh supply.

I got from Benares the other day 3 doz. porter, a warm English blanket, a rezai, and a country "choga". The weather is very cold and chilly now and a jolly warm blanket is uncommonly nice. I take a great deal of exercise both morning and evening and my appetite is something astonishing.

Well, I have now filled my sheet, and told all the news I had, so I will now dispatch this letter to the post office and hope it may soon reach you safe and sound. When you write to my uncles or any of my numerous well-wishing friends, give my best love to them and say I hope ere many months are over to be once more at home. I trust and expect that in my next letter I shall be able to tell you that we are ordered down country. Give my very best love to dearest auntie and Emmie, and believe me to remain dearest Father and Mother,

Ever your most affectionate son
Hugh P. Pearson

Letter No. 60

Buxar Barracks
Sunday 26th December 1858

My very dearest Father and Mother,

In 3 months more I hope to be once more on the wide ocean and I am happy to say there is every chance of our being so. We expect daily to receive the orders for volunteering, and of course the next step will be to go down country. We left the Rhotas Hills about 10 days ago and arrived at Buxar all safe. The district is now entirely clear of rebels, and all the troops (with the exception of a few Seikhs) have been withdrawn, and are now occupying Doomraon, Buxar and Chowsa. The Hd.Qrs. of the 84th and 5 companies of the regiment are here, and the rest are divided between the other two places I have mentioned.

Colonel Seymour now commands, and he is now getting us all into order. We have a very busy time indeed of it, what with parades twice a day, committees and boards of all sorts, orderly duty, courts martial, company's accounts, and Non-Effective accounts etc, in fact all sorts of duties. The Colonel is very strict indeed on duty, and thoroughly understands his work; whilst off duty he is as jolly and nice a man as I ever saw. I am sure I shall like him very much. Every duty now is performed in shell jackets etc. and in fact every thing is carried on in strict accordance with the standing order of the regiment, even to dining in uniform. Lieut Brownrigg has joined us, and also Asst. Surg. Jenkins. The former is a fine strapping fellow, and will be I imagine a man after my own heart; the latter I do not know sufficiently to be able to form an opinion.

I am happy to say that I shall be able to send home to Cox in a few days about £90. This is compensation for kit destroyed at Cawnpore and I intend to make it up to £100 and buy another kit when I get home. It is possible that I shall send home £50 more in a few days' time but this I am not yet sure about. Wolseley, Browne and Pratt have exchanged; the former into the 98th, the latter into the 69th, and Browne into the 97th. Du Vernet's step is not yet filled up owing to Crohan's not having yet passed the necessary examination for his company. However, I hope ere this he has been gazetted.

My No.59 left Hatta on the 15th inst. and on the 20th I had the extreme delight of receiving your No.42 dated 1st Novbr. I stopped the "Friend of India" long ago so I suppose it is a mistake.

Yesterday I had a great chum of mine to dine with me and we made merry over a bottle of "Simkins" together, both wishing that we might eat our next Xmas dinner in the bosoms of our families. The day before yesterday all the troops at Buxar paraded to witness the presentation of the Victoria Cross to Lieut. and Adjt. Lambert of ours. We were all of opinion that he got it "uncommon easy". I have just seen the ribbon for the Indian Medal, and think it will look very well on my buzzim especially with 2 clasps on it. What thinks mother? I have also treated myself to one of Hart's Army Lists, and expect it daily from Calcutta. We have a great deal to do now, in making up accounts and putting the companies straight, and have always two parades a day. Jones' wound is getting on nicely, though the bullet is still in his leg; he is now able to walk about a little with a stick.

December 27th. Poor Lightfoot has just heard of the death of his father General Lightfoot and is very sad and melancholy about [it]. I believe the old man had more clasps than anyone in the service: he had 14 on his Peninsular medal alone.

The Colonel has gone this morning to Doomraon to inspect the accoutrements of the men there, and this afternoon my company is to be inspected by him to see that their new accoutrements fit properly. We are all up to our ears in work and it is only at intervals that I can spare time to write to you. I have just been paying off all my Calcutta debts amounting in all to Rs.95. As soon as my company's accounts are squared and there is less work, I shall study to pass for my company, however this will not be for a month or so.

I shall now send this letter off, short though it is, or it will not be in time for the mail. Give my best love to Aunty, Emmie, and all my relations when you write, and believe me to be, my very dearest Father and Mother,

Ever your affectionate son,
Hugh Pearce Pearson

Letter No. 61

Barracks, Buxar
New Year's Day 1859

My dearest Father and Mother,

I cannot begin this letter better than by wishing you all a happy New Year, and many more of them, adding at the same time that I hope I may be with you on this day next year. My last letter was sent off on the 27th ult. and since then nothing very unusual has occurred.

The Colonel, in speaking to us this morning, said we should probably arrive in England about June, but I should say April or May would be nearer the time of our arrival at home. The order for volunteering has not yet come, though the Colonel expects it daily. We are still over head and ears in work, making up accounts, issuing new clothing and accoutrements, and drilling. Two days ago I was on a court of Inquest on the body of Commander White of the Indian Navy who, in a drunken fit, tumbled off a table into the river and was drowned. I contrived to get leave yesterday to go over to Chowsa for a day's shooting, but I did not see a bird.

I have just been treating myself to a copy of the "Journal of an English Officer in India" by Major North of the 60th Rifles. It begins at the time when the little column under Major Renaud left Allahabad on the 30th June 57 and describes all our doings from that time till the relief of Lucknow by Sir Colin Campbell. It is a very truthful little book and its only fault is its shortness. I also got a "Hart's Army List" to the end of September. I see they have got me down in it as "wounded" so I suppose this is your alteration. I shall not forget to ask the Colonel for permission to go home overland, and I think I shall get it too. At any rate I have a better claim than any of the present subalterns, however this will do when we get to Calcutta. Well dearest Father and Mother I have told you all the news I have at present so I shall put this bye till another day.

(Sunday 2nd). Last night a letter was received by Seymour dated Allahabad Head Qrs. Camp. 29th Decbr. 58 which said:

> "It having been arranged that H.M.'s 2nd Battn. Military Train, 10th and 84th Regts. shall be immediately placed under orders for England, I am directed to state that the volunteering from these corps will take place on or immediately after the 1st February next, under orders which will be communicated hereafter. I have the honor to be, etc, etc."

We are to be inspected shortly by Brigadier Douglas C.B., then volunteer, and the remnant of the regiment march or go by river down country. The volunteering is to take place (as per the above letter) on the 1st prox. and the Colonel expects to leave this with what remains of the regiment about the 15th Febry., arrive in Calcutta (or wherever we are sent to) about the end of Febry., and embark for home about the end of March. At the latest I expect we shall spend our next Midsummer's Day in England. This is indeed joyful news. It has been long expected, but has at last arrived. When Willis left us, he said he would give us a step for £500. Oakley is now writing to offer it to him so that will (if Crohan gets Du V's step) leave me third. Young Horan is going to exchange and I dare say two or three more will too. I shall now put this bye for the present.

(Wednesday 5th) The detachment of ours at Doomraon came in this morning, and the one at Chowsa is to come to-morrow, so the regiment will once more be all together. We are shortly to be inspected by Brigadier Douglas, and every body is now hard at work getting things ready to receive him. I am sorry to say there is not a chance of my being able to come home overland as, according to the new rules, no passage money is to be allowed. Field Officers are not on any account to be allowed to go home overland, and other officers are not to be allowed either unless it is of the greatest importance to themselves or their families: when they get leave they are to pay their own passage.

I have just seen Crohan's promotion. This makes me 4th lieutenant, and if Willis accepts Oakley's offer of £500 I shall get another step. I have just sent £90 to Parry to be transferred to my credit at Cox's. I shall very likely send £50 more soon, but am not yet certain. I received your No.38 dated 22nd August on the 3rd of this month. It has been a long time in coming. I also received a nice kind letter from Mrs Kenny which I enclose, and one from Mr Wratislaw which I will send when answered. Pratt left us yesterday. He has gone to join his new regiment, the 69th.

I have now told you all the news, and shall at once send this letter off, trusting you will forgive the shortness of it when you read the good news it contains. Directly any thing of importance in the shape of news comes I will write again, even though it should be only a line. Remember me kindly to all my uncles, aunts, and cousins when you write, and tell them how soon I shall be at home. Give my very best love to dear Emmie & Auntie, and accept the same my dearest Father & Mother,

from your most affectionate boy
Hugh P. Pearson

Letter No. 62

Buxar. Stud Stables
January 19th 1859

My dearest Father,

My last letter was posted here on the 6th inst. and took the glad tidings of our coming home. It is seldom that I allow so much time to elapse between my letters, but I am at present studying hard for the examination for my company and intend to go up on the arrival of the regiment at Calcutta.

I see in Thacker's Overland of the 17th December that George's name stands at the head of the list of candidates for commissions at Sandhurst. I am delighted to see that he has got on so well. I suppose in the next gazette I shall see his appointment to some regiment. We are to volunteer on the 1st prox. and we shall be on our way to Calcutta by the 10th. I see the arrival of the ship "Plantaganet" with troops is announced. Very likely part of the Regiment will go home in her.

I received your No.44 on the 15th inst. and was glad to hear you all continued in health. You say in your letter that it will be a great shame if I do not get two clasps. I am happy to say there never was any doubt on the subject, and of course I shall get two, one for the relief and one for the capture of Lucknow. I sent £91 0. 0. to Parry to be forward to Cox & Co. and yesterday received Parry's receipt for it. I shall continue to write to you up to the day I embark, and shall tell you all about the vessel I go in etc. If I can discover when we are to land I will also mention it, and then you can come and meet me. Directly I get home I shall put in for 3 or 4 months leave, and I think I shall get it as I am the best entitled to it amongst the present subalterns.

(21st Jany.) Yesterday morning I had a tusk pulled out. It gave me great pain, and underneath the fangs was found an abscess. I also had a touch of fever. This morning I have taken a good big dose of calomel to put me all straight again.

Yesterday morning the Military Train arrived here on their way to Ghazipore where they are to volunteer. We are to volunteer on the 1st and by the 10th shall be on our way down.

The following extract from Field Force Orders by Brigadier Douglas was published in orders last night:

> "The Military Train and H.M.'s 84th Regiment being about to leave the Shahabad Field force on their return to England, the Brigadier takes this opportunity of recording his high appreciation of the services rendered to their country by these gallant corps which have been almost uninterruptedly in the Field throughout the Rebellion. Their gallant conduct and bearing in many hard fought fields previous to their coming under the Brigadier's command have been conspicuously noticed by Lord Clyde, Sir James Outram, and other distinguished leaders, and since they have been attached to the Shahabad Field Force the duty that has devolved upon them has been arduous and harrassing in the extreme, and the cheerful, willing and soldier-like manner in which it has been performed the Brigadier is satisfied could not have been surpassed, and merits his warmest acknowledgements."

> "To Lieut Col. Seymour, Major Lightfoot, Captain Wyatt and all the officers and soldiers of these fine regiments Brigadier Douglas offers his best wishes, and bids them all a hearty farewell."
> By order
>   (signed)
>   H. H. Stevenson, Major Major of Brigade"

Dr Jackson of ours and I have had some very good shooting at Chowsa 6 miles from here. The first day we got 4½ couple of duck and 1 teal; and we went again two days after and bagged 6½ couple of fine duck. We are all very anxious for the 1st of February to come, and the days go by very slowly in consequence. I suppose by this time Emily has gone to her new school in France. She says in her letter that Aunty is going with her, but you do not mention it in yours, so I suppose it is merely to see her comfortably settled.

Buxar is exceedingly dull and I have told you all the news there is. I am now going to continue my reading for the examination, so shall send this off at once. I shall write again directly after the volunteering.

Give my love to dearest Mother, Aunty and Emily and accept the same,
                    my dearest Chaper
                        from your most affectionate boy
                            Hughie

Letter No. 63

Buxar, Stud Stable
January 30th 1859

My very dearest Father and Mother,

The time is now rapidly approaching when I shall see you all again, and the days appear to me like weeks, so anxious am I to be at home. We are to volunteer on the 1st and two following days, and the order says that as soon as possible after volunteering we are to proceed to Calcutta to embark for Europe. The Colonel says he expects to leave Buxar about this day week or at the latest on the 12th. We are to go down the river in steamers, and so are the Military Train, but the 10th march down, and the 32nd go by bullock train. Lightfoot leaves this on the day after to-morrow, having obtained leave to proceed overland, paying his own passage.

I have been busy lately making up the men's accounts and studying for my approaching examinations, but I found time for two days shooting last week. The first day Jackson, Gregory and I went out and brought home 3 wild geese, 4½ couple of duck and 1½ couple of teal. Jackson and I went by ourselves on Friday last, and bagged 1 wild goose, 2 couple of duck, 4 and a half couple of teal, and 2 couple of curlew. The first day, I shot two geese right and left, but only got one, and the other two fellows each shot and bagged one. The wild fowl shooting here is magnificent. Indeed our 2nd day's bag proves how good it must be. The wild geese and curlews were most delicious eating, and of course the duck and teal were also.

We have lately had examinations for subalterns three times a week and it has been a great help to those of us who are about to go up for our companies. An order came yesterday which says that returns are immediately to be sent in to the authorities at Calcutta of the officers, men, women, children, and amount of baggage which are going home, in order that tonnage may be taken up for us. It is expected that we shall be on our way home from India about the end of the first week in March. I have drawn my six months donation batta, but find that instead of Rs. 730 8. I am only allowed Rs. 547! They have only allowed me ensign's batta, because I served in that rank going in with Havelock. They have cut every one in the same way and it is of no use complaining. I have not sent any of this 547 Rs. home as I shall require most of it for my expenses in this country, and for my outfit for the voyage. Of course I shall have to get a supply of warm clothes for going round the Cape, and a suit or two of decent clothes to appear in when I land at home, but I shall leave all my underclothing for dear mother to purchase out of the Rs. 910 (compensation) which I sent home a short time ago for that purpose, as I know she understands such things better than I do.

I fully expect to find everything of mine eaten by white ants or destroyed by the wet, but there are several things such as my gun and rifle barrels, iron work of my spring cot, etc. etc. which I shall be able to save out of the wreck. There is of course a bare possibility that my things, or some of them, may have escaped entirely, but I am prepared for the worst. I shall now put this bye for the present and shall report progress as matters proceed.

Feby. 2nd One day of our volunteering is over and 146 men have extended their services in India. To-day 50 more will do the same, and tomorrow as many more. Altogether we shall I suppose leave behind in India between 250 and 300 men. Last night we had a grand dinner for the purpose of wishing "good bye" to Major Lightfoot, and had speech making and singing till a late hour. This morning at 8 o'clock he left for Ghazipore from which place he will dak down to Calcutta, and if he is in luck will catch the steamer which leaves Calcutta on the 9th inst. and which arrives at Southampton about the 15th or 16th prox.

The Colonel expects to see Oakley's name in the gazette which arrives tomorrow for his company. If he gets it I shall be 3rd senior lieutenant. Magrath, if he chose to make application, could get his company just for the asking and I should then be in a very comfortable position. Everyone here says that if I chose to apply for my promotion they could not refuse me, but I would much rather wait for a year and get it in the 84th. I should not exactly like to be promoted into any regiment out here and have to come out again. Besides, I am very happy under my present commanding officer, who evidently takes an interest in me, and as to the officers, they are the best and most jolly set of fellows I ever had the luck to come across. I am now as happy as any man on this earth, and as to sickness, how could one be sick with the prospect of seeing dear and well known faces again in three short months?

If you have not already ceased writing to me, I think you had better do so immediately as I shall be half way home ere this reaches you. We expect an English mail here to-day, and as I shall not post this till the day after tomorrow, I shall be able to answer your letter (that is to say if there is one). I shall now put this bye to wait the results of the postman's visit to the fort.

(Friday 4th) The volunteering is now over and upwards of 240 men have gone to other regiments. At least 50 will go from the depots down country, and altogether we shall I dare say leave 300 men in India.

I to-day received your No.45 and was glad to hear you are all well, and that my sword had arrived. I also heard from Aunt Pearson giving me the news of George's examination, but I had already seen his name at the head of the list in "Thacker's Overland". I now see in the Overland of Jany. 3rd that he has got his cornetcy in my uncle Key's Regiment, and right glad I am to see he has begun his career in life so well as he seems to have done. I only hope he may have the same good fortune in getting speedy promotion as I have had.

The Colonel has written up to say he is all ready to move, and he seems to think that he (with 2 companies and his staff) will leave this about next Wednesday. I see in the gazette of the 31st Decbr. that Innes is promoted, and that we have old Joe La Presle back into the regiment as surgeon. We have also two new ensigns.

Remember me kindly to Dr. Bird and tell him that as I intend visiting Felstead etc. once more I will not fail to see him also. I suppose from dear Emmie's letter she is by this time in France; however, you must have her back for two or three months to meet me on my return home. I am greatly afraid of missing the mail: indeed I have run it much closer than I ought in my anxiety to let you have the latest news. I shall not write again now till I reach Calcutta. Good bye. Give my very best love to dearest Aunty and Emmie, and to all at Bourton when you write, & accept the same my beloved Father & Mother,

from your affectionate son

Hugh P. Pearson

P.S. Do not write again.

Letter No. 64

Stud Stables, Buxar
February 19th 1859

My dearest Father,
I had hoped that we should have left this ten days ago, but owing to the shallowness of the river many of the steamers have grounded, and great delay has ensued in consequence. For the last three days a steamer has been expected which is to take down our three first companies. She is sure to arrive to-day, and four or five others are close behind her, so I think by this day week we shall all be on our way.
Two companies of H.M.'s 6th have been here some days. They came from Azimghur to take our places. The officers are a capital set of fellows, and I am constantly down with them. The 10th and 32nd marched down weeks ago, and are now more than half way to Calcutta. The Madras Fusiliers passed through Calcutta, and the Governor General gave them a grand speech, and saluted them with artillery etc. They then embarked for Madras. The English Mail of the 17th is in, and I was much disappointed to find no letter from you: however, it matters little now, as I shall be with you in 3½ months time.
I went out shooting yesterday with the 6th fellows, but only got 2 couple of duck and one snipe. The colonel is very ill of dysentery, but I sincerely hope he will soon be all right. There is no news here, and nothing to do. I am going to send this off now, short as it is. Indeed I should not have written at all if it had not been that I did not like to let a mail go without letting you know I was well. Good bye. Love to dearest Mother, Aunt, and Emmie, and accept the same, best of fathers
From your affectionate son
Hugh P. Pearson

Letter No. 65 [missing]

Letter No. 66

"Dum Dum", near Calcutta
March 17th 1859

My own dearest Father and Mother,
Here I am again once more after an absence of exactly two years to a day. I have capital news for you and instead of keeping it as a surprise at the end of the letter as was my first intention; my impatience makes me tell it now. The best news is that I am "COMING HOME OVERLAND'. There! now it is out and I feel much better. Fourteen of the officers of the 84th are coming home overland, and I am one. We go in the P. & 0. Company's steamer "Hindostan" which I believe is to leave Calcutta on the 30th April. This, however, is not settled, and the only sure thing is that I am to go overland with (of course) my passage paid for me. The reason is that there is no accommodation for officers in the sailing vessels. The "Tudor" 1300 tons has been taken up for us (the regiment) and they are now making arrangements for our departure.
The next piece of good news is that I have got all my heavy baggage from the Agents, and it is only very slightly damaged. The only box which is in the least injured is the bed box, and fortunately I had not many valuables in it except my

bed, gun, and rifle. My drawers are in most perfect preservation, and of course everything inside too: the cases are slightly broken, but not much. The bed was in rather a rusty state, but I got 3 coolies to work with sand at it, and it is now as good as ever. All my underclothes, blankets, sheets etc. etc. are as they came from the makers' hands. My gun was rather badly rusted and also the rifle, but I have had them both well cleaned. I am sorry to say that the rust has eaten deeply into the breech of the gun, but I am going to take it to a gun maker in Calcutta to-morrow and see what can be done. Every one admires it and I could sell it for whatever I chose, but I would not take its weight in gold for it. My watch was a bit bulged, but I have sent it to a first rate jeweller in Calcutta who will soon put it right.

I went into Calcutta two days ago and ordered myself a suit of clothes, and bought a few other things. For the last few months I have been saving a little money to buy a few things I fancy when I came down, so I bought a copy of "Mecham's sketches of Lucknow" and also "Sketches of Lucknow" by Major McBean. These are both as a present for you, and you will, I know, often look at them and think of the time your darling lad was there. I had heard a deal of "Mecham's sketches", and expected to see something good, but I must say they far exceeded anything that I imagined. Everything in them is so truthfully delineated, and so entirely free from exaggeration that I often look at them and can imagine easily that I am once more in the several places they represent. They are in my opinion worth ten times what I paid for them (Rs.25), Mr McBean's are also exceedingly truthful but are on a smaller scale. They are well worth what I gave (Rs.8).

I have also got a present for you dear Father, which I procured on my arrival in India, but I am not going to tell you what it is till I place it in your hands. After having kept the secret so well for two years it would not do to tell you now. Now you need not say, foolish boy! for I have been saving these £25 for the sole purpose of buying something nice for each of you, and as I made up my mind to do so, I did it. I am going again into Calcutta to buy something nice for dear Aunty and Emmy. I am now, you know, an enormously rich man and can afford to do all these little (what you would call) extravagant things!!

When in Calcutta I went to Wilson's Hotel and treated myself to a thing I resolved I would do when I was starving in Lucknow, namely a big dish of sausages, and Simkin iced to wash it down with! Oh! I have not been living on garbage for two years for nothing, and I made up my mind sometime ago that I deserved a delicious dinner, and I had a regular "uncommoner".

The day before yesterday your No.46 was put into my hand, and right glad I was to see your dear handwriting once more. I hope ere long to see those dear hands that write all the letters I have looked so anxiously for during the time I have been out in India. In my desk I found your No.1! What stirring events have happened since that was written and rec'd. This day two years (St. Patrick's Day) we were in the P.& O. steamer "Bentinck" on our way from Rangoon to Bengal! I shall now put this bye till another day.

(Sunday 20th) No changes have been made in our arrangements for going home and I hope to get off in the steamer which leaves Calcutta on the 9th prox. The Colonel goes in the P&O. steamer "Nemesis" which sails on the 23rd inst. and Gregory our asst. surgeon goes with him to take care of him as he is still dangerously ill. So many passages are allowed in each steamer, and as there are many officers of other regiments to go as well as ourselves, we can only get our share of the vacant berths. I sincerely hope I may be able to get off by the 9th of April steamer, but perhaps not till later.

Parry & Co. my agents have "gone smash", and I stand to lose Rs. 100 or so: I am afraid I shall have to draw on Cox for a 100 or 200 Rupees, but I won't if I can help it. Several officers have joined us, among whom are Saunders our surgeon, Captn. Hudson, Lieut. Stewart, who exchanged with Wolseley, and Ensign Knox.

Last night I went to an entertainment given by a rich native Baboo, to which many ladies and gentlemen were invited. It commenced with some first rate singing by a professional named Farquarson, who sang some of Russell's songs in a masterly way. The band of the 3rd Buffs played most exquisitely in the interval, and the evening finished with a dance. Plenty of champagne was provided, and of course eatables to match. I and an Asst. Surgeon of ours Jenkins went in one gharry (cab) and on the way we must needs race with another gharry that overtook us. The consequence was we found ourselves wheels uppermost in a ditch with one of the ponies about to give up the ghost. I found my head in the pit of Jenkins' stomach and flatter myself he was most hurt. We each got a lift in passing coaches, and arrived without further mishap at our destination.

I find I shall have to send my heavy baggage round the Cape, or else pay fearfully for bringing it overland. I therefore intend bringing my chest of drawers, gun cases and portmanteau with me and putting my bed box and No.4 with one of the ships which takes our regiment. I have sent my gun, rifle, and watch to be put in order at Calcutta. I forgot to mention that the 10th have sailed.

And now my very dearest Father and Mother, I must wish you good bye for the present. Pray give my very best love to dearest Emmie and Aunty, and believe me to remain now, as ever,

Your most affectionate son
Hughie

P.S. I shall yet eat my Midsummer's day dinner in Jersey.

Contemporary of photographs of the Residency at Lucknow © York and Lancaster Regimental Museum. 1998.83

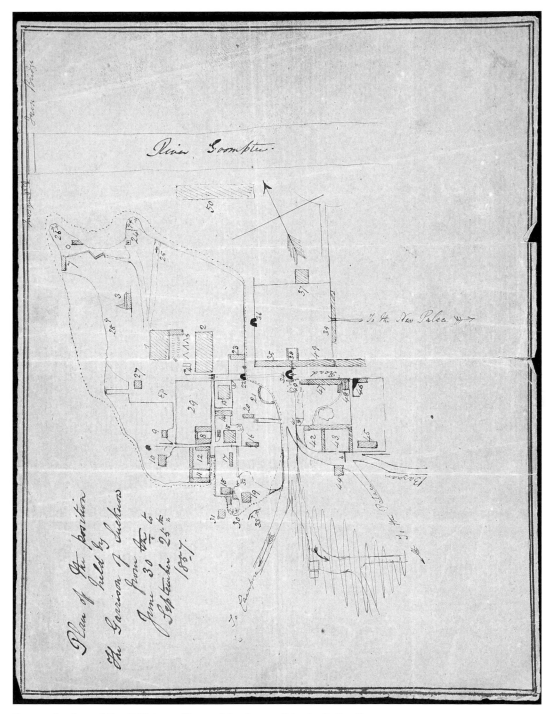

Pearson's plan of the British positions at Lucknow. Private Collection
See key on page 160

References

1. The Residency
2. The Hospital
3. The Church
4. The Magazine
5. Place where the horses were picketed
6. Tents for shot and shell
7. Innis's bungalow
8. Begum Cotee (where the ladies and wounded were)
9, 10. Houses occupied by officer etc
11. Brigade Mess
12. Buildings in which the half casts stopped
13. Gubbins's house
14. Occupied by natives etc
15. The Post Office + P.O. battery
16. Stables
17, 18 Buildings occupied by artillerymen
19. Anderson's post
20, 21. Occupied by natives
22. Bailey Guard gate
23. Sikh Square (* denotes a breach made by the enemy)
24. The Redan battery
25. A 24pr howitzer to protect the road
26. A battery
27. Small summer house
28. An 18pr gun
29. A collection of buildings, squares etc
30. The Cawnpore battery
31. A house occupied by the enemy & commanding the Cawnpore battery (blown up by our mine during the siege)
32. One 18 pr gun
33. A battery of the enemy
34. The Clock Tower (here had a 32 pr and a 12 pr carronade)
35. Old buildings occupied by the enemy & loopholed
36. A large gate with towers
37, 38, 39. Houses occupied by the enemy
40. Mosque occupied by enemy 60 yds from Bailey Gd.
41. A gun of the enemy
42, 43, 44 Houses occupied by the enemy
45. The Jail
46. A battery of the enemy
47, 48, 49, 50 Occupied by the enemy

The doted line ... denotes the boundary of our position; the marks /// denote a building; the blank space inside the entrenchments are gardens, walls etc

Photograph of the Officers of the 84th Regiment in the 1870s. Lieutenant Pearson is standing fourth from the left. © York and Lancaster Regimental Museum (A372)

Major-General Sir Henry Havelock
© Board of Trustees of the Armouries

Lieutenant-General Sir James Outram
© Board of Trustees of the Armouries

Portrait of General Sir David Russell
© York and Lancaster Regimental Museum
(775.79)

Portrait of Colonel & Mrs Lightfoot
© York and Lancaster Regimental Museum
(199867.2)

Portrait of Major Hardy
© York and Lancaster Regimental Museum
(1998.67.5)

Portrait of Major Rolleston
© York and Lancaster Regimental Museum
(1998.67.18)

Portrait of Captain Willis (standing)
© York and Lancaster Regimental Museum
(1998.83.210)

Portrait of Captain Snow
© York and Lancaster Regimental Museum
(1998.83.151)

An engraving of the British base at Alum Bagh, near Lucknow. From *Sketches and incidents of the siege of Lucknow / from drawings made during the siege by Clifford Henry Mecham* (London, 1858). © Board of Trustees of the Armouries

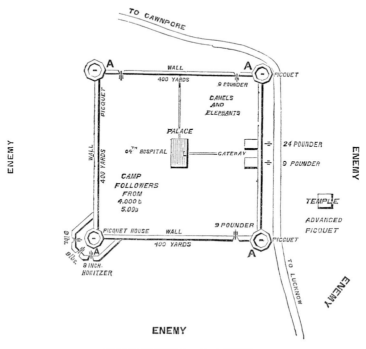

PLAN OF ALUMBAGH, NEAR LUCKNOW.

A plan of Alum Bagh. From the *Illustrated London News* (16 January 1858) © Board of Trustees of the Armouries

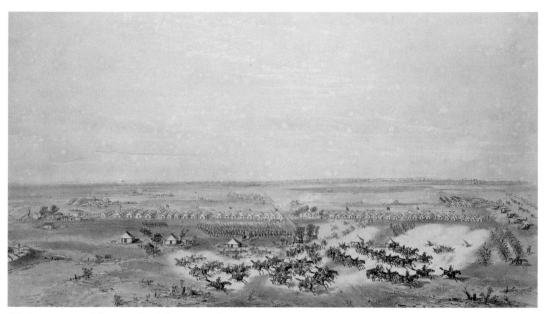

Contemporary lithograph of General Outram's force at Alum bagh. © York and Lancaster Regimental Museum (693.79)

Contemporary lithograph of Martiniere College © York and Lancaster Regimental Museum (693.79)

Commentary on the letters

1st un-numbered letter, 14 August 1857

Pearson writes that he was much pressed for time 'owing to my not yet being dismissed drill' (in modern terms, 'passing off the square'). Despite having held an ensign's commission in the Army since 9 May 1857, and previously been a lieutenant in the Militia, it seems that he had not previously actually served with either, as he was still learning foot drill at this time.

The new iron bridge at Rochester, which had taken six years to complete, was formally opened on Wednesday 13 August 1857 with much civic pomp and a dinner in the Corn Exchange. The new bridge was decorated for the occasion and a display of fireworks took place on the old bridge (subsequently demolished) in the evening.

2nd un-numbered letter, 19–20 August 1856

The review to which Pearson refers was intended to demonstrate the procedures for respectively attacking and defending fortifications, conducted by officers of the Royal and East India Company's Engineers. About 2,700 men were involved, of whom 1,000 were sappers (the Royal Corps of Sappers and Miners, who provided skilled military labour had been amalgamated with the previously all-officer corps of Royal Engineers earlier in the year), 600 were Royal Marines, and the rest came from the Provisional Battalion (Pearson's 'P.B.s'), consisting of the various depot companies and other minor units forming the Chatham garrison. The accidental springing of the mine was not reported in the Press. Spectators seem to have been impressed by a different explosion, that of a 50-lb charge of gunpowder submerged in St Mary's Creek and set off by a voltaic battery'.

'Cane and Co.' (Crane and Sons) were the Irish Army Agents of the 57th Foot. This regiment's usual firm of Agents was the well-known firm of Cox and Co, but on embarking for the Mediterranean in 1853 it had left its depot company at Fermoy. In his preceding paragraph, Pearson is referring to drafts from the depots of the regiments he lists here, rather than the depots themselves, which remained in the UK.

3rd un-numbered letter, 28 August 1856

Lieutenant Drage's failed attempt to exchange with 'an Indian Regt' was with one of the British Army's regiments serving in India, not with one of the East India Company's regiments, who belonged to a completely different Army. Exchanges between these two forces was not possible, as the Company's officers did not hold the Queen's commission.

The summer of 1856 was remarkable for a heat wave in southern England, blamed by the local authorities for an increase in the mortality rate. Pearson does not say where his thermometer was placed, but if he was in the Main Guard of Chatham Dockyard, surrounded by brick buildings and flanked by areas of hard standing, the oven-like conditions thus created may well account for these extreme figures.

5th un-numbered letter, 28 December 1856

Lieutenant Saunders of the 84th was in command of that regiment's draft in the troopship *Agincourt*. He later died very bravely at Kanpur. There are no good natural harbours on the south-east coast of India, and ocean-going ships had to anchor off-shore while passengers and cargo were taken to and from the shore through the surf in local boats. Catamarans, though the term is nowadays applied to any multi-hulled vessel, were originally rafts of three logs separated by spreaders, and their name is a corruption of the Tamil for 'tied tree'. *Masuli* or *Masula* boats were another vessel characteristic of this region. They were made of planks sewn together with coir yarn, a construction giving the pliability to withstand the shock of the local surf, which can have breakers running from 10 to 16 feet (or 3 to 5 m) high.

Letter 1, 1–5 January 1857

At this time there were more than 3,000 miles of railway planned or under construction in India, but only a few hundred, starting at the three presidential capital cities and seaports of Calcutta, Madras and Bombay, had actually been opened. On reaching the end of the line troops had to march to their inland destinations as previously.

The 29th Foot, at this time stationed in Rangoon, were intended as reinforcements for ,'the Persian War', the Gulf War then in progress against Iran, but the success of the British expedition led by Sir James Outram of the Bombay Army meant that the Iranians were about to agree on an armistice.

The brahminy kite, *haliastur indus*, also known as the red-backed sea eagle or white-headed sea-kite, lives in coastal watery places ranging from South Asia to southern China, the Philippines and north-eastern Australia. A medium-sized bird of prey, it eats small animals and fish snatched up in its talons. It also scavenges from road verges, rubbish tips, and elsewhere. In India it is sacred to the god Vishnu (hence its name, from Brahman, a member of the priestly class of Hindu society).

Letter 2, 15 January 1857.

The 12th Lancers, under the command of Pearson's uncle, Lieutenant Colonel Thomas Hooke Pearson, had from embarked the UK for Madras in August 1856, a few weeks before the infantry drafts in *Agincourt*.

Letter 2a, 15 January 1857)

The Lesser Florican, *sypheotis indica*, described here by Pearson is a small bustard. It is now extinct in southern India, and only rarely found in the rest of the sub-continent, mostly due to the reduction of its grassland habitat, though it seems that even in 1857 it was uncommon.

The rate of exchange between sterling and the Company's rupees fluctuated from time to time, not least because the pound sterling was coined in gold and the rupee in silver. In 1857 the rate was roughly ten rupees to the pound. There are 16 annas in a rupee, with four pice or pies in an anna, and there were 20 shillings in a pound, with 12 pence in a shilling, abbreviated respectively to Rs, a. p. and £.s.d. The monthly pay of an ensign serving in the United Kingdom was nearly £8, equal to Rs.80, less than half of what was paid in India, where the cost of living was in fact cheaper. Rangoon, Pegu, and the mouths of the Irrawadi had only recently become possessions of the East India Company, following the 2nd Burma War (1852–53) and as *batta* (campaign allowance) was still being paid, Pearson's income was actually the same as an ensign of the East India Company's infantry on full allowances.

Letter 3, 6 March 1857.
Most of the large animals mentioned by Pearson in this and other letters are now endangered or extinct in much of their former range, due to loss of habitat and the depredations of so-called sportsmen. The Asiatic bison or gaur, *bos gaurus*, is the largest of all the wild oxen and can measure up to 7 feet (over 2 m) high at its shoulder hump. Only a few hundred survive in Burma (Myanmar) under government protection in game reserves. The wild buffalo, *bubalis arni*, can reach up to 6 feet (almost 2 m) high. The spotted deer or chital, *axis maculata*, is still common in Bangla Desh, Nepal and southern India. The sambar or garau, *rusa aristotelis*, misnamed 'elk' by the trophy-hunters, is the largest South Asian deer. The bears to which Pearson refers were probably a variety of sun-bear, *helarctos eurspilus*. The great cats, tiger, leopard or panther, and cheetah preyed upon domestic cattle, and the wild pigs damaged crops, so hunting them for sport was encouraged by the authorities.

The great pagoda at Rangoon is the Shwe Dagon, said to date from the time of the Buddha, and is much revered as a symbol of strength.

Letter 4, 12 March 1857.
Lieutenant George Blake of the 84th, whose diaries form the basis of his grandson Captain (RN) Lionel Dawson's *Squires and Sepoys*, confirms this account of the regiment's mobilisation. In the morning of 13 March, the same date as given by Pearson, he saw a large steamer (the East India Company's *Lord William Bentinck*) coming up the river and heard from his servant that it was rumoured that they were to sail immediately for Calcutta. This was soon confirmed when the officers were told they had until 4pm to get their companies ready to embark in light marching order. In fact *Bentinck* had to take on coal and water and was not in all respects ready for sea until the next morning.

Letter 6 [7]; 20–21 April 1857
Blake refers to torrential rain on the night of 19 April, when the 84th arrived at Chinsura for the third time, late at night, with the tents a foot deep in water, prior to the execution of Jemadar Iswari Pande. '*The next day* ', Blake noted '*... we had nothing to do and I, and several others, went to see the prisoner. He was in the guard tent of the 53rd, heavily ironed, and four sentries posted. On our entering, he got up, salaamed, and seemed very civil*'.

The 'adjutants' that Pearson saw in Calcutta were large storks of the species *leptoptilus dubius*. These birds, which can stand up to 5 feet (about 1.75 m) high, were so named because their precise and stiff-legged gait was thought to resemble that of the officers who are responsible for regimental discipline and turn-out. They are commonly found near water and protected on account of their value as carrion-eaters. Pearson's shooting at them from the steamer taking him up-river to the scene of operations (*Letter 14; 22 June 1857*) was contrary to standing orders at most stations.

Letter 8, 28 April 1857
Blake refers to the delay in the arrival of the death warrant for the execution of Jemadar Iswari Pande, probably the source of the rumour, mentioned by Pearson, that there would be a reprieve. Blake times the arrival of the execution detail at 4.00 pm, which (after allowing time for the condemned man's speech from the scaffold) accords with Pearson's time of 5.30 p.m. for the actual time of death.

Letter 13, 16–30 May 1857
Neither the 2nd Bengal Native Infantry (Grenadiers) nor the 70th Bengal NI joined the mutiny. The bandsmen of sepoy regiments were recruited from Eurasian Christians.

Troops from Calcutta were hastened up-country in the way that Pearson describes, first by rail 100 miles to Raniganj where the line ended, then by road in either 'ekkas' (post-chaises) capable of carrying two men, or bullock carts (corresponding to the covered wagons of the American West) that could carry six, but travelled at only a mile and a half in the hour. Lady Canning, wife of the governor general, wrote that it was like sending reinforcements in teaspoonfuls. The first sixteen men of the 84th covered the 250 miles from Raniganj to Varanasi (Benares) in five days.

The Second China War, 'the Arrow War', had begun in October 1856. The large British force en route to that theatre was diverted to Bengal as emergency reinforcements after the extent of the Mutiny became clear. The China campaign (in conjunction with the French) was resumed in 1858, after the restoration of British control in India.

Letter 14, 22–28 June 1857
The previously loyal sepoys at Varanasi mutinied on 4 June 1857, fearing they would be attacked by the troops arriving from Calcutta, and many Europeans took refuge in the Mint. The mutineers abandoned the city, but for a short time British authority in the surrounding countryside collapsed. Pearson's account of Blake's rescuing local Europeans is confirmed by Blake's own narrative. The mutiny of the 6th Bengal Native Infantry at Allahabad took place on 6 June, with many casualties among their officers and European residents in the city, who were attacked by criminal gangs. The British held out in the fort until the arrival of troops from Varanasi on 11 June. All accounts confirm Pearson's references to the heavy incidence of cholera among the 1st Madras European Fusiliers, the looting of Allahabad by both sides, and to the punitive village-burnings and hangings that marked the British line of march. He was, however, in error with his news of events at Delhi, where the King (newly proclaimed Mughal Emperor) reigned until the British stormed the city, 14–20 September 1857.

Letter 15, 6–9 July 1857
Pearson's report of the events at Kanpur (Cawnpore) is substantially accurate. Five Europeans (three officers and two soldiers) escaped in the one surviving boat. Of the latter, one, a Bengal Artilleryman, died of cholera later in the campaign and the other, Private Sullivan of the 84th, became the custodian of the Cawnpore memorial. This, a marble angel, designed by the sculptor Carlo Marochetti, and set within a colonnade and garden into which only Christians were admitted, became a place of pilgrimage for British soldiers serving in India until the achievement of Independence in 1947. Captain Mowbray Thompson, one of the survivors, mentions in his account that, after having been given shelter by a friendly land-holder, the first British troops they met were a party of the 84th under Lieutenant Woolhouse.

Letter 16, 19 July 1857
Pearson's account agrees with other reports of the battle on the outskirts of Kanpur, on 16 July 1857. The death of Captain Currie is thus described by Major Francis Maude, Royal Artillery, in his Mutiny memoirs, as follows: '*turning to young*

Captain Currie, who had just come up with us and taken command of the detachments of the gallant 84th Regiment, he [Havelock] said to him "Young as you are, Sir, if you come out of today's affair with credit, I promise you your promotion to major." Currie bowed and smilingly thanked the General. But by a strange chance one of the first round shot – a 24-pounder – carried away nearly the whole part of poor Currie's body, inflicting a ghastly wound. Yet he lingered for nearly three days'. Havelock may well have intended to promote Currie by brevet, since at this time there were ten captains senior to him in the 84th. The anaesthetics available to military surgeons in this campaign were chloroform and opium, the latter a valuable crop on which the government of India relied for much of its revenue. British casualties in this battle amounted to one officer, five soldiers and one sepoy killed or mortally wounded, and another 101 of all ranks wounded.

The references here and elsewhere to 'grape-shot' are probably a misnomer for 'canister', a close-range projectile consisting of a metal container packed with musket-balls. The container disintegrated when fired and the balls spread out in a pattern in much the same way as from a shot-gun. Grape-shot by this period was primarily used with naval ordnance. In the same way, soldiers continued to use the term 'shrapnel' to mean shell splinters, long after shrapnel shells (a more modern form of canister, designed to burst in the air at long range) were replaced by high explosive shells. War correspondents continue to misuse this word in their reports even at the present day.

Nana Sahib, the Raja of Bithur, was the adopted heir of the last Peshwa (hereditary prime minister and chief of the Maratha Confederacy) Baji Rao II. In 1817 Baji Rao was defeated and his dominions annexed by the British. He was exiled to Bithur in the North West Provinces of Bengal, and awarded an annual pension of eight lakhs of rupees to support himself and his household for the rest of his life. To the chagrin of the Indian Finance Department, he lived until 1852, after which the pension and the extra-territorial privileges of his lands at Bithur were discontinued. Nana Sahib appealed to the East India Company's Court of Directors, but was told the decision must stand. He remained on polite terms with the British officers at Kanpur, many of whom enjoyed his hospitality, and when the mutiny first broke out, he offered them his aid. The subsequent revolt of the sepoys at Kanpur led him to place himself at their head, with the aim of becoming the new Peshwa. The accusation that he deliberately tricked the British into surrendering on a false promise of safe conduct, is unproven, and he certainly sent orders to stop the killing of women and children when he heard what was going on. Nevertheless, once the survivors were in his custody, he became responsible for their safety under both Western and Indian laws of war. Even if he did not personally order the subsequent massacre, he did not seek to punish the perpetrators, and his name is indelibly stained with this atrocity. He was never brought to justice by the British, but escaped to Nepal, where he was said to have died from fever, or been killed by a tiger, though occasionally unconfirmed sightings of him were reported, the last in India as late as 1892.

Letter 17, 1 August 1857
All other accounts agree with Pearson's narrative, including the preference of the sepoys for fighting with musketry from behind walls, the effect of the monsoon rains and the adverse climatic conditions, and the incidence of cholera, a disease caused by the ingestion of food or water contaminated with infected faecid material. The cause was unknown at this time. 'Sun-stroke' was either what is

now diagnosed as heat exhaustion or heat stroke. 'Boned' seems to have been a euphemism for looted. A corresponding term in World War II was 'liberated'.

Lieutenant Dangerfield was not awarded the Victoria Cross.

Letter 20, 20–26 August 1857
The practice of auctioning the personal effects of officers and men who died while serving overseas was a long-established one, and continued well into the 20th century. It was usual for bidders to offer inflated prices, knowing that the proceeds would go to benefit the deceased's dependants. The rapidity of the onset of symptoms of cholera, described here by Pearson with his usual accuracy of observation, is characteristic of this disease.

Complaints about the parsimony of the Government of India were as common as are those about HM Treasury, though in this case it could be argued that compensation for the cost of carriage hire was one of the items for which the issue of *batta* was intended as compensation. Military officers commonly regard such allowances as permanent additions to income and are reluctant to apply them to the purpose for which they are made, or to lose them when they are no longer justified.

Letter 21, 4 September 1857
The massacre at Jhansi, in which nearly 60 European men, women and children were put to death after surrendering on 8 June 1857, was the largest after the two at Kanpur.

Chumpo, the small dog from Central China, resembles very closely the Pekingese or 'little lion dog'. It is generally held that such animals were reserved to the Chinese Emperors and did not become known to Europeans until a number of them were acquired during the destruction of the Summer Palace at Peking (Beijing) by Anglo-French troops in 1860.

The transfer of the 84th from the Madras to the Bengal establishment allowed the regiment's rear party to be moved to Calcutta from Rangoon.

Letters 22–25, 17 September–11 December 1857
This group of letters covers the advance to Lucknow, the rush through the city streets to reach the Residency where the British were besieged; the subsequent defence until they were relieved by Sir Colin Campbell; the withdrawal to Kanpur, leaving a brigade outside Lucknow in the Alam Bagh; the loss of British stores at Kanpur when the force left to hold the city was defeated by the mutineers of the Gwalior Contingent; and Campbell's arrival there in the nick of time. Pearson and the 84th were in the force under Outram that fought its way to the Residency, expecting to rescue the original garrison and its women and children, only to find itself trapped there until Campbell's arrival. Pearson confirms all accounts of the privations endured by soldiers and civilians alike. Most other diarists, like Pearson, mention the shortage of soap and the limited rations.

The mining and counter-mining to which he refers were conducted on the insurgent side by mutineers from the Bengal Sappers and Miners and by local militia, badly armed but skilled at tunnelling, the retainers of local land-holders who had joined the revolt. The counter-mines, under officers of the Bengal Engineers, were dug by Indian labour and by volunteers from the 32nd Foot, whose ranks included tin-miners from Cornwall and lead-miners from Derbyshire. La Martiniere College, named after its founder, a French adventurer in the service of an earlier King of Awadh, was a solidly-constructed building that played an important part in the fighting at Lucknow. Its masters and senior boys fought as volunteers in the defence of the Residency, and the younger ones served as messengers and domestic helpers. It remains to this day one of the premier schools in India.

Secundra-baugh, Heron Khana and *Dil Koosha* are Pearson's unconventional renderings respectively of *Sikandar Bagh* (Alexander Garden), *Harn Khana* (Deer House or Park) and *Dilkhusha Bagh* (Garden of the Heart's Delight), all scenes of desperate street fighting during the various operations at Lucknow.

The Residency derived its name from its previous function as the headquarters of the British Resident (a post corresponding to ambassador) in Lucknow, prior to the British annexation of the kingdom of Awadh in 1856. It then became the base of 'the Chief Commissioner of Oudh', the head of what had become a new British province. The whole complex covered an area about the size of Windsor Castle.

Thomas Kavanagh was a member of the uncovenanted or locally-recruited junior branch of the Bengal Civil Service. Covenanted civil servants, the 'twice-born' elite of the Company's service, were so described because they were bound by covenant not to accept bribes, and in return were paid so handsomely that they did not need to. Kavanagh, one of the only two civilians to be so decorated (both members of the Bengal Civil Service),was awarded the Victoria Cross for his conduct in passing through the enemy lines in disguise and subsequently guiding the relieving force through the city streets to the Residency.

Letter 26, 20 December 1857

Pearson's father, as his son tells him, was not the only one to comment on the dearth of senior officers present in the field with the 84th. Major Maude noted (not entirely accurately) in his memoirs that 'The two colonels were absent. The senior major was invalided before, and the junior major fell ill soon after, the beginning of the outbreak. Of the captains, the senior (who by the way was 62 years of age) was *en route* to join; Radcliffe was quartered at Chatham; Seymour was on the Staff; Hughes and Lightfoot were in England. Besides these, three other officers were on the Staff, and several on sick leave in England...this roll of absentees among officers is one rarely matched at the commencement of a campaign'.

Pearson later revised his favourable opinion of Willis and his unfavourable one of Snow. Nevertheless, Willis commanded the regiment very creditably during the first advance into Lucknow, leading them through the street fighting after first telling them, in his own words, that their comrades in front (the company inside the Residency) 'were anxiously expecting relief, and the poor wives and families in Calcutta looked to us to succour their husbands and fathers'. When Campbell later arrived, Willis was detailed to lead a storming party of the 84th into the Harn Khana, a duty he gallantly performed despite his suspicion (subsequently confirmed) that the mine intended to breach the wall did not go far enough forward. He later wrote that, when it was sprung, 'away we rushed, followed by the men...cheering away as hard as we could – there is nothing like shouting on these occasions'.

Pearson's criticisms of the behaviour of some British regiments at Kanpur (when Windham was defeated by the Gwalior Contingent), at Chinhut (after which Sir Henry Lawrence was driven back into Lucknow) and Ara are all justified by the reports of these actions, though they mostly resulted from a combination of faulty tactics and poor logistics. He was nevertheless mistaken in reporting that after the rout at Kanpur the commanding officer of the 82nd Foot had been sent home in disgrace. Its senior officer, Lieutenant Colonel Edward Blagden Hale, with two of its companies, had been with Campbell at Lucknow, and returned to Kanpur with him in time to rescue Windham. The companies left at Kanpur were commanded by Major (Brevet Lieutenant Colonel) David Watson, who succeeded Hale as CO when the latter was promoted to brigadier in October 1858. The officer casualties in this action amounted to 7 killed, 15 wounded and 2 missing (total 24), not 17 killed as Pearson says. Brigadier Wilson, one of those he correctly lists as killed, was colonel not of the 78th Highlanders, but of the 64th Foot.

Letters 27–28, missing
Both these letters were despatched with letter 26 on 25 December 1857.

Letter 29, 1 January 1858
The 9,000 Ghoorkas (Gurkhas) were an allied contingent under the personal command of Jang Bahadur, chief minister (in effect, ruler) of Nepal. He had mobilised an army to aid the British when the Mutiny first broke out, but Canning, declined this offer of help, partly because he did not wish it to appear that the British needed it, and partly because he feared that Jang Bahadur had designs on districts of Awadh bordering Nepal. Now, with Campbell needing more troops for a three-pronged advance to recover Lucknow, Canning invited to Jang Bahadur to lead his Gurkha army into Awadh. For reasons of diplomacy, Campbell agreed to delay his attack on Lucknow in order to give Jang Bahadur time to arrive and share in the glory (and the loot).

Letters 30–35, 8 January–21 March 1858
This group relates to the period in which Campbell gathered his reinforcements and drove the insurgents out of Lucknow. The Military Train mentioned by Pearson was the newly raised successor of the ill-fated Land Transport Corps, and was primarily intended to operate with horse-drawn wagons. To improve its social status, it was made a 'purchase' corps, and its junior subalterns given the rank of cornet, as in the cavalry, rather than of 2nd lieutenant or ensign. Its 2nd Battalion was part of the British expedition en route to China on the outbreak of the Mutiny, and was diverted with it to India. There was no requirement for British transport personnel, but a desperate need for British cavalry, and as many members of the battalion had previously been in the cavalry, it was remustered as light dragoons, using the horses and equipment of disarmed regiments of native Bengal Light Cavalry. Critics of the corps maintained that it thereafter became too cavalry-minded, instead of concentrating on its role as a logistic service, but it long remained an unpopular choice among junior officers, who dubbed it the Moke Train (from the slang word for a donkey). Its successor, the Royal Transport Corps, now part of the Royal Logistics Corps, was likewise vulgarly known as 'the donkey-wallopers'.

The 'Moulvee' or Maulavi Ahmadullah Shah, a wandering holy man, first came to British notice at Faizabad early in 1857, when his followers killed a number of policemen who had tried to arrest him. He was held responsible and was sentenced to death for preaching sedition, but due to legal delays was still in prison when the sepoys at Faizabad mutinied and released him on 8 June. He took command of them and subsequently became a leading figure among the insurgents at Lucknow, though he was a Sunni and the royal family there were Shi'as. A man respected equally for his piety and his courage, he condemned the slaughter of women and children as contrary to the teachings of Islam and a distraction from the aims of the revolt. During Campbell's final attack on Lucknow, he and his men were among the last to hold out, after which he continued to operate successfully against the British elsewhere in Awadh. With a price of Rs 50,000 on his head, he was killed on 5 June 1858 while trying to enter the fort of the pro-British Raja of Pawayan.

The little cannon that Pearson took as a souvenir of the fighting at Lucknow remains in the possession of his family.

The escape of the insurgents from Lucknow was a matter of some controversy. Certainly the British cavalry were in the wrong place when the insurgents abandoned the city, and never caught up with their main force. It is also possible that Campbell made little effort to stop them, expecting that with the last major centre of resistance back in British hands, they would abandon the fight and disperse to their homes.

Letters 36–40, 2 April–14 May 1858
Pearson and the 84th formed part of the column that pursued Kunwar (Koor, or Koer) Singh from Awadh back to his home territory around Jagdispur, Bihar. A much-respected Rajput nobleman at this time in his seventies, Kunwar Singh had fallen into debt through the many charitable and religious expenses expected of men in his position and was in danger of being forced to sell his ancestral lands to meet British revenue demands. When the sepoys at Dinapore (many of whom came from villages on his estates) mutinied, they placed themselves under his command, and successfully ambushed a company of the 10th Foot sent to attack them. They then besieged a small group of Europeans at Ara but were defeated by a relieving force that pursued them to Kunwar Singh's stronghold at Jagdispur. Driven from Bihar, Kunwar kept the Dinapore mutineers in the field, and was later appointed governor of the south-eastern districts of Awadh by the insurgent government at Lucknow. He subsequently fell back to Bihar, fighting a series of well-conducted rearguard actions and crossing the Ganges in a brilliant deception plan, after spreading reports that for lack of boats he would ford the river with relays of elephants. At the crossing, he was wounded in the forearm by artillery fire from the pursuing British, but still fought his way back to his ruined home at Jagdispur.

Pearson faithfully reports the defeat of Captain Le Grand and the 35th Foot, in the same area that a detachment of 10th had been ambushed and routed the previous year. Kunwar Singh is said to have cut off his useless hand and thrown it into the Ganges as a sacrifice. He died of his wounds the day after his last victory. The surviving officer of the 35th mentioned by Pearson as an old friend from their time at Chatham was Lieutenant Richard Parsons, who always insisted that, despite everything, the British would have won if Le Grand had handled his command properly.

Letters 41–49, 31 May–26 July 1858
With major operations over, Pearson's attention turned to a reprise of his part in them, and to the prospects of promotion. The summary of his services that

Pearson and his brother officers were ordered to prepare for the Army List probably relates to *Hart's Army List*, a private publication founded in 1839 and containing many details not included in the official Army List, contributed by the individual officers or their families.

Dum Dum was the great arsenal and ordnance depot near Calcutta, and gave its name to the dum-dum bullet that was intended to expand on hitting its target. This kind of bullet was later banned by international conventions on the humanitarian conduct of warfare.

The 'Bengal Hurkaru' was an English-language newspaper based at Calcutta with an editorial line reflecting the opinion of most Europeans in Bengal that the government was acting with insufficient energy. Along with all other newspapers, English as well as vernacular, it was made subject to Press censorship to prevent reports of British weakness, troop movements, sepoy atrocities (mostly wildly exaggerated) and stories likely to stir up inter-racial tension. The 'Hurkaru' had its license withdrawn for a week in September 1857 until its editor was dismissed by his proprietor.

The 32nd were given the distinction of becoming a regiment of light infantry, but in their case the whole regiment (or what remained of it) was inside Lucknow throughout the entire siege, whereas the 84th had at first only one company there.

Having endured the cold weather at the Alam Bagh, the 84th continued in the field in the north Indian plain for a second year, enduring first the extreme summer heat and then the rains of the monsoon. The hot weather was notorious for trying men's tempers and may have played a part in the onset of the brawl between Lieutenants McGrath and Oakley (*Letter 42, 13 June 1858*). A generation earlier such an event would inevitably ended in a duel, for although duelling was always against the law, it was the only socially acceptable way for a gentleman to answer a blow. The custom gradually died out when Queen Victoria and her consort made their disapproval clear. Under Queen's Regulations that still remain in force, any officer who considers himself to have been insulted by another is obliged to report the circumstances to his commanding officer. This gives additional force to the statement by Lightfoot, who was commanding the 84th at this time, that he would 'never associate with a man who has been kicked and thrashed without reporting it'. The words 'Oakley actually took no notice of it' are less easy to explain. Possibly this is a slip for O'Brien, who as a senior captain might have been expected to take some action.

In writing that the English ladies at whom he stared in Baksar (Buxar) were the first he had seen for a year, Pearson seems to forget the large number inside the Residency, whom he had last seen when they were escorted out at the end of November. Many of these wore their best gowns and bonnets for the occasion, some with white gloves and even, it was suspected, a little rouge. Mrs Maria Germon, the young wife of an officer of Bengal Native Infantry, took a more practical line. Fearing that her boxes would not get through, she put on three pairs of stockings, three chemises, three pairs of drawers, six petticoats, four flannel waistcoats, and a dressing-gown skirt and plaid jacket, all under a dress and jacket she had made from her riding habit. Unsurprisingly, she had to be helped onto her pony by a group of amused officers.

Gwalior was the capital city of the pro-British Maharaja Sindia, a leading Maratha prince whose temporising policy delayed the departure of the Gwalior Contingent (a force maintained by the British out of his revenues, but not part of his own army) to join the insurgent forces around Kanpur for several critical months in 1857. Defeated by Campbell on his return from Lucknow, the insurgents remained in the field and at the end of May 1858 made a sudden descent on Gwalior, declaring that they would rule the state in the name of the new Peshwa, Nana Sahib. Sindia was forced to take refuge with his British friends at Agra, but a British force defeated the insurgents outside Gwalior city on 17 June and restored Sindia to his throne a few days later. Among the insurgent casualties was Lakshmi Bai, Rani of Jhansi, the Boadicea of India. When the sepoy garrison at Jhansi mutinied in June 1857, some 60 Europeans, including women and children, were put to death after surrendering. This was the largest single massacre during the Mutiny apart from those at Kanpur, and many on the British side held the Rani responsible.

Letters 50–58, 6 August–17 November 1858
These cover the final three months of the war as far as the 84th were concerned. Low intensity operations continued, with lives lost to disease or the effects of heat or in occasional skirmishes. Pearson had the chance to return to his passion for game shooting. He refers to the spotted deer and the 'sambre' (the sambar or gaur of which he had written a year earlier); the black buck, *antilope cervicapra*; and the 'nylghu', *boselaphus tragocamelus*. This animal, more conventionally spelt nilghai or nylghau, is commonly known as the blue bull, but despite its name (which literally translates as 'blue cow') it is actually the largest of the South Asian antelopes and still flourishes in India's national parks.

The sicknesses that afflicted so many of his brother officers and men (sometimes fatally) included the cholera and dysentery that had caused such heavy casualties during the campaigns of the previous year. The 'neuralgia in the head and inflammation of the brain' suffered by Paymaster Donelan was probably meningitis, still a potentially life threatening illness. Erysipelas, an airborne infection of the skin, is not fatal in itself and is nowadays easily treatable by antibiotics. However, its common name 'St Anthony's Fire' indicates the intensely painful irritation that drove sufferers to scratch and tear at affected areas, causing wounds that (especially in the crowded military hospitals of the mid 19th century) became infected and led to death through blood poisoning. The 'miasma' from decayed vegetation in swampy areas was thought at this time to be the cause of the malarial (lit. 'bad air') fevers commonly contracted during the rainy season. It was not for another fifty years that medical scientists discovered that the disease was spread by the anopheles mosquito that flourished in those conditions.

Anwar Singh (Pearson's 'Ummar Sing') kept up a guerrilla war despite the efforts of British flying columns to run him to earth in his native hills and jungles. He was eventually driven out by the use of mounted troops under the command of Major Sir Henry Havelock, VC, the son of the hero of the relief of Lucknow, but was still at large when the war ended. The offer of amnesty to all who had not been involved in the murder of Europeans was included in the Queen's Proclamation of 1 November 1858, which announced the transfer to the British Crown of the East India Company's possessions, obligations and servants, guaranteed the existing position of the Indian princes and expressly prohibited any interference with the religious practices of the country.

The Indian Mutiny Medal was unusual in that it was awarded only to those who had been present under arms in an engagement, rather than merely serving in the theatre of operations. On this principle, Pearson gave a medal to the older of his two pet monkeys, but not the younger one. 290,000 men were awarded the Indian Mutiny Medal. Pearson was among those awarded bars for the Defence of Lucknow (granted not just to the members of the original garrison, as he at one time feared, but to the reinforcements that arrived under Outram and Havelock) and for Lucknow, the subsequent capture of the city by Sir Colin Campbell (Lord Clyde).

The comet mentioned in letter 56, 8 October 1858, is very probably Donati's comet, first recorded on 2 June 1858 by the Italian astronomer Giovanni Battista Donati. It should have been visible to Pearson's family in the Channel Islands. Comets were generally regarded by portents of some forthcoming disaster in Europe as they were in India.

Letters 59–66, 10 December 1858–20 March 1859
This final group covers the 84ths anticipation of returning to the United Kingdom after 16 years' service in the East Indies. With hostilities over, there was a return to peacetime standards of dress and discipline. Pearson lists the various exchanges, departures and promotions that took place among the regiment's officers at this time, and refers to the large number of men who volunteered for transfer to regiments that were remaining in India. The departure of from the 84th of Colonel Russell on becoming a major general allowed several consequential promotions. Russell later became the colonel of its successor, the York and Lancaster Regiment, formed by the amalgamation of the 65th and 84th Foot and the 3rd West York (Light Infantry) Militia.

The King of Delhi, whom a detachment of the 84th escorted on his way to Calcutta, was Bahadur Shah Zafar II, the last of the Mughal emperors. His dynasty had for 50 years been merely the shadow of a great name, protected and subsidised by the East India Company, which in theory derived its authority in India from Mughal grants. An indecisive character then in his eighties, he was persuaded to place himself at the head of the mutineers when they invaded his palace and declared the restoration of the Mughal Empire. When the British recovered Delhi, he surrendered on a promise that his life would be spared. After a trial of doubtful legitimacy before a military tribunal, he was convicted of treason and rebellion against the Company and sentenced to exile for life. With a small family retinue, he reached Calcutta on 4 December 1858 and embarked for Rangoon, where he died in 1862.

Pearson's 'GT Road' or 'GTR', the famous Grand Trunk Road of northern India, was built by the Mughal emperors. It links Calcutta to Varanasi and the other great cities along the Ganges before passing into the Punjab and ending at Peshawar, below the Khyber Pass. It still forms a vital highway of northern India and Pakistan

Lieutenant Clifford Henry Mecham (1830–65) of the Madras Army was adjutant of the 7th Oudh Irregular Infantry at the time of the Mutiny, and saw active service in and around Lucknow. His *Sketches and Incidents of the Siege of Lucknow*, the accuracy and artistic merit of which continue to be much admired, was published on 1 October 1858 by Day and Son, London. The work consists of a loose-leaf volume with a title page and sixteen plates of tinted lithographs, most with two subjects on each, and further pages of descriptive notes by George Couper, Secretary to the Chief Commissioner of Oudh.

Colonel Seymour, a well-liked and efficient commanding officer, did not survive the dysentery that killed so many other officers and men in this campaign. Despite the attentions of Assistant Surgeon Henry Gregory, he died on 3 April 1859.

Pearson's reference to going home by 'the overland route' does not mean that he intended travelling through the wilds of Central Asia and Iran, or even through the Ottoman Empire, which at this time still included Arabia and much of the Balkans. The term meant sailing fom India, through the Red Sea, to the Isthmus of Suez, and then proceeding by land through Egypt (an Ottoman province) to the Mediterrnean. The Suez Canal, which cut the journey time between England an India from six months to six weeks, was not completed untl 1869.

Biographical summaries of individuals mentioned in Pearson's letters

p after a rank indicates promotion by purchase. Names in brackets are the spellings sometimes used by Pearson.

ANSON, Hon Augustus Henry Archibald, 3rd s of 1st Earl of Lichfield; b Colwich, Staffs, 5 Mar 1835; ens *p*, 44th Foot, 27 May 1853; 2nd lieut, Rifle Bde, 2 Dec 1853; lieut, 8 Dec 1854; capt *p*, 6 Jul 1855; 84th Foot, 8 Jan 1856 (with the intention of joining them in India in order to serve as ADC to his uncle, Lieut Gen the Hon George Anson, C-in-C, India, who d of cholera, 27 May 1857); 7th Hussars, 24 Aug 1858; bt maj, 28 May 1859; bt lieut col, 23 Jul 1870; ret, 31 Jul 1873. Served in Crimean War 1854–56 and Indian Mutiny, awarded Victoria Cross; 16 mentions in desps; fought 34 single-handed engagements, killing 28 men; MP for Lichfield 1859–68. Described by the future Field Marshal Sir Garnet Wolseley, with whom he shared a tent during the Mutiny campaign, as an indifferent horseman and a bad swordsman, he secured an attachment to the 9th Royal Lancers and became ADC to Maj Gen Hope Grant, serving at capture of Delhi and the final relief of Lucknow. A prize sword was instituted in his memory at the RMC, Sandhurst, a fore-runner of the Sword of Honour at the present-day RMA Sandhurst.

AYTON, Henry Abraham Whitmore; ens, 2nd W India Regt, 14 Aug 1846; lieut, 13 Oct 1846; active service against slavers, Gambia, W Africa May 1849; 84th Foot, 1 Aug 1851; staff duty in Turkey during Crimean War; d of wounds, 28 Nov 1857.

BARRY, Robert; b Dublin, 17 Mar 1828; ens *p*, 97th Foot, 17 May 1850; 84th Foot 9 Jul 1850; lieut, 2 Feb 1855; wounded, 25 Sep 1857; capt, 10 Sep 1858; ret by sale of commn, 30 Mar 1867.

BATEMAN, Hugh Osbourne; ens *p*, 43rd Foot, 6 Mar 1856; lieut *p*, 24 Aug 1858; capt, 1 May 1864; served in New Zealand War.

BERKELEY, Charles Assheton Fitzhardinge; ens *p*, Scots Fusilier Guards, 27 May 1836; lieut *p*, 12 Aug 1837; lieut in the regt and capt in the Army, 14 Apr 1843; served on staff of Lt Gen Sir George Berkeley in the Kaffir War, 1847; bt maj, 15 Sep 1848; capt and lieut col, 13 Dec 1850; wounded at the battle of the Alma, 1854; col, 19 Jun 1855; 32nd Foot, 1857; COS and Mil Sec to Sir J Outram at Lucknow and the Alam Bagh 1857–58; d of wounds received while leading Hodson's Horse at the recapture of Lucknow, Feb 1858.

BIDDULPH, George; b Birdingbury, Warwicks, 19 Jan 1811; cdt, Bengal Native Inf, 1827; ens, 5 Nov 1828; lieut, 2 Oct 1831; capt, 10 Jul 1846; maj, 10 Jun 1853; lieut col, 1857; served in the Sikh Wars; kia Lucknow, 17 Nov 1857.

BINGHAM, G W Powlett; ens *p*, 64th Foot, 16 Feb 1838; lieut, 8 Apr 1838; capt *p*, 12 Sep 1848; maj, 2 Nov 1852; lieut col, 10 Dec 1856; col, 1862; served in Persian War 1856–57 and during Indian Mutiny.

BLAKE, George Pilkington; b Thurston Hall, Suffolk, 1833; ens *p*, 74th Foot, 5 Nov 1852; lieut *p*, 84th Foot, 29 Jul 1856; capt, 100th Foot, 17 Sep 1858; Military Train, 9 Nov 1858; ret by sale of commn, 18 Dec 1860; lieut col, Loyal Suffolk Hussars Yeo, 26 Aug 1876; d 1915. He was a noted horseman, with ample funds to secure good mounts, and his experience of horsemastership made him an ideal officer for the Military Train, which relied on horse-drawn wagons for its transport of army supplies. He left the Regular Army at the insistence of his future father-in-law, when he married. He later became Master of the Surrey Union Foxhounds.

BODKIN, James B; 2nd lieut, Land Transport Corps, 23 Nov 1855; cornet, Military Train, Feb, 1857; lieut, 2 Feb 1858; served at capture of Lucknow and subsequently in Eastern Awadh and Bihar; ret by sale of commn, 1860.

BOMFORD, John North; served in ranks in Bengal 1842–56; ens, 29th Foot, 29 Feb 1856; lieut, 23 Jun 1858; capt, 25 Mar 1862; ret by sale of commn, 1868.

BOULTBEE, Edward J; ens, 15th Foot, 13 Apr 1858; lieut *p*, 4 Jan 1861; d 1864.

BRETT, Edward B; lieut, W Essex Militia, 11 Mar 1854; ens, 28th Foot, 30 Nov 1855; lieut, 5 Jan 1860; capt, 1 Apr 1870; to half pay list, 26 Apr 1870. Neither the Navy List nor the East India Register show a Midshipman Brett at this time.

BROWNE, Henry George; ens, 32nd Foot, 31 Aug 1855; lieut, 15 Oct 1856; cmnd gren coy at battle of Chinhut and subsequently in the Residency at Lucknow; twice wounded; awarded Victoria Cross; capt, 100th Foot 1858; maj, 1 Feb 1868; to half-pay list, 23 Dec 1868; later bt lieut col; changed name to Gore-Browne, 1915.

BROWNE, Henry; b St Bride's, Co. Durham, 8 Sep 1814; served in ranks 31–Dec 1827–8 Nov 1849; ens, 84th Foot, 9 Nov 1849; lieut, 15 Aug 1852; adj, 27 Jul 1855; severely wounded, Unao, 29 Jul 1857; capt, 4 June 1858; 97th Foot, Dec 1858; d 27 Dec 1871.

BROWNRIGG, Henry Latham; b Dublin, Ireland, 6 Jul 1831; ens, 89th Foot, 25 May 1855; lieut, 17 May 1857; 8th Foot, 13 Apr 1858; capt *p*, 5 Apr 1864; maj *p*, 5 May 1869; bt lieut col, 1 Oct 1877; lieut col, 19 Dec 1877; served in Indian Mutiny; d Dover, 28 Jun 1879.

BURTON, Robert Graves, MD; asst surg, 24 Feb 1854; served with 77th Foot in the Crimea; with 6th (Inniskilling) Dgns in India 1858; resigned 1863.

CAMBRIDGE, HRH George, 2nd Duke of; b 26 Mar 1819; Queen Victoria's cousin; bt col, 3 Nov 1837; Gen C-in-C of the British Army, 15 July 1856; field marshal 9 Nov 1862; d 17 Mar 1904; was C-in-C longer than any other occupant in the history of this appointment, doing much to protect the Army from the military reformers. His care for the ordinary soldiers under his command is exemplified by Pearson's description of the way he took charge of the rescue party at Chatham on what was one of his earliest tours of inspection as C-in-C.

CAMPBELL, Sir Colin; cr Baron Clyde, Jul 1858; b Glasgow, 1792; ens, 78th Hdrs, 26 May 1808; Coruna; lieut, 9th Foot, 28 June 1809; Walcheren; Peninsular War; capt, 60th Foot, 3 Nov 1813; 21st R Scots Fus, April 1821; maj *p*, 26 Nov 1825; lieut-col *p*, 1835; 98th Foot; 1st China War; col, 23 Dec 1842; 2nd Sikh War and Punjab frontier; Crimean War; maj gen, 20 Jun 1854; lieut gen, 4 Jun 1856; C-in-C, India, 11 Jul 1857; gen, 14 May 1858; field marshal, 9 Nov 1862; d Chatham, 14 Aug 1863.

CANNING, Charles John; 2nd Visct (succ 1837) and 1st Earl (cr 1862), b 1812; Whig politician; MP 1836–37; under-sec of state, Foreign Office, 1841–46; chief commr for woods and forests, 1846; postmaster gen, 1853; gov gen of India, 1855–61, becoming also the first viceroy of India when govt was transferred from the E I Coy to the British Crown in 1858; d 1862.

CHAMIER, Stephen Henry Edward; cdt, E I Coy Mil Sem, Addiscombe, 1851–53; 2nd lieut, Madras Artillery, 11 Jun 1853; served in Pegu campaign, 1856 and Indian Mutiny, 1857–58 (inc Windham's engagement at Kanpur); 1st lieut, 27 Apr 1858; RA, 1861; capt, 29 Feb 1864; maj, 11 Oct 1864; lieut col, 17 May 1774; col, 17 May 1879; maj gen, 26 Feb 1885; lieut gen, 27 Oct 1886.

CHUTE, Pierce, b Listowel; Cornwall, 24 Jun 1831; ens p, 84th Foot, 17 May 1850; lieut p, 7 Sep 1852; wounded at Lucknow, 25 Feb 1858; capt, 2 Jul 1858; d 21 Aug 58.

CLARK, Francis; ens p, 24th Foot, 11 Apr 1845; lieut p, 9 Oct 1846; served in the Sikh Wars; capt p, 26 Dec 1851; 4th Foot (in Mauritius), May 1857; India, Sept 1857; d 1859.

CLERY, Cornelius Francis; ens, 32nd Foot, 5 Mar 1858; lieut p, 3 Jun 1859; adj, 1863–66; capt p, 16 Jan 1866; to half-pay list as maj, 20 Mar 1878; lieut col, 29 Nov 1879; col, 21 May 1904.

COCHRANE, William Edward; Madras Civil Service; apptd 1838; Dep Collector of Sea Customs in 1856-7.

CROHAN, Harry Bermingham; b Marylebone, London, 6 Oct 1839; ens, 84th Foot, 1 Jun 1855; lieut, 7 Dec 1855; capt p, 19 Nov 1858; 38th Foot, Dec 1861; ret by sale of commn, 14 Mar 1868.

CURRIE, Eugene; b Qulon, Madras Presidency (Kollam, Kerala), 9 Nov 1822; ens p, 97th Foot; 16 Sep 1851; 84th Foot, 30 Sep 1851; lieut p, 27 Oct 1853; capt p, 3 Aug 1855; d of wounds, Kanpur, 20 Jul 1857.

DE CARTERET; In 1857–58 the only officer of this name in either the British Army List or the East India Register was Lieut Havilland J de Carteret, 79th Hdrs, with which he served in the Crimea. The regimental history lists him among those embarking with the 79th from Dublin for India in Jul 1857.

DELAFOSSE (DELAFORCE), Henry George; ens, 53rd Bengal Native Inf, 9 Dec 1854; lieut, 23 Nov 1856; survivor of the Kanpur massacre, 1857; capt, 101st Foot (R Bengal Fus), 21 Jun 1861; bt maj, 12 Sep 1861; maj, 10 Jan 1872; bt lieut col, 4 Mar 1872; lieut col, 22 Sep 1875; col, 1 Oct 1877; King's Own Borderers, 30 Nov 1881; ret on pension.

DONELAN, Henry; b Halifax, Nova Scotia, 14 Oct 1814; served in the ranks, Feb 1830–Dec 1854; quartermaster, 84th Foot, 15 Dec 1854; paymaster, 6 Aug 1856; served with the 84th in all its actions during the Mutiny campaign; d Baksar (Buxar), Bihar, 28 Aug 1858.

DOUGLAS, John; ens p, 79th Foot, 6 Sep 1833; lieut p, 8 Jul 1836; capt p, 8 Jun 1841; bt maj, 1 Nov 1842; maj p, 24 Dec 1852; bt lieut col, 20 Jun 1854; lieut col, 13

Aug 1854; cmnd 79th Hdrs at Balaclava and Sebastopol; col, 1 Aug 1857; cmnd column in Bihar counter-insurgency ops, 1858; half pay list, 1 Oct 1859.

DOYLY, Capt; the only officer of this name in either the British Army List or the East India Register at this time was Maj John Walpole D'Oyly, 11th Foot, promoted from capt, 13 Jul 1858. This regt was not in India on that date but was en route from Australia to the UK. Possibly Pearson's "Captain Doyly" is a mis-spelling of a similar name or he was a retired officer of the British or Company's service or even a former sea captain.

DRAGE, William Henry; ens, Essex Rifles Militia, 14 Oct 1854; lieut, 15 Jun 1855; ens, 85th (Bucks Vols) King's Lt Inf, 9 May 1856; lieut, 4 Mar 1861; adj, 1863; capt, 52nd Lt Inf, 3 Aug 1872; maj and ret, 13 Sep 1879. The 85th served in Mauritius from 1853 to 1856, when it moved to Cape Colony, South Africa. It returned to the UK in 1863.

DRIBERG, William Charles; b Point de Galle, Ceylon, (Sri Lanka); ens, 84th Foot 11 Dec 1857; lieut, 10 Sep 1858; capt p, 19 Apr 1864; ret by sale of commn, 18 Apr 1865.

DU VERNET, William; b Colombo, Ceylon (Sri Lanka), 8 Sep 1825; ens, 50th Foot, 22 Mar 1844; shipwrecked in troopship *Runnymede*, Andaman Is., Nov 1844, surviving 54 days before rescue; served in Sikh War; wounded at Aliwal, 28 Jan 1846; lieut, 29 Jan 1846; 67th Foot, 29 Dec 1846; capt p, 13 Apr 1852; 43rd Foot, 20 Sep 1853; 84th Foot, 26 Dec 1854; ret by sale of commn, 23 Jul 1858.

EDDY, George Henry; ens, 11th Foot, 29 Aug 1826; lieut, 75th Hdrs, 20 Feb 1835; paymaster, 84th Foot, 28 Apr 1846; d of "sunstroke", 11 Apr 1858.

EYRE, Vincent; b Portsmouth, Hants, 23 Jan 1811; cdt, E I Coy Mil Sem, Addiscombe, 1827–28; 2nd lieut, Bengal Artillery, Dec 1828; 1st lieut, 1837; served in 1st Afghan War and was one of the hostages surviving the retreat from Kabul; cmnd arty, Gwalior Cont; maj, 1854; at the outbreak of the Mutiny he was commanding a troop of horse artillery at Rangoon, and subsequently played a leading part in the relief of Ara and succ to the command of the artillery in the siege and capture of Lucknow; mentioned in desps; lieut col and bt col, Dec 1858; maj gen, Oct 1863; d Aix-le-Bains, France, 22 Sep 1881.

FORSTER, Seaton Ralph; b Bedford, 11 Jul 1834; ens, 48th Foot, 23 Nov 1855; 84th Foot, 2 Feb 1858; lieut, 17 Sep 1858; 76th Foot, 4 Nov 1859; ret by sale of commn, 12 Mar 1861.

FRANKLYN, Charles; ens p, 84th Foot, 17 Jul 1823; lieut p, 8 Apr 1826; capt p, 10 Jul 1828; maj p, 28 Dec 1838; lieut col, 16 Sep 1845; bt col, 20 Jun 1854; brig, Feb–Mar 1858; maj gen, 1860; d 5 Aug 1861.

FRANKS, Sir Thomas Harte; ens p, 10th Foot, 7 Jul 1828; lieut p, 31 Oct 1831; capt p, 1 Mar 1839; maj p, 3 Apr 1846; lieut col p, 7 Jun 1849; col, 20 Jun 1854; maj gen, 20 Jul 1858; d 1862; cmnd 10th Foot in Sikh Wars; deployed to Jaunpur and Azamgarh late in November 1857 with 2,300 British troops and 3,200 Gurkha allies to protect these districts, along with Varanasi and the surrounding opium crop against insurgents from Lucknow. These troops subsequently became the Fourth Division of Campbell's army in the reconquest of Awadh, and joined him at Lucknow, after fighting a number of engagements en route, in time for the final assault. They then returned eastwards in pursuit of insurgents who had escaped from the city and followed them into Bihar where Franks cmnd in counter-insurgency ops.

GIBAUT, Alfred; b Jersey, 20 Jun 1836; ens p, 84th Foot, 9 Jun 1854; lieut, 11 Jun 1855; kia while trying to extinguish some burning sacks in a trench, Lucknow, 6 Oct 1857.

GILSON, Alexander Daniel; ens, 22nd Foot, 23 Mar 1855; lieut, 16 Jul 1858; not listed after 1861.

GORDON, Dundas W; cdt, E I Coy Mil Sem, 1851–52; lieut, Bengal Artillery, 1853–58; cmnd dets of artillery and heavy guns in the advance to relieve Lucknow and at the Alam Bagh; mentioned in desps; kia by a round shot at Alam Bagh, 9 Jan 1858.

GRANT, Sir James Hope; b Bridge of Earn, Perthshire, 22 Jul 1808; cornet p, 9th Lancers, 29 Aug 1826; lieut p, 26 Feb 1828; capt p, 29 May 1835; maj, 22 Apr 1842; bt lieut col, 28 Nov 1849; lieut col p, 29 Apr 1850; col, 28 Nov 1854; maj gen, 15 Jan 1858; lieut gen, 1860; gen, 1872; served in 1st China War; Sikh wars; Indian Mutiny, cmnd cav bde at Delhi, Kanpur, Lucknow, Bihar; C-in-C, 2nd China War; C-in-C, Madras, 1862–65; QMG, British Army; d London, 7 Mar 1875.

GREGORY, Henry Patrickson; b Finglas, Dublin, Ireland; asst surg, 84th Foot, 31 Dec 1857; 81st Foot, 15 Feb 1861; staff, 31 Mar 1863; d 26 Jul 1864.

GRIFFIN, Thomas; b Gosport, Hants, Mar 1825; served in ranks Mar 1840–Feb 1858; ens, 84th Foot, 2 Feb 1858; lieut, 4 Apr 1859; instr of musketry, 4 Oct 1861; capt, 14 Oct 1866; k by a fall from his mule over a precipice, Kingston, Jamaica, 21 Jul 1867.

HAMILTON, Joseph; lieut, Land Transport Corps, 6 Jul 1855; to half-pay list, 1 Apr 1857 (when LTC was replaced by the Military Train); quartermaster, 1st Bn, 8th Foot, 16 Apr 1858; d Baksar (Buxar), Bihar, Sep 1858.

HANBURY, (later Sir) James Arthur, MB; b Co Meath, Ireland, 13 Jan 1832; asst surg, 30 Sep 1853; 84th Foot, 29 Sep 1854; staff, 31 Dec 1857; 45th Foot, 13 June 1859; surg, 63rd Foot, 1863; served in the Second Afghan War and at Tel-el-Kebir, Egypt; ret as surg maj gen, 1892; d June 1908.

HARDY, Frederick; b Cork, 25 Dec 1830; ens p, 84th Foot 23 Nov 1849; lieut p, 6 June 1851; capt, 27 Nov 1857; maj p, 21 Nov 1862; bt col, May 1874, col of the York and Lancaster Regt, 1903.

HARFORD, Charles Joseph; cornet p, 12th Lancers, 16 Jan 1846; lieut p, 27 Oct 1848; capt p, 29 May 1856; 85th Foot, 1860; ret by sale of commn, 1860.

HARRIS, George Francis Robert, 3rd baron (succ.1845); b Throwley, Faversham, Kent, 14 Aug 1810; Christ Church, Oxford (contemporary with Dalhousie, Canning and Elgin, all of whom later became gov-gens of India); gov, Trinidad, 1846–54; gov, Madras, 1854–59; sent troops from Madras to Bengal during the Indian Mutiny; courtier; d Throwley, Nov 1872.

HART, George F; ens, 29th Foot; 16 Oct 1855; lieut, 20 Jan 1857; ret by sale of commn, 1860.

HAVELOCK, Sir Henry, 1st baronet (cr 1857); b Ford Hall, Bishopwearmouth, Sunderland, 5 Apr 1795; 2nd lieut, 95th Foot (Rifle Bde), 20 Jul 1815; lieut, 13th Light Inf, 24 Oct 1821; capt, 5 Jun 1838; maj, 4 Oct 1842; lieut col, 30 Apr 1851; col, 20 Jun 1854; maj gen, 1857; d of dysentery, Lucknow, 24 Nov 1857; served in 1st Burma War, 1st Afghan War, Sikh Wars, Persian War, cmnd adv to relieve Lucknow, Jun–Sep 1857.

HAVELOCK, Sir Henry Marshalman, 2nd baronet (succ 24 Nov 1857); ens, 18th Foot (R Irish Regt), 31 Mar 1846; lieut, 32 Jun 1848; capt, 9 Oct 1857; maj, Jan 1858; lieut col, 26 Apr 1859; col, 17 Jan 1868; maj gen, 18 Mar 1878; Lib MP, 1874–81, 1885–92, 1895–97; served in Persian War and Indian Mutiny; ADC to his father at Lucknow, 1857; awarded Victoria Cross and numerous mentions in despatches; wounded; cmnd Indian cavalry force in pursuit of Kunwar and Anwar Singh, Bihar, and credited with adoption of mounted infantry in successful counter-insurgency operations; New Zealand War; killed by a Pathan (Pushtun) extremist while accompanying a parliamentary commission to Punjab NW frontier, 30 Dec, 1897.

HELY, Mrs; probably the wife of Egbert Charles Septimus Hely (q.v.). At this time it was unusual for subalterns to marry, though the Helys might have married before he joined the Regular Army at the age of 26.

HELY, Egbert Charles Septimus; b O Porto, Portugal, 1 Jul 1830; lieut, 1st Surrey Militia, 10 Jan 1856; ens, 84th Foot, 8 Jul 1856; arrived India, Dec 1856; lieut, 26 Sept 1857; capt p, 21 Nov 1862; ret by sale of commn, Apr 1865.

HODSON, William Stephen Raikes; b Gloucester, 19 Mar 1821; Trinity Coll, Cambridge, 1840–44; lieut, Guernsey Militia, 1845; ens, 2nd Bengal Native Inf (Grens), Sept 1845; 1st Bengal European Fusiliers; adj, Corps of Guides, Punjab Irregular Force, 1847; civil employ; commdt, Guides, 1852; int staff, May 1857; raised and cmnd Hodson's Horse (irregular Indian cav) May 1857; capt, Sep 1857; bt maj; d of wounds, Lucknow, 15 Mar 1858; served in Sikh Wars and Indian Mutiny, Delhi, Lucknow; arrested King of Delhi, 21 Sep 1857; captured and executed Mughal princes, 22 Sep 1857; the subject of controversy over this and other episodes in his career; regarded variously as an heroic man of action or a ruthless freebooter.

HORAN, Charles Thomas; b Belgaum, Bombay Presidency (now in Karnatika), 29 Jul 1839; ens, 84th Foot, 17 Nov 1857; lieut, 7 Sep 1858; ret by sale of commn, 24 Mar 1863.

HUDSON, James; b Bessingby, Yorks, 6 Mar 1838; ens p, 97th Foot, 3 Mar 1854; lieut, 9 Feb 1855; capt, 25 Jun 1858; 84th Foot, 28 Dec 1858; maj p, 25 Apr 1868; lieut col, 7 May 1877; ret by sale of comm., 15 Aug 1877; served in Crimea 1855–56 and Indian Mutiny, Aug 1857–Sep 1859.

HUMPHREY, Robert Fraser; b Stonehaven, Kincardine, 30 June 1838; ens, R Aberdeenshire Militia, 1 May 1855; ens, 84th Foot, 29 Feb 1857; lieut, 28 June 1857; capt, 11 Nov 1863; 59th Foot; half-pay list, 7 Aug 1867; ret by sale of commn, Jan 1869.

IMPETT, John; ens, 71st Highland Lt Inf, Apr 1814; served at Waterloo, June 1815; lieut *p*, 5 Oct 1820; capt, 74th Highlanders 30 Jan 1835; bt maj, 9 Nov 1846; bt lieut col 20 June 1854.

INGLEFIELD, Henry Hope A' Court; ens *p*, 14th Foot, 12 Mar 1852; lieut, 6 Jun 1854; served with this regt in Crimea; capt *p*, Military Train, 9 Jan 1857; d 1859.

INNES, Francis William, MD; asst surg, 84th Foot, 10 Feb 1837; surg, 2 Feb 1849; supt surg, Lucknow, 21 Jul 1857–Mar 1858; surg maj, 1 Oct 1858; ret as Insp Gen of Hospitals, 1873.

JACKSON, Sir Robert William; asst surg, 90th Lt Inf, 26 May 1854; served at Sebastopol; 84th Foot, Jun 1858–Oct 1859; served in Ashanti War; ret as Dep Surg Gen, Dec 1882.

JENKINS, William Henry; b Hove, Sussex, 29 Mar 1831; asst surg, 24th Foot, 24 Sep 1855; 84th Foot, 23 Apr 1858; 14th Foot, 22 Oct 1861; staff, 9 Oct 1863; served at Scutari and in Crimea; with 59th Foot in 2nd China War, Aug 1857–Oct 1858; Indian Mutiny, Aug 1858–Oct 1859; resigned, 9 Oct 1865.

JONES, Henry Shaw; b Naples, 1 Aug 1836; ens *p*, 84th Foot, 25 Aug 1857; lieut, 24 Aug 1858; wounded, 14 Oct 1858; d suddenly at Pembroke Dock, 14 Apr 1864.

KAVANAGH, Thomas Henry; b Mullingar, Co Westmeath, 15 Jul 1821; joined Bengal Uncovenanted Civil Service 1849; awarded Victoria Cross for gallantry at Lucknow; asst commr, Awadh; d Gibraltar 11 Nov 1882.

KEATS, William McGeachy; b Wyveliscombe, Somerset, 18 Oct 1824; ens *p*, 75th Hdrs, 14 Oct 1842; lieut *p*, 21 Apr 1846; 84th Foot, 26 Mar 1847; capt, 7th R Fus, 26 Sep 1857; ret by sale of commn, 21 Feb 1860.

KENNAN, Thomas H P; b Fort St George, Madras, 26 Jan 1824; ens *p*, 84th Foot, 27 October 1846; lieut, 12 Apr 1850; served in India and Burma, Aug 1847–Feb 1857, ret by sale of commn, Aug 1857.

KENNY, Edward; ens, 89th Foot 1813; later Lt Col; served in the Peninsular War; father of Lieuts Edward and Henry Kenny (q.v.).

KENNY, Edward Courtenay Geils; b Greenock 14 Dec 1830; ens, 57th Foot 2 Jan 1848; lieut *p*, 28 Dec 1849; 84th Foot, 19 April 1850; d on passage from Rangoon to Madras, 19 Feb 1856.

KENNY, Henry Thomas William Oxley; b at sea 3 Aug 1839; ens, 84th Foot, 15 Jan 1856; lieut, 21 July 1857; d of cholera, Kanpur, 24 Feb 1857. Pearson met him at Chatham while they were waiting to embark and the two became close friends.

KERR, Lord Mark; younger s of 6th Marquess of Lothian; b 12 Dec 1816; ens *p*, 13th Lt Inf, 19 Jun 1835; lieut *p*, 14 Sep 1838; capt *p*, 26 Jun 1840; maj *p*, 25 Jul 1851; lieut col *p*, 30 Dec 1853; col, 28 Nov 1854; cmnd 13th Lt Inf in Crimea and Indian Mutiny (Bihar campaign); maj gen, 6 Mar 1868; lieut gen, 13 Jul 1876; gen, 11 Nov 1878.

KNOX, John Hunter; b Dublin, Ireland, 25 Jun 1840; ens, 94th Foot, 30 Mar 1858; 84th Foot, 10 Sep 1858; lieut *p*, 8 Feb 1861; 14th Hussars, 26 Nov 1861; capt, 2 Oct 1866; maj, 15 Jun 1876; lieut col, 15 Jun 1881; col, 15 Jun 1885; d 25 Oct 1885; served in Indian Mutiny and Transvaal War.

LA PRESLE, Joseph Thomas; b Kilkenny, SE Ireland, 25 Feb 1820; asst surg, 66th Foot, 22 Dec 1846; 84th Foot, 16 Aug 1850; surg, Rifle Bde, 14 Jan 1859; d Marri, Punjab, 8 Sept 1864.

LAMBERT, George; b Markethill, Perthshire, Dec 1819; served in ranks, 84th Foot, June 1840–11 Dec 1857; awarded Victoria Cross for conduct at Unao and adv to Lucknow; wounded at relief of Lucknow; ens, 2 Dec 1857; adj, 2 Jul 1858; lieut, 17 Sep 1858; d Sheffield, 10 Feb 1860.

LANCE, William Henry Joseph; ens, Bengal Native Inf, 18 Sep 1849; lieut, 7 Feb 1851; bt capt, Bengal Staff Corps, 18 Sep 1861; capt, 10 Aug 1862; maj, 18 Sep 1869; lieut col, 18 Sep 1875; col, 12 Jun 1878; ret on pension.

LAWRENCE, Sir Henry Montgomery; b Ceylon (Sri Lanka), 28 Jun 1806; cdt, E I Coy Mil Sem, Addiscombe, 1820–22; 2nd lieut, Bengal Artillery, 10 May 1822; lieut, 5 Oct 1822; capt, 10 Feb 1840; maj, 23 Sep 1850; lieut col, 18 May 1856; brig gen, May 1857; served in 1st Burma War, 1st Afghan War, Sikh Wars and Mutiny; President of the Punjab Commission, 1849–53; agent to gov-gen, Rajputana; chief commr, Oudh, 1857. Noted for his sympathy towards Indian nobles and landholders whose position was adversely affected by the advent of British rule; d of wounds, Lucknow, 4 Jul 1857.

LE GRAND, Arthur; ens *p*, 35th Foot, 5 Sep 1843; lieut, 16 Apr 1845; capt, 6 Jan 1854; kia near Jagdispur, Bihar, 23 Apr 1858.

LIGHTFOOT, Thomas; b Kingston, Upper Canada, 27 Dec 1820; ens, 84th Foot, 1 Jan 1838; lieut *p*, 30 Oct 1840; capt, 26 Jun 1851; bt maj, 24 Mar 1858; maj, 2 Jul 1885; lieut col, 4 Apr 1859; bt col, 4 Apr 1864; maj gen, 1 Oct 1877; ret as hon lieut gen, 27 Dec 1882; cmnd 84th Foot at Alam Bagh, capture of Lucknow, and subsequent campaign.

LIGHTFOOT, T; ens, 45th Foot, Aug 1797; lieut, Mar 1800; capt, Dec 1804; lieut col, May 1814; col, May 1836; maj gen, Nov 1841; lieut gen, Dec 1851; col of 62nd Foot; served in Netherlands and Peninsular War; Army Gold Medal with two clasps; Army Silver Medal with eleven clasps; d 1858; f of above.

LIVESAY, William; ens, 43rd Foot, 26 Oct 1855; lieut *p*, 3 Apr 1857; capt, 30 Apr 1864; maj, 19 Jun 1876; lieut col, 19 Jun 1883; col, 1 Jun 1888; ret on half pay, 1 Jun 1889; served in the Indian Mutiny and New Zealand War.

LUGARD, Sir Edward; ens, 31st Foot, 31 Jul 1828; lieut *p*, 31 Oct 1831; capt, 30 Dec 1843; bt maj, 3 Apr 1846; bt lieut col, 7 Jun 1849; col, 20 Jun 1854; maj gen, 20 Jul 1858; lieut gen, 12 Jan 1865; gen, 24 Oct 1872; served in 1st Afghan War, Sikh Wars, Persian War, Indian Mutiny; chief commr, Army Purchase Commission, 1877.

McCARTHY, William Justin; ens, 15 Jun 1815; half pay, 25 Feb 1816; 2nd lieut, Ceylon Rifle Regt, 29 Mar 1827; lieut, 57th Foot, 30 Sep 1830; capt, 29 Mar 1844;

84th Foot, 13 Aug 1845; bt maj, 23 Mar 1855; maj, 27 Nov 1857; bt lieut col and ret, 2 Jul 1858.

McGRATH, Frederick Augustus; ens *p*, 84th Foot, 7 Dec 1855; lieut, 16 Jun 1857; capt, 25th Foot, 13 Dec 1859; 81st Foot, 15 June 1860; ret by sale of commn, 1867.

M'MASTER, Valentine Munbee, MD; b Trichinopoly, S India, 16 May 1834; asst surg, 27 Mar 1855; surg, 14 Mar 1868; served with 78th Hdrs in Persia and Indian Mutiny; awarded Victoria Cross for rescuing and treating wounded men under fire at Lucknow, Sep 1857; later served in India with 6th Inniskilling Dgns and 18th Hussars before rejoining 78th Hdrs, with whom he was serving when d at Belfast, 22 Jan 1872.

MADIGAN, J A; b Belgaum, Bombay Presidency, 25 Apr 1820; ens, 71st Foot, 16 June 1837; 4th Foot, 10 July 1837; lieut *p*, 14 Dec 1838; capt, 24 Jan 1850; 84th Foot, 25 Oct 1850; murdered in Pegu, while detached for construction of telegraph line, 1856.

MAUDE, Francis Cornwallis; gent cadt, RMA, Woolwich, 9 Mar 1844; 2nd lieut, RA, 1 Oct 1847; 1st lieut, 30 Jun 1848; 2nd capt, 13 Dec 1854; bt maj, 19 Jan 1858; capt, 26 Apr 1860; ret, 29 Aug 1866; arrived in Bengal at the beginning of the Indian Mutiny in cmnd of a company of artillerymen formed from units in Ceylon (Sri Lanka), the first elements of the RA to serve in India since the Seven Years War; cmnd artillery in Havelock's Lucknow campaign; awarded Victoria Cross.

MAYBURY, Richard; b Killarney 20 Mar 1827; ens 31st Foot, 9 Nov 1855; lieut *p*, 84th Foot, 17 May 1856; d of fever, Benares (Varanasi) 15 Jun 1857. Pearson claimed he had starved himself to save money.

MECHAM (MICHAM), Clifford Henry; b 1830; ens, 27th Madras Native Inf, 20 Jan 1849; lieut, 23 Nov 1856; adj, 7th Oudh Irregular Inf, 1856–57; served with distinction at def of Lucknow and subsequent campaigns; 3 mentions in desps; capt, Madras Staff Corps, 11 Oct 1862; commdt, 6th Bengal Cav, 17 Apr 1863; d 1865; a talented artist, noted for his published Sketches of the Siege of Lucknow.

NASON, Henry; 2nd lieut, Land Transport Corps, 28 Jun 1849; lieut, 1 Aug 1853; capt, 3 Feb 1856; Military Train, Feb 1857; served in Awadh and Bihar; kia, Oct 1858.

NEILL, James George Smith; cdt, Madras Army, 1826; ens, 1st Madras Eur Regt (later Fus), 5 Dec 1826; lieut, 7 Nov 1828; capt, 2 Feb 1843; maj, 25 Mar 1850; lieut col, 1854; col, 1857; brig gen, 1857; served in 2nd Burma War and Crimean War; noted for his policy of severity during the operations to relieve Kanpur and Lucknow, and for his insubordinate attitude towards Havelock (q.v.); kia Lucknow, 26 Sep 1857.

NEWCASTLE, 5th Duke of; Henry Pelham Fiennes Pelham-Clinton, by courtesy Earl of Lincoln prior to succ Jan 1851, b London, May 1811; Tory politician; commr for woods and forests, 1841–45; chief sec for Ireland, 1846; sec of state for war and the colonies, 1852–54; for war, 1854–55; for the colonies, 1859–64; d Oct 1864.

NORTHEY, STEWART; ens *p*, 25th Foot, 18 Jan 1839; lieut *p*, 21 May 1841; ret, 1852; adj and capt, Essex Rifles Militia, 22 Sep 1852 – 6 Mar 1866.

NUNN, John Joshua; ens *p*, 90th Lt Inf, 25 Aug 1854; lieut, 9 Feb 1855; kia Lucknow, 24 Sep 1857.

OAKLEY, George John Arata; b Hyderabad, S. India, 10 Apr 1836; ens, 1st Foot 14 May 1853; 84th Foot, 28 Oct 1853; lieut *p*, 16 May 1855; wounded in the head by a musket ball, Lucknow, 25 Sep 1857; capt, 4 Apr 1859; 68th Foot, 23 Sep 1859; ret by sale of commn, 27 Jul 1866.

O'BRIEN, David; b 1827; ens, 2nd W India Regt, 22 Nov 1844; 84th Foot, Mar 1844; lieut, 20 May 1846; capt, 21 Jul 1857; bt maj, 24 Mar 1858; 4th W India Regt, 30 June 1865; d 27 May 1866; cmnd No 9 Coy, 84th Foot, in the garrison of Lucknow through the entire siege.

OLPHERTS, Sir William; b Dartry, Co Armagh, 8 Mar 1822; E I Coy Mil Sem, Addiscombe, 1837–39; 2nd lieut, Bengal Artillery, 11 Jun 1839; 1st lieut, 17 Jun 1831; capt, 3 Mar 1853; bt maj, 19 Jan 1858; bt lieut col, 24th Mar 1858; lieut col, 18 Feb 1861; bt col, 26 Feb 1864; col, 17 Jul 1872; maj gen, 23 Jun 1878; lieut gen, 1 Oct 1877; gen, 31 Mar 1883; served in ops in Burma, Central India, Gwalior, Sind Frontier; Sikh Wars, Central Asia; Indian Mutiny; cmnd artillery in def of Lucknow and at Alam Bagh; awarded Victoria Cross.

OUTRAM, Sir James; b Butterley Hall, Derbyshire, 29 Jan 1803; cdt, Bombay Army, 1819; lieut and adj, 1/12th (later 23rd) Bombay Native Inf, 1820; served on staff and as political officer, 1st Afghan War; Upper Sind Frontier; maj, 1839; bt lieut col, 1843; def of Hyderabad; commr in Sind; pol agent, Gujerat, Satara, Baroda; resident at Lucknow, 1854 and chief commr, Oudh, 1856; local lieut gen and comd, Persian War, 1856–57; re-appointed chief commr, Oudh, and given cmnd of Lucknow relief force, but waived rank to allow Havelock (q.v.) to remain in cmnd until they reached the Residency; lieut gen, 1858; def of Lucknow and Alam Bagh; capture of Lucknow, 1858; member of gov gen's council, 1858–59; ret, 1860; d Pau, Navarre, 11 May 1863; bur Westminster Abbey; known as the "Bayard of India" from his chivalry and achievements as a soldier and diplomat.

PAKENHAM, Robert Maxwell; b Longford Lodge, Co. Antrim, 10 Apr 1834; ens, 43rd Foot, 6 Jul 1852; lieut *p*, 8 Sep 1854; capt *p*, 26 Sep 1856; 84th Foot, 16 Mar 1857; kia Lucknow, 25 Sep 1857.

PARSONS, Richard; ens *p*, 35th Foot, 9 May 1856; lieut *p*, 15 May 1857; capt *p*, 16 Mar 1870; 36th Foot, 17 May 1876; maj, Worcs Regt, 1 Jul 1881; lieut-col, 19 Dec 1886; ret as lieut-col.

PEARSON, George John Hooke; b 1841; gent cdt, RMC, Sandhurst, 1857–58; cornet, 15th Hussars, 31 Dec 1858; lieut *p*, 25 May 1860; capt *p*, 17 Sep 1861; ret by sale of commn, 1873.

PEARSON, Hugh; *see* Introduction, paras 5 and 6.

PEARSON, Hugh Pearce; *see* Introduction, paras 5, 6, 7 and penultimate para.

PEARSON, Thomas Hooke; cornet *p*, 11th Lt Dgns, 14 May 1825; lieut *p*, 1 Aug 1826; capt *p*, 16 Aug 1831; maj, 19 Jun 1846; lieut col, 20 Jun 1854; col, 26 Oct 1857; maj gen, 6 Mar 1868; lieut gen, 1 Oct 1877; gen, 1 Jul 1881; served at taking of Bharatpur and in Sikh Wars.

PEEL, Jonathan; 5th s of Sir Robert Peel, b Bury, Lancs, 12 Oct 1799; 2nd lieut *p*, Rifle Bde, 15 June 1815; lieut, 3 Dec, 1818; capt *p*, 71st Hdrs, 3 Dec 1818; maj *p*, Gren Gds, 7 Nov 1822; lieut col *p*, 53rd Foot, 7 Jun 1827; bt col, 23 Nov 1841; maj gen, 20 Jun 1854; lieut gen, 7 Dec 1859; ret, 4 Aug 1863; MP 1826 – 68; sec of state for war, Feb 1858 –Jun 1859, Jun 1866 – Dec 1870; d 13 Feb 1879.

PEEL, Sir William; 3rd s of Sir Robert Peel; b 2 Nov 1824; midshipman, RN, Apr 1838; lieut, 13 Mar 1844; cdr, 27 Jun 1846; capt, 10 Jan 1849; awarded Victoria Cross for services with naval bde at Sebastopol; cmnd HMS *Shannon*, 1856; led naval bde to Lucknow; wounded, 9 Mar 1858; d of hospital-acquired smallpox, 27 Apr 1858.

PENTON, John; b Calais, France, 27 Nov 1829; ens *p*, 84th Foot, 6 June 1851; lieut *p*, 13 Sep 1853; capt, 22 Aug 1858; maj *p*, 89th Foot, 1864; lieut col, 28 Mar 1874; col, 28 Mar 1879; maj gen, 26 Oct 1886. At the storming of the Harn Khana, 13 Nov 1857, he rescued his CO, Captain Willis (q.v.) from a mine crater and was first through the breach; brig gen, 2nd Afghan War.

POOLE William; b Keyworth, Leics, 4 Jan 1834; ens, 84th Foot, 27 Jul 1855; lieut, 20 Feb 1856; d of wounds, Lucknow, 28 Sep 1857.

PRATT (PEATE), Roberts Torrens; b Bengal 7 Oct 1834; ens, 84th Foot, 11 Jun 1852; lieut *p*, 9 Jun 1854; capt, 24 Aug 1858; 69th Foot, 12 Nov 1858; d 2 Aug 1867.

PRATT, Thomas Simson (f of above); a veteran of the Napoleonic and 1st China Wars; col, 11 Nov 1851; maj gen, 26 Oct 1858.

RADCLIFFE, William; b Douglas, Isle of Man, 17 Jul 1810; ens *p*, 87th Foot, 27 Sep 1831; lieut *p*, 24 Apr 1835; capt *p*, 7 Jun 1844; 84th Foot, 5 Feb 1847; bt maj, 18 Dec 1855; maj, 18th Foot, 13 Apr 1858; lieut col, 75th Foot, 26 Oct 1858; col, 7 Dec 1863; maj gen and ret, 9 Dec 1864.

RAIKES, Thomas; ens, 1st Madras Fus, 25 Dec 1840; lieut, 24 Jan 1845; capt, 4 Mar 1854; bt maj, 24 Mar 1858; maj, 102nd Foot (R Madras Fus), 1 Jan 1862; lieut col, 30 Jul 1862; col, 30 Jul 1867, maj gen, 1 Oct 1877; served in 2nd Burma War, def of Lucknow and subsequent campaign.

REED, Matthew Benjamin George; b circa 1801; ens, 4th W India Regt, 26 Feb 1818; to half-pay list, 8 Sep 1819; 70th Foot, 18 Sep 1823; lieut, 19 Nov 1825; capt *p*, 84th Foot, 26 Feb 1836; maj, 16 Sep 1845; bt lieut col, 24 Jun 1854; ret as col, 4 Jun 1858. Commanding the 84th at the beginning of operations in 1854, he led one wing in the march towards Varanasi, but then returned to Calcutta, medically unfit for active service.

RENAUD, Sydenham G C; 1st Madras Fus; bt capt, 1852; capt, 1853; bt maj 1857; a veteran of the 2nd Burma War, he served as second-in-command of his regt in the initial advance towards Kanpur and was noted for his severity in dealing with mutineers and other insurgents; d of wounds, 15 July 1857.

ROLLESTON, Cornelius Charles; ens, 84th Foot, 20 May 1842; lieut, 7 Jul 1845; capt, 2 Feb 1855; mentioned in desps, 1858; maj, 11 Nov 1864; ret by sale of commn, Apr 1864.

RUSSELL, David; b 27 May 1809; cornet, 7th Lt Dgns, 10 Jan 1828; lieut, 1 Oct 1829; capt, 5 Apr 1833; 84th Foot, 10 Apr 1835; maj, 7 Jul 1845; lieut col p, 10 Dec 1847; bt col 28 Nov 1854; brig Nov 1857; wounded, relief of Lucknow; cmnd bde at Alam Bagh and capture of Lucknow; mentioned in desps; maj gen, 3 Sep 1862; lieut gen, 25 Oct 1871; col of the York and Lancaster Regt 1872, d 16 Jan 1884.

SANDWITH, Benjamin; b Wexford, SE Ireland, December 1827; gent cdt, RMC, Sandhurst, 1842–45; ens, 84th Foot, 19 Dec 1845; lieut, 15 Aug 1849; served in advance to Lucknow 1857; actg field engr during def of Lucknow; kia, 21 Nov 1857; mentioned in desps.

SAUNDERS, Frederic John Gothliepe; b Glanmire, Co.Cork, 5 Apr 1826; ens p, 57th Foot, 29 Dec 1846; 84th Foot, 2 Mar 1850; lieut, 3 Jul 1850; served in the Turkish Contingent, Crimean War; commanded No.9 Coy, 84th Foot, during siege of Kanpur; captured when the garrison was massacred after marching out on a promise of safe conduct, he demanded to be taken before the insurgent leader, Nana Sahib, and killed or wounded several of that prince's bodyguard before being overpowered. He was then crucified and repeatedly ridden over by enemy cavalry who cut him to pieces with their swords.

SAUNDERS, Richard Westrops, MD; asst surg, 22 Jan 1858; served in India with 23rd R Welsh Fus; later on staff in UK and with 16th Foot from 1861 until resigned in 1865.

SIDDALL, John; vet surg, Bengal, 17 Jul 1844; sub asst, Stud Dept, Central Provinces, Baksar (Buxar), Bihar, 1852.

SEATON, Sir Thomas; b East Bergholt, Suffolk, May 1806; cdt, Bengal Army, 1821; ens, Bengal Native Inf, 4 Feb 1823; lieut, 1 May 1824; capt, 3 Apr 1834; maj, 17 Nov 1852; lieut col, 27 Jun 1857; bt col, 13 Oct 1857; col, 1st Bengal Eur Fus, 14 Jan 1858; ret, 3 Jun 1859; hon maj gen; d Paris, 11 Sep 1865; served at siege of Bharatpur, 1st Afghan War, def of Jalalabad, Indian Mutiny.

SEYMOUR, Charles F; b 1820; gent cadet, RMC, Sandhurst, 1833–37; ens, 84th Foot, 9 Jan 1838; adj, 10 May 1839; lieut, 29 Aug 1839; capt p, 10 Dec 1847; asst adj gen during siege and capture of Lucknow, mentioned in desps; maj, 4 Jun 1858; lieut col, 10 Sep 1858.

SHEEHEY, William; ens p, 64th Foot, 22 Nov 1850; lieut, 20 Jan 1854; served at Sebastopol as a volunteer (promoted for distinguished service); capt, 41st Foot, 16 Nov 1855; 81st Foot, Apr 1856; d of cholera, 6 Sep 57.

SMITHETT, Hamilton; cdt, El Coy Mil Sem, Addiscombe, 1853–55; 2nd lieut, Bengal Artillery, 8 Jun 1855; 1st lieut, 21 Apr 1859; RA, 1861; 2nd capt, 24 Mar 1865; maj,

25 Sep 1872; lieut col, 1 Feb 1880; col, 1 Feb 1884; maj gen, 15 Sep 1885; ret, 1885; served in Indian Mutiny.

SNOW, Walter C E; ens, 84th Foot, 11 April 1842; lieut 22 April 1844; capt, 9 Jan 1855; ret by sale of commn, 8 Feb 1861.

STABB, Henry Sparke; ens *p*, 32nd Foot, 29 Apr 1856; lieut *p*, 1 Aug 1856; capt, 5 Nov 1861; maj, 8 Mar 1875; lieut col, 29 Jun 1881; col, 29 Jun 1885; d while commanding the troops in Natal during the Zulu rebellion, 1888.

STEWART, Andrew; b Banbridge, Co Down, 5 May 1836; ens, 98th Foot. 26 Feb 1856; lieut, 7 May 1858; 84th Foot, 17 Jan 1859; 64th Foot, 22 Dec 1863; resigned, 9 Sep 1854.

TAYLOR, Warington; lieut *p*, 29th Foot; killed Pearson's pet kitten at Chatham where he may have been waiting, to embark to join his regiment. He is unlikely actually to have done so as he ret by sale of commn before the end of 1857.

WALLACE, Robert; formerly in Madras Army; senior major, Essex Rifles Militia, 1855–57.

WAY, Charles Gregory; ens, West Essex Militia, 2 Jan 1856; ens, Bengal Native Inf, 1857; one of the eight ensigns newly-arrived from England ("griffins" in Anglo-Indian slang) who were killed in the notorious "massacre of the griffs" during the mutiny the 6th Bengal Native Inf at Allahabad, 6 June 1857. Lewis John Way, his uncle, was capt in the W Essex Mil, 1852–60.

WEST, James Alexander; b Edinburgh, 24 Apr 1808; ens *p*, 84th Foot, 6 Jul 1826; lieut, 28 Feb 1828; capt, 8 Apr 1842; bt maj, 20 Jun 1854; maj, 7 Feb 1855; bt lieut col, 27 Nov 1857; ret, Nov 1857; d Feb 1880.

WETHERALL, Sir George August; b 1788; lieut, 7th R Fus, 29 Jul 1795; served as capt on staff of his f, Gen Sir Frederick Wetherall, at Cape of Good Hope, 1807 and Java, 1819; counter-insurgency ops, Canada, 1837; col of 84th Foot, Jun 1854; lieut gen, 8 Sep 1857; gen, 23 Oct 1863; gov, RMC, Sandhurst, Feb 1856 until d Apr 1868.

WHEELER, Sir Hugh Massy; b Clonbeg, Co Tipperary, 30 Jun 1789; cdt, Bengal Army, 1803; ens, Bengal Native Inf, 17 Mar 1805; lieut, 5 Apr 1805; capt, 1 Jan 1819; maj, 18 Jul 1829; lieut col, 27 Jun 1835; col, 1 Apr 1846; maj gen, 20 Jun 1854; served in 1st Afghan War and Sikh Wars; cmnd Cawnpore Div, 30 June 1856; besieged 6–25 Jun 1857; kia 26 Jun 1857.

WHITEHEAD, Frederick George; formerly capt, 42nd R Hdrs; senior major, Essex Rifles Militia, 1857–69.

WHITTOCK, George Frederick Tod; b Moulmein, British Burma (Myanmar), 5 Dec 1827; ens *p*, 4th Foot, 11 Dec 1846; 84th Foot, Aug 1847; lieut, 26 Jun 1851; capt, 13 Apr 1858; on staff of his f, Maj Gen Sir George Whittock, commanding Sagar Field Force, Central India campaign, 1858; ret by sale of commn, 31 Aug 1866.

WILLIAMS, Montgomery; b Bath, Somerset, 22 Aug 1837; ens *p*, 69th Foot, 22 Jul 1856; 84th Foot, 14 Aug 1857; lieut, 29 Nov 1857; capt *p*, 21 Feb 1860; 19th Foot, May 1860; maj, 100th Foot, 1878; ret as col, 1894.

WILLIS, Frederic Arthur; b Kensington, Middx, 16 Jul 1827; ens 27th Foot, 27 Sep 1844; lieut *p*, 8 May 1846; capt *p*, 16 Jan 1852; 84th Foot, 29 Apr 1853; commanded regt at Unao, Kanpur and Lucknow, Aug 1857–Jan 1858; bt maj, 24 Mar 1858; maj, 38 Foot, 4 Apr 1859; bt lieut col, 26 Apr 1859; lieut col *p*, 22 Dec 1863; col 21 May 1865; maj gen, 26 May 1870; 26th Foot; lieut gen, 19 Mar 1886; 5th Fus; ret, 1 April 1891.

WILSON, Nicholas; ens, 64th Foot, 31 Oct 1809; lieut, 7 Oct 1813; capt *p*, 24 Oct 1821; maj *p*, 30 Dec 1828; bt lieut col, 4 Aug 1848; col, 20 Jun 1854; kia as brig, Kanpur, 28 Nov 1857.

WINDHAM, Sir Charles Ash; b Felbrigg Hall, Norfolk, 8 Oct 1810; gent cdt, RMC, Sandhurst, 1823–26; ens, Coldm Gds and lieut, Army, *p*, 30 Dec 1826; lieut and capt, *p*, 31 May 1833; bt maj, 9 Nov 1846; capt and lieut col, *p*, 29 Dec 1846; maj, 9 Nov 1846; lieut col (unattached), 29 Jun 1854; col, 20 Jun 1855; maj gen, 8 Sep 1855; lieut gen, 5 Feb 1863; served in counter-insurgency ops, Canada, 1838–42 and Crimea 1854–56, where he gained a reputation for dash and courage, esp in leading a storming party during the failed attack on the Redan; hailed as a national hero; served in Indian Mutiny; blamed for making sortie from Kanpur contrary to orders and suffering subsequent heavy losses in men and material, Nov 1857. Given no further command in the field; C-in-C, Canada, Oct 1867 until d at Jacksonville, Florida, 2 Feb 1870.

WOLSELEY, Sir George Benjamin; b 11 Jul 1839; ens, 22nd Foot, 18 Sep 1857; 84th Foot, 9 Oct 1857; lieut, 24 Aug 1858; capt, 103rd Foot, 21 Mar 1868; 104th Foot, 25 Mar 1871; 105th Foot, 31 Oct 1871; 65th Foot, 12 Feb 1873; maj, 16 Feb 1878; bt lieut col, 22 Nov 1879; lieut col, 1 Apr 1889; maj gen, 16 July 1892; lieut gen, 1 Apr 1900; served in Indian Mutiny, 2nd Afghan War, Burmese, Egyptian and Sudan campaigns; ret, May 1906.

WOOLHOUSE, Edward; b Kanpur 29 Aug 1832. ens *p*, 84th Foot; lieut, 24 Aug 1855. He was wounded at the entry to Lucknow on 25 September 1857 where he lost an arm, but survived to become capt, 16th Foot, 7 Sep 1858 and command a company of gentlemen cadets at the RMC, Sandhurst, in August 1862, from which he ret as maj, 4 Nov 1864.

WYATT, James Henry; ens *p*, 27th Foot, 20 Sep 1844; lieut *p*, 26 Jun 1846; Military Train, 1856; capt *p*, 3 Aug 1859; bt maj, 26 Apr 1859; maj, 26 Dec 1863; lieut col, 1 Apr 1870; ret, 21 June 1871; served in Indian Mutiny at Lucknow, Awadh and Bihar.

Glossary of Indian terms

atcha (*achchha*)	good (said of a thing or in response to a command)
ayah (*aya*)	Indian nursemaid or lady's maid
baboo (*babu*)	master (title of respect), a learned person
backsheesh (*bakhshish*)	gratuity, donation, reward
bagh	garden, a large walled enclosure
bahadoor (*bahadur*)	hero, paladin, (in titles, the gallant)
bandy	covered cart or carriage (from the Tamil *vandi*)
banghy (*bahngi*)	shoulder-pole with slings at each end for carrying boxes
batta, battah	allowance paid as compensation for additional expenses incurred during a campaign or subsequent occupation
bheesty (*bhisti*)	water-bag bearer
bobbery	Anglo-Indian corruption of the exclamation bap re 'Oh father', hence a fuss or nuisance.
budmash (*badmash*)	evil-doer, criminal, villain
buggy (*bagghi*)	gig (two-wheeled light passenger vehicle)
bunda (*bandar*)	monkey. The word is best known to most English-speakers as the 'bandar-log' or monkey people, in Rudyard Kipling's *Jungle Book*.
butcha (*bachcha*)	child
cassid, kossid (*qasid*)	messenger, despatch-carrier
chatty (*chatti*)	porous earthenware water-container, cooled by the process of evaporation
chit, chitty (*chitthi*)	letter, written note
choga	a cloak
chupatti (*chapati*)	a thin loaf of unleavened bread
coolie, coolly (*quli*)	manual labourer
dauk, dawk (*dak*)	mail, post
decoit (*dakait*)	bandit, one of a gang committing robbery with violence
dhirzee (*darzi*)	tailor
dhol, dhole (*dal*)	Indian pea, pulse
dingy, dinghy (*dengi*)	small boat, skiff, ferry-boat
dobie (*dhobi*)	washerman
doolie (*doli*)	covered litter or stretcher
dour (*daur*)	forced march, raid, sudden attack
ekka	contraction of *ikka gari*, a single horse cart (from *ek* meaning 'one'), a two-wheeled post-chaise
gharry (*gari*)	light horse-drawn carriage
ghi (*ghee*)	clarified butter, extensively used in South Asian cookery and Hindu religious observances
gingall, jingall (*janjal*)	heavy musket, fired from a wall or other mounting
gram, gramm	Indian chick-pea, any kind of pulse intended as animal feed (from the Portuguese *grao*). The Urdu term is *chana*
hackery, hackory, etc	two-wheeled ox-cart (Anglo-Indian, prob from the Urdu *chhakra*)
hauk (*hank*)	a crying or calling out; a driving of beasts by shouting ('au' pronounced as in 'laugh'; the *n* is nasalised

hurkaru (*harkara*)	courier (used as the title of a Bengal newspaper)
huthee (*hathi*)	elephant
jemadar (*jama'dar*)	Indian lieutenant. The term has other meanings and is no longer used as a military rank
jheel (*jhil*)	lake, marsh, swamp
kaisah (*kaisar*)	emperor
kerait (*karait*)	the common krait, *bungarus caeruleus*, a very venomous snake, measuring up to 3 feet or 1 metre long.
ket, khet (*khet*)	cultivated field, crops
khaki	dusty, drab (of a colour)
khana	dwelling-place, department
koodawan (*khudawand*)	master, lord, your worship (form of address to superiors)
moonshi (*munshi*)	a writer or scrivener; a teacher of Indian vernacular languages; a title of respect
palanquin	garbled synonym for palkee (q.v.). The nasalised suffix *in* forms a plural, but the word has passed into English as a singular noun, just as in recent times has Taliban, the plural of *Talib*, a seeker or follower (especially of religious doctrines)
palkee (*palki*)	covered litter or sedan chair, carried by four or six men
pariar, pariah (*pariayar*)	a low-caste Hindu in southern India, and by extension a social outcast of any kind. Pariar or 'pi' dogs, generally yellow and about the size of English retrievers, commonly live as scavengers on the outskirts of South Asian settlements
puckah (*pakka*)	genuine, proper, authentic
lac (*lakh*)	a hundred thousand
loot (*lut*)	plunder, booty
mahout (*mahut*)	elephant driver
maidaun (*maidan*)	a plain, especially a level area used for military drill (*ai* is pronounced as in 'my', *au* as in 'laugh')
mohur (*mohar*)	gold coin, worth Rs.15 in the East India Company's currency
nautch (*nach*)	a dance
nujeeb (*najib*)	lit. a 'hero' or 'volunteer'
otta (*ata*)	flour, meal
otto (*attar*)	essence (esp of rose petals)
pauckally (*pahkali*)	a cleaner (household servant)
Ram-Sammee	from Ram or Rama, the seventh incarnation of Vishnu according to Hindu teaching, and Sammee (*swami*), an idol or image, and hence a religious procession or celebration. The term entered colloquial English as a synonym for a noisy gathering
rezai (*razai*)	quilt, coverlet
rung (*rang*)	colour, tint
sahib (*saheb*)	gentleman, Mr, Sir (honorific form of address)
salaam (*salam*)	greeting, obeisance, salute (lit. 'peace')
sammee (swami)	term of respect, lord, master, etc, especially accorded to Hindu religious teachers, or to the image of a Hindu deity

sepoy (*sipahi*)	Indian regular soldier
Seikhs (*Sikhs*)	This community, predominantly from the Punjab, was formed from believers in a peaceful synthesis of Muslim and Hindu teachings, but developed martial traditions in response to religious persecution by the Mughal emperors. In 1857 many Sikhs were already serving in the Bengal Army, and during the Mutiny campaign many more joined, partly to pay back the Hindustani sepoys who had conquered the Sikh kingdom of Lahore for the British in the 1840s, partly because the mutineers stood for the restoration of Mughal rule, and partly attracted by the prospects of loot.
shekarri (*shikari*)	Indian hunter or tracker
simkin	champagne (Anglo-Indian mispronunciation)
sowar (*sawar*)	Indian cavalry trooper (lit. a rider)
syce (*sais*)	a groom, a servant who attends to horses
tulwar (*talwar*)	Indian broadsword
tat (dim. of *tattu*)	pony, small riding horse
tiffin	light midday meal or luncheon. Although the word is associated with Anglo-Indian culture, it does not derive from any South Asian language but from a Northern English dialect, in which it means a sip or small draught of liquor
tope (*topu*)	grove, orchard, clump of trees. Originally a South Indian term.
wallah (*vala*)	doer, person, inhabitant, (used as last element of compounds)
zenana (*zanana*)	women's quarters, harem, seraglio. It is said that the origins of all disputes derive from *zar* (gold), *zamin*, (land) or *zanan* (women)

Select Bibliography

Barnes, R M 1950 *A history of the regiments and uniforms of the British Army.* Seeley, Service & Co.

Broeld, WG Jr 1986 *Crisis of the Raj: The revolt of 1857 through British lieutenants' eyes.* University Press of New England, Hanover, New Hampshire and London

Bruce, A 1980 *The purchase system in the British Army 1660–1871.* Royal Historical Society, London

Burrows, J W 1929 *The Essex Regiment. Vol 4. The Essex Militia.* Southend-on-Sea, Essex T A Association

Dalrymple, W 2006 *1857 The last mughal. The fall of a dynasty.* London, Bloomsbury

Dawson, L 1960 *Squires and Sepoys, 1857–1958* [Mutiny letters of Captain George Blake, 84th Foot]. London, Hollis & Carter

Germon, M 1870 *Journal of the siege of Lucknow.* London, Privately published

Harris, J A 1858 *A lady's diary of the siege of Lucknow.* London, John Murray

Heathcote, T A 2007 *Mutiny and insurgency in India, 1857–58. The British Army in a bloody Civil War,* with a foreword by Richard Holmes. Barnsley, Pen and Sword Military

Hibbert, C 1978 *The Great Mutiny: India 1857.* London, Allen Lane

Holmes, R 2005 *Sahib. The British soldier in* India *1750–1914.* London, Harper Collins

Hunter, W W 1893 *The Indian Empire: Its peoples, history and products.* London, Smith, Elder & Co.

Raikes, G A 1910 *Roll of officers of the York and Lancaster Regiment 1756–1884.* Revised R E Key. London, William Clowes & Son

Saul, D 2003 *The Indian mutiny 1857.* London, Penguin

Sen, S N 1957 *Eighteen fifty seven.* Calcutta and Delhi, Government of India, Publications Division

Taylor, P T O 1996 *A companion to the Sepoy mutiny of 1857.* Delhi, OUP

Wilson, T F 1858 *The defence of Lucknow: T F Wilson's memoir of the Indian mutiny, 1857.* London, Smith, Elder, and Co. Reprinted 2007 with new introduction by Saul David. London, Greenhill Books

Wylly, H C 1930 *The York and Lancaster Regiment, 1758–1919. Vol I.* Privately published

Index of Letters

Index of Letters (continued)

Index